MANCHESTER METROLINK

DAVID HOLT

Published by Platform 5 Publishing Ltd., Lydgate House, Lydgate Lane, Sheffield S10 5FH, England.

Printed by Nuffield Press, Hollow Way, Cowley, Oxford, OX4 2PH.

ISBN 1 872524 36 2

▲ Metrolink car No 1008 on a driver training run crosses the River Irwell at Radcliffe, accelerating for the long straight climb to Whitefield. Holcombe Hill, topped by the monument to Sir Robert Peel, can be seen rising behind Bury in the distance.　　*Peter Fox*

▼ This remarkable picture shows Car A of Metrolink vehicles 1009 and 1010 stranded in the snow on the Brenner Pass between Italy and Austria on 3rd January 1992. The destination displays 'Bury' and 'Sorry Not in Service' are oddly approppriate. The convoy, which included a BR Class 465 car body destined for Metro-Cammell, was en route from Firema's Casaralta plant near Naples and had been diverted from the normal route via Mont Blanc because of Christmas traffic restrictions in France. The picture on page 51 testifies to 1009's safe arrival.　　*Mrs Giuliana Moro*

CONTENTS

▶ "It's great to be back – Trams return to Manchester" say the roof boards on Metrolink No 1007, proudly carrying the same fleet number as Manchester's "last" tram (next page). No 1007 is seen here making an early morning call at the High Street tram stop on Monday 27th April 1992, the day it became the first tram to carry fare-paying passengers through Manchester's streets after a 43 year gap.   *Author*

1. EARLY DAYS

HISTORICAL BACKGROUND

In the heyday of Manchester's fine municipal electric tramways you could travel cheaply all the way across Lancashire from Rochdale to Liverpool via Piccadilly Gardens, using the interlinking tracks of several different undertakings. Now Metrolink is re-introducing electric public transport to Manchester's streets, 26 years after the last trolleybus ran in 1966 and 43 years after the trams finished in 1949. To understand the origins of Metrolink we need to look much further back to the Manchester of a century and more ago.

Though served so well by first-generation tramways, Manchester had always suffered from heavy rail's failure to reach the heart of the city centre, a handicap inherited from mid-Victorian times. In those far-off days commuters accepted longish walks as part of their journeys, for the simple reason that alternative personal door-to-door transport was not available to them.

The railway companies, thanks to their market dominance, had no commercial need to buy expensive city-centre land for their termini, even if the city fathers had allowed them to. Neither could costly tunnelling be justified − so the railway stations ended up on the edge of the city centre, where they remain to this day. Through services used peripheral routes, though companies were not always keen to establish links with their rivals.

Throughout the present century traffic flows on the city's streets have been consistently heavy. Only the nature of the traffic has altered, from slow-moving commercial and public transport vehicles in the first half of the century to the faster-moving motor traffic of more recent times.

Starting as long ago as 1839, various schemes to construct both heavy rail and, later, tramway tunnels across the city centre were proposed but never materialised. Then, from the nineteen-thirties onwards, a developing obsession with road-only transport (cars and buses) led steadily towards abandonment of existing fixed public transport infrastructure (tramways, trolleybus routes and some railways) on a devastating scale.

By the early 'sixties, three factors were conspiring to make it unfashionable even to mention railed transport in British city streets; Dr Beeching's ruthless pruning of the railways was fresh in people's minds and so was the final demise of the last British city tram system (Glasgow 1962), added to which the love affair with the motor car was gaining ground alarmingly. In an ironic twist of history Manchester's first tramway abandonment, in 1930, featured the

Manchester's "last" tram − for the time being at least − ran on 10th January 1949. Here it is at the end of its journey outside Birchfields Road depot, a building which many years later was to play an important part in the birth of Manchester's new trams, one of which (previous page) bears the same fleet number − 1007 − as the "last" tram. Metrolink's ghostly white livery seems poignantly appropriate when one contemplates this scene. Author's collection.

"Circular" 53 route, which happened to run right past the future site of the city's second-generation tramway headquarters at Queens Road, of which more later. In 1949 Manchester became the first major British city to deliberately lose its trams. Now, in 1992, Manchester is in the vanguard of the British tram's revival. The Phoenix has risen from the ashes − but back in the early 'sixties there was still a long way to go.

THIRTY TRAMLESS YEARS

The SELNEC (South East Lancashire and North East Cheshire) Highway Plan of 1962, the year when the British city tram was laid to rest for the time being, was manifestly road-oriented. The tram, never rejected on the Continent, was by the nineteen-sixties decidedly "old-fashioned" here, and any mention of it was likely to be met either with derision or with patronising dismissal. A great many British people, including politicians, were suffering from a kind of paranoid xenophobia left over from wartime days which made them scornful or ignorant of developments overseas. Few wanted to know that car congestion was damaging British urban public transport and fuelling a vicious circle of more car usage.

SIXTIES EXTREMITIES

So far did road-traffic dominance go in the 'sixties and early 'seventies that moves were even being made to keep people away from the city's surface by means of overhead walkways; this being one of the recommendations of Professor Colin Buchanan's "Traffic in Towns" report of 1963. Manchester's County Hall (now Westminster House), Arndale Centre and Piccadilly Plaza incorporated parts of just such a walkway, and the surviving footbridges across Corporation Street and Deansgate near to the Cathedral were also to have linked into it.

London's Barbican gives us a vision of what it would have been like if carried through. Bleak windswept piazzas overlooking roaring traffic canyons might or might not have been right for the City of London, but time has proved how out of place the concept would have been in Manchester; the short stretch of Deansgate between Blackfriars Street and Victoria Bridge Street, with its minimised provision for pedestrians at street level, remains as a stark reminder of an arrested malaise.

The 'sixties was a fertile time for such extremities; it is instructive for us to recall that the popular, if tongue-in-cheek, "Thunderbirds" puppets rode on monorails rather than on light rail vehicles. And so the monorail became the common man's composite answer to every urban transport problem, though even in those hairbrained days there were those who could see a less fictitious way forward.

MARTIC − AN IDEA BEFORE ITS TIME

In the middle 'sixties, undaunted by brash talk of non-conventional solutions, local representatives of the Light Railway Transport League (now the LRTA) put forward the "Martic" (Manchester Area Rapid Transit Investigation Committee) scheme for LRT in Manchester in response to light rail's exclusion from the range of options being considered in the SELNEC Transportation Study, set up in 1965 (see below). Martic foreshadowed Metrolink technologically and was cleverly promoted as "Duorail" to emphasise its mature distinction from the trendy glistening monorail. The proposed north-south route would have connected two large out-of-town overspill estates, Langley and Wythenshawe, via an on-street city centre section.

Unfortunately public opinion, bombarded with talk of moving pavements and magnetic levitation, was not yet ready for anything as rational as "Duorail" and so the proposal lapsed, though not before it had helped sow seeds of light rail awareness in the city. The City Council put forward similar ideas in the late 'sixties, promoted as "Duorail" to distinguish the technology from the sci-fi systems superficially popular at the time. This proposal lapsed partly because the onset of the county-wide PTE threatened to exhaust it of City kudos, and partly because of Picc-Vic.

PICC−VIC − A FAILED INITIATIVE

In the unfavourable late 'sixties climate for public transport, ways

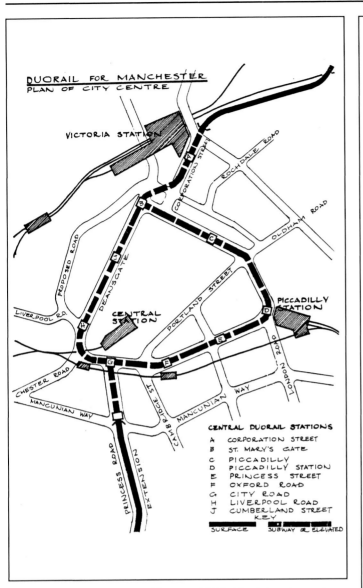

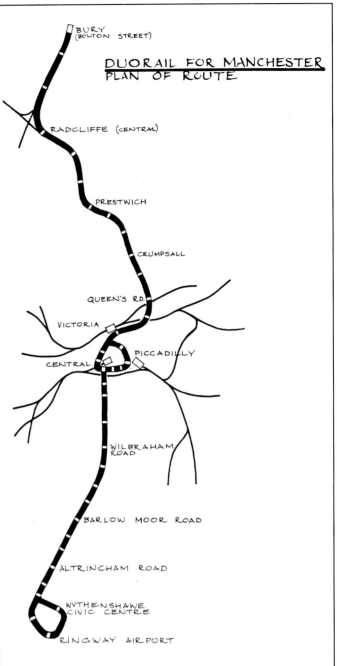

These two maps, reproduced from a mid-60s Martic brochure, show how closely in that scheme anticipated Metrolink. One variation is the nature of the Airport rail link, now being implemented not as LRT but as a BR spur from the Styal line. It is interesting to observe that G-MEX was at the time of the Martic proposals still in existence as Central Station, enjoying frequent express services to London St. Pancras.

were being sought by planners and politicians to come to terms on a county-wide basis with the car's escalating greed for space and resources. In 1965 the SELNEC Transportation Study was initiated, setting out to establish a strategic transport plan for the region. This exercise, bringing in the Department of the Environment, was complemented by the 1969-established Passenger Transport Executive's statutory Long Term Plan for the next 25 years and, later, by the Transport Policies and Programme submissions of the Metropolitan County Authority.

The main feature of the 1973-published Long Term Plan was the Picc–Vic proposal, a complete public transport package based on linking Piccadilly and Victoria stations by rail tunnel complete with three new stations under the city centre. Liverpool's Merseyrail and Tyneside's Metro are comparable schemes; if it had come to fruition, Picc–Vic in its entirety would have provided a 50 mile heavy electric rapid transit system for the Manchester region and plenty more besides.

As with the Tyneside Metro, integration of buses with rail was a cornerstone of Picc–Vic. Furthermore, the plans included provision for fill-in light rail services and electrified heavy-rail reinstatement (later dropped from the plans) of the lifted line from Radcliffe to Bolton, together with earmarking of proposed bus-only roads and reservations for possible future conversion to LRT.

One local LRT member put forward remarkably prophetic light rail proposals to complement Picc–Vic; he suggested conversion of the Oldham Loop line to LRT with on-street links across and into

the City centre and even an on-street extension to the centre of Rochdale via Drake Street.

Parliamentary Powers for Picc–Vic were obtained by the PTE in the SELNEC Act 1972. Under this Act, ownership of the new tunnel and stations would have rested with the PTE with operation undertaken by BR under a long-lease arrangement, though other options were provided for in the legislation. Encouraged by Tyneside's success in securing the allocation of £49.1M for its Metro and Liverpool's in securing £16.2 Million for Merseyrail, Greater Manchester PTE applied for Government grant aid for Picc–Vic at the end of July 1973.

Had a grant been forthcoming, tunnelling for Picc–Vic would have started in September 1973. However, after some intermediate rebuffs the Minister for Transport Industries pulled the project up short in August 1974 by announcing that funding could not at that time be made available, citing high cost and insufficient benefits of the tunnel section as a reason. It must also be remembered that the country was not in the best of economic health at the time. Thenceforward, cost projections for Picc–Vic steadily crept up both because of inflation and because of lessons learned from the Tyne and Wear Metro's tunnel construction, which began in October 1974; November 1974 figures gave the grant-eligible capital cost of Picc–Vic as £114 667 000 spread over 9 years, of which £55 870 000 would have been for the tunnel section. By 1977 the total figure had gone up to £160 Million.

Northbound
First train | Second train
BOLTON | OLDHAM

Royal Exchange

« way out

The Picc·Vic Project

GMC ▥

▲ The Picc-Vic scheme was strongly pursued in the mid-'70s. The front cover of GMPTE's attractive Picc-Vic brochure featured an artist's impression of a train calling at the projected Royal Exchange underground station. Provision for this station was actually made during construction of the Arndale Centre's foundations.

▼ The city centre map shows the tunnel's intended route between Piccadilly BR and Victoria — hence the name "Picc-Vic". Royal Exchange, convenient for shops and offices, would have become a busy stop.

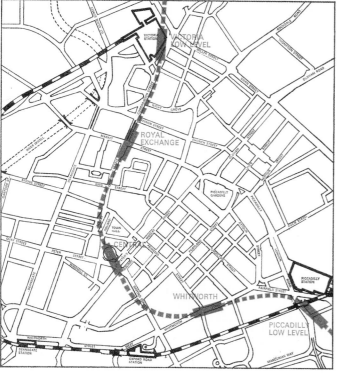

PICC – VIC'S DEMISE

Even though the PTE and the new Greater Manchester County Council worked strenuously in continuing to promote Picc – Vic, the country's mid-70s economic problems finally brought dismayed acceptance in 1977 that the momentum had gone and that economic circumstances were unlikely in the foreseeable future to favour approval of the project as it stood. Nevertheless, some peripheral elements of the scheme did get completed; these included the splendid Bury and Altrincham bus/rail interchanges and the electrification of the Buxton line as far as Hazel Grove. Platforms 1–4 at Victoria Station were cleared away in preparation for Picc – Vic and the adjacent Manchester Arms pub was demolished. Less visibly, part of the basement of the city's new Arndale Centre was built with provision for one of the proposed subterranean Picc – Vic stations.

Picc – Vic's final demise fell to a limited extent in line with trends elsewhere; during the Amsterdam Metro's construction rising costs, environmental damage and related unrest had led the Dutch Minister of Transport to announce in 1976 that no more new underground rail lines would be approved in the Netherlands; Rotterdam's East – West metro had already been endorsed. Exemplary results have since been accomplished at ground level using upgraded and new surface tramways benefitting from vital political commitment. Meanwhile, beneath the earth's surface, crime on some of the world's underground railways was starting to increase steadily.

POST PICC – VIC: THE PROBLEMS REMAIN

Post Picc – Vic in the late '70s, Greater Manchester Council and its Passenger Transport Executive were left with an increasingly-onerous duty under Section 20 of the Transport Act 1968 to support essential though for the most part unprofitable and unimproved local rail services. Manchester was by then the only major British city without adequate cross-city rail links. Section 56 of the 1968 Act allowed the Government to make grants towards the cost of new rail infrastructure projects promoted by PTEs. The Act's provisions, which had once helped spawn Picc – Vic, now set in motion a sequence of events which eventually led to the development of the Metrolink scheme.

Still charged under Section 9 of the Transport Act to "secure and promote the provision of a properly integrated and efficient system

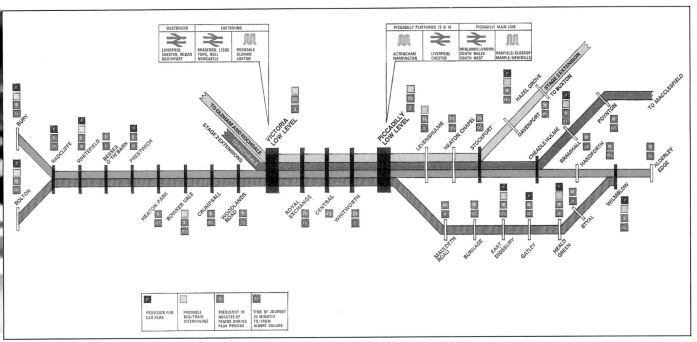

	WESTBOUND	EASTBOUND	
	🚆 LIVERPOOL CHESTER, WIGAN SOUTHPORT	🚆 BRADFORD, LEEDS YORK, HULL NEWCASTLE	♒ ROCHDALE OLDHAM ASHTON

PICCADILLY PLATFORMS 13 & 14		PICCADILLY MAIN LINE	
♒ ALTRINCHAM WARRINGTON	🚆 LIVERPOOL CHESTER	🚆 MIDLANDS, LONDON, SOUTH WALES SOUTH WEST	♒ HADFIELD/GLOSSOP MARPLE/NEW MILLS

P		5	25
PROVISION FOR CAR PARK	PROBABLE BUS/TRAIN INTERCHANGE	FREQUENCY IN MINUTES OF TRAINS DURING PEAK PERIODS	TIME OF JOURNEY IN MINUTES TO/FROM ALBERT SQUARE

The diagrammatic map of the proposed routes shows how the scheme would have funnelled commuter rail services into the tunnel section to achieve city-centre penetration as well as cost-saving cross-city operation.

of public transport with due regard to town planning and traffic and parking policies'' (to which the words ''Westminster permitting'' might well have been added), the PTE started looking afresh for a way forward. The problems afflicting the local rail network were briefly: rolling stock, signalling and electrification system obsolescence, lack of a north – south link penetrating the city centre and duplication/separation of Piccadilly and Victoria stations, not to mention an increasing thirst for Section 20 local authority funding – £19 million per annum in the mid-80s, currently (1991/2) standing at £28 Million. These figures have always been substantially higher than those expended per passenger for bus services. There was cross-party local political support for averting the threat of forced closure of some local railway lines, perhaps accelerated by damaging service economies forced on the PTE by spending cuts – altogether a prospect which no-one relished at local level.

One proposal considered was the Castlefield Curve. This relatively low cost scheme would have linked Victoria and Piccadilly stations via a new viaduct crossing through the throat of the historic Liverpool Road station, now a flourishing museum site. This scheme came to nothing; the benefits did not justify the cost, mainly because central area access would not have been directly improved.

NETWORK NORTHWEST

Then in 1980 British Rail revealed plans for a new length of railway between Windsor Bridge and Oldfield Road in Salford, which rather than directly linking the two disconnected stations, would make it possible to run Provincial and Inter-City trains more easily through Manchester in a north-westerly direction. The Windsor Link, as it was called, offered relatively little in terms of improving Section 20

supported services, though it would make it easier to reach the Oxford Road side of Manchester from the Bolton direction as well as facilitating some more or less esoteric transfer journeys.

A related scheme, first proposed in recent times by the publisher of this book when he worked for British Rail was the Hazel Grove Chord, designed to provide through services from Sheffield and beyond to Liverpool and the north-west – again with relatively few obvious benefits for local commuters, whose rather stale slice of the early 'eighties cake was confined to the proposed re-equipping of the 1500 V d.c. Manchester – Glossop/Hadfield line with 25 kV a.c. electrification and second-hand trains; this took place at the end of 1984.

Though concentrated more on improving long-distance services, the Windsor Link and Hazel Grove Chord initiatives did have implications of a more local nature. Part of the strategy behind them lay in British Rail's intention under the ''Network NorthWest'' plan to concentrate its principal long-distance services at Piccadilly and to retain Victoria only for some Provincial and local services. The plan as put forward under a joint BR/DTp policy document in 1981 was to have been strengthened by 25 kV electrification from Manchester to Preston and Blackpool.

IMPLICATIONS FOR LOCAL TRAINS

A great many of the trains using the improved network would have to pass along the double-track railway through Piccadilly Station Platforms 13 and 14, Oxford Road station and Deansgate station (formerly Knott Mill and Deansgate) before reaching Castlefield Junction, where the line towards Warrington and Altrincham and beyond splits from the line towards the Windsor Link and Eccles and beyond.

This congested length of railway, running on viaduct between large

▶ One of the reasons for prompting the Picc-Vic scheme and, after it, Metrolink, was the obsolescence of the electrification system and of the rolling stock on the popular Bury line, which connected Manchester Victoria with Bury; this is one of the line's two-car slam-door Class 504 trains Nos. 65460/77181 calling at Heaton Park on Saturday 13th July 1991. Metrolink's new lifts are already under construction in the background. *Peter Fox*

buildings and across busy roads, would need prohibitively expensive quadrupling if it were not to form a bottleneck constricting the new services. The alternative was to divert some local traffic away from it to release more capacity for Provincial and Inter-City traffic, and that is partly what gave British Rail the incentive to seek city-penetrating diversion of some services as a realistic way forward.

BACK TO TUNNELS?

In the context of all this rationalisation it was easy to envisage the insertion of city-centre tunnels such as those featured in the Picc – Vic scheme, together with uniform electrification at 25 kV of the remaining commuter railways feeding into Manchester. All the region's suburban and commuter trains could in abstract theory then have burrowed under the city to enhance their appeal, but in reality nothing of the kind was achievable without grossly excessive expenditure.

The Moorgate dead-end tube disaster had raised questions about the feasibility of phased tunnel construction, and it would not have been possible to run existing trains through the tunnels because of their non-retention toilets and swing doors – not to mention questions of curves, gradients and station lengths. Consequently all tunnel rolling stock would at that time have had to be new, apart from possible second-hand acquisitions like the Class 303 sliding door stock cascaded from Glasgow for the Glossop/Hadfield line.

Any services sharing tracks in the suburbs with freight or with longer-distance passenger trains, or making timetable connections, could threaten disruption of intensive short-headway tunnel operation by introducing random knock-on delays. Taken together with variable dwell times at busy underground stations, this may have imposed constraints on the numbers and variety of services which could be fed through city-centre tunnels.

LIGHT RAIL OBJECTIVES

It is worth at this point reviewing the motives of the different participants in the study group. British Rail had its own concerns about the coreless nature of Manchester's existing rail system; after all, an Inter-City or Provincial network without local access of matching quality is as disadvantaged as a tree without good roots. The same would in time apply to the planned heavy rail link to Manchester Airport. As far as the city-centre was concerned, the introduction of the "Centreline" bus link between Piccadilly and Victoria stations in July 1974 did go some way towards providing better city-centre access, but it could never be expected to bring the full benefits of effective rail penetration. In any case, there was still quite a long walk from Piccadilly Station's busy Platforms 13 and 14 to be undertaken before one stepped off railway premises and proceeded towards the city centre.

In 1982 a joint Rail Study Group was set up bringing together British Rail, the Greater Manchester Council and Greater Manchester Passenger Transport Executive, with technical assistance from consultants Mott, Hay and Anderson. The objective was to develop a long-term strategy for the County's local rail network in the light of British Rail's proposals for its Inter-City and Provincial networks. The existence in those days of the Metropolitan Counties, with their statutory duty to produce Structure Plans, was what made County-wide initiatives like the study group possible and it is difficult to imagine today's less elegant metropolitan structure and less orderly means of public transport administration generating the same level of co-operation and unity of purpose.

The PTE and GMC were, for their part, faced with providing increasing revenue support for train services which were failing to show a reasonable rate of return in terms of benefit to the community. Stopping short of the city centre, life-expired and increasingly unreliable trains could not offer the prospect of catering for much more than a small proportion of local public transport journeys (around 5% in 1985) or passenger mileage (around 15% in 1985) in the region even if they were replaced with new rolling stock. Added to that, wide station spacing in some residential areas was denying the trains some much-needed patronage.

The City of Manchester, with an interest in 55% of City property, was represented on the Rail Study Group through GMC. Anxious to maintain its status as a regional centre, Manchester was in the early 'eighties facing the threat of loss of economic activity partly due to developments springing up around the formative outer motorway ring and on "green-field" sites. Without counter measures, urban decay could easily set in; the 1981 Toxteth riots in Liverpool had been a frightful warning of what might happen. Another threat to the regional core took the form of increasing traffic congestion resulting from unchecked private car use. Gridlock seemed a real possibility

and did indeed happen on one later occasion.

Traffic congestion costs businesses money; snarled up in traffic, company cars and vans clock up staggering total costs in terms of drivers' paid time which ought to be put to much more productive use. Ambulances, fire appliances and police vehicles caught up in traffic might run up high costs in terms of loss of life or property, and there is the direct cost and burden on the health service of road traffic accidents. By 1990 the annual cost of road traffic congestion was estimated by the CBI to be £15 billion.

A 1982 survey amongst local businesses indicated that they saw the need for good access for both business and commerce to the city-centre both to attract and retain staff by widening the labour catchment area and to ensure that customers could continue to be attracted. This was also brought out in a report "Capital of the North – the Business Service Sector in Inner Manchester/Salford", published by Roger Tym & Partners in 1981, which suggested rapid transit for improving the rail system.

Certainly something was needed to draw economic activity inwards, counteracting the forces pulling it away and at the same time providing an attractive alternative to individual car transport. It was obvious that the answer must take the form of some kind of improved public transport; the Rail Study Group was set up to identify the right means of providing it.

The population of the City of Manchester was around 450 000, but 150 000 people travelled daily by all forms of transport to work in the city centre. Improved rail links were seen as essential for Manchester to be sustained as a vibrant regional centre.

THE OPTIONS

Broadly, the Rail Study Group set out to look at two alternative ways forward. One option was the phased construction of a system of cross-city tunnels linking a network of local lines electrified uniformly at 25 kV – in effect a heavy rapid transit or metro system. The other option embraced two further alternatives: Light Rail Transit (a mouthful of a new name for tramways), and busways. Both of these latter two strategies had similar objectives, namely the linking of radial rail alignments via existing streets or via new tunnels across the regional centre.

The reason for looking at light rail or busway tunnels as well as surface alignments across the city centre was that they would cost considerably less than those needed for heavy rail. They would be able to feature sharper curves and steeper gradients than those needed for heavy rail, enabling them to be fitted in more easily and cheaply under the city. Putting light rail underground would make it less environmentally intrusive than on-street light rail but at the same time would hide the service, lengthen door-to-door journey times because of the added time taken to reach underground stations and introduce all the negative personal security aspects of underground places.

As it has turned out, tunnelling has not been resorted to although going underground remains an optional way of upgrading light rail services in the future, taking advantage of light rail's phased construction capabilities. The five existing lines considered suitable for a basic light rail network were all carrying well-used rail services which GMC wished to retain and improve. A sixth line brought the extent of the proposed network to some 100 km; the full network's projected cost at 1982 prices was £100 million.

THE ROUTES

Working geographically clockwise from the north, the first eligible line we come to is the Manchester Victoria to Bury line which was originally (and paradoxically) electrified by the Lancashire and Yorkshire Railway Company in reponse to tramway competition. This line was perhaps the prime candidate for conversion to LRT. With its unique and worn-out side-contact third-rail 1200 V d.c. current collection system it operated in splendid isolation of other railways in the area, having its own depot, trains and, to a large extent, staff. Passengers on the Bury line enjoyed the most reliable commuter service in the country thanks partly to self-containment but mainly to the method of current collection. The shrouded side-contact third rail, patented by John Aspinall in 1916, resisted icing up and was also safer than an exposed live rail.

On the same side of Manchester another contender was the Victoria to Oldham and Rochdale "loop", exclusively operated by PTE-supported diesel multiple units then nearing the end of their life expectancy. Moving on in a clockwise direction, the next line completely dedicated to PTE-supported services after cessation of the Woodhead services in 1981 was the Manchester Piccadilly to Glossop and Hadfield line, then still operating at a non-standard 1500 V d.c. Next, a little further south, came the DMU-operated line to Marple and Rose Hill from Manchester Piccadilly, important because of the poor road network in the areas it served.

The Altrincham line, the fifth line considered by the study group, was another suburban route originally electrified in response to tramway competition. It was built by the Manchester South Junction & Altrincham Railway (a joint undertaking owned by the Midland and Great Central Railways) and was electrified at 1500 V d.c. in 1931. The line always showed quite strong LRT characteristics of its own due to its visible penetration of residential areas coupled with closely-spaced stations and frequent service.

In earlier days, track quadrupling and the use of separate city terminus facilities meant that longer-distance trains to Liverpool via Lymm (since axed) and Chester (since diverted) could run separately from the ''Altrincham electrics'' over much of the line's length. Latterly, only the Chester trains shared the remaining pair of tracks with the Altrincham trains, and they have now in turn been re-routed via Stockport in connection with the Windsor Link scheme. Altrincham trains, now 25 kV, were the only services still using the line between Deansgate Junction (betwen Timperley and Navigation Road) and Cornbrook Junction. They ran onward through Oxford Road and Piccadilly stations to either Hazel Grove, Alderly Edge or Crewe.

A sixth alignment was looked at by the study group; the old Midland main line from Manchester Central to London St Pancras was then still in use between Old Trafford and Hough End by BR for freight traffic and for occasional passenger diversions. Beyond Hough End lay an abandoned trackbed stretching all the way to East Didsbury and a little beyond, though not unfortunately all the way to Stockport; the BR trains veered left at Hough End − site of the old Chorlton Junction − to continue to Gorton and beyond. Reinstated and converted to LRT as far as East Didsbury and added to the other five lines, this route would balance up the projected network. Connection with the Altrincham line would be made close to Old Trafford (now Trafford Bar) station.

CITY-CENTRE SURFACE LINKS

In the city centre three completely double-tracked street-running alignments, totalling 2.71 route kilometres, would radiate from a triangular junction centrally located in Mosley Street beside Piccadilly Gardens. At each of the extremities of the three street sections, interfaces with existing railway alignments were proposed. At G-MEX the tracks would climb onto the former Central Station viaduct which would carry them on via Cornbrook towards Altrincham and East Didsbury. At Victoria the tracks would meet end-on with the existing Bury line, linking in also with the line to Rochdale via Oldham.

The third arm of the delta-shaped city-centre layout would enter Piccadilly Station's undercroft area which would take it diagonally across to a point where it would rise up on the Glossop side of the station to meet the tracks of the Glossop/Hadfield and Marple/Rose Hill lines. Thus each arm gave two suburban railways surface penetration of the city centre. In time, the Bury and Altrincham lines together with the complete city-centre layout would come to be known as Phase 1. The form which the initial city-centre proposals took remained substantially unaltered; the alignment of each of the three arms will be described in more detail later.

Bury to Manchester and Altrincham to Manchester were chosen for conversion and interlinking in the first phase because between them they were sufficiently robust to support the installation of the city centre section, which once in place could accommodate services arising from the implementation of future phases.

The phased basis on which the full six line network was planned was consistent with the Transport Supplementary Grant mechanism then in use for allocating central government funds to eligible local public transport schemes. Incorporated in the GMC's Transport Policies and Programme submission, an acceptable phased project would qualify as a ''named scheme'', guaranteeing the allocation of further funds to maintain the continuing phased development of the entire project until its completion.

▶ The Bury line had been electrified in 1916 at 1200 V d.c. by John Aspinall in response to electric tramway competition. One of the original trains is seen here on 29th May 1955 calling at Bowker Vale station. The unique wood-shrouded side-contact third rail can be seen in this view. *A.C. Gilbert*

The drawing below shows a cross section of Aspinall's shrouded side-contact third rail assembly.

▶▼ The other local BR route chosen for early conversion to light rail was the Altrincham line, electrified in 1931 at 1500 V d.c. from Manchester Oxford Road to Altrincham. This shows one of the original 3-car LMS trains in dark green livery arriving at Oxford Road's platform in the early 1960s. It is interesting to compare the track layout here with the post-Network NorthWest arrangement. *N.R. Knight*

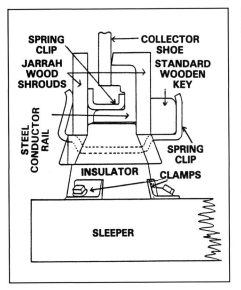

WHAT IS LIGHT RAIL?

Not being a rigid concept, light rail defies attempts to closely define it. Nevertheless it is conventional to quote figures in works of this nature so as to give some sense of dimension to light rail's place in the scheme of things. Passengers per direction per hour (ppdph) is the relevant statistic.

Buses can cater economically for passenger flows up to and including about 6000 ppdph. For greater demands, it is difficult to justify expensively-segregated urban railway ("metro") construction for passenger flows of fewer than 15 000 ppdph. We can see straight away that this leaves a big 6000 – 15 000 ppdph gap; this is the gap which light rail can fill. Because of its cheaper non-segregated construction and its less labour-intensive operation, light rail can cater economically for passenger flows of between 2000 and 20 000 pphpd. This makes the mode very versatile; bare statistics, however, can't on their own give us a clear understanding of light rail's relevance.

When light rail succeeds in increasing patronage substantially, as it usually does, its capacity can be progressively increased until the system either metamorphoses vertically downwards into a segregated underground metro system or grows laterally into a more comprehensive set of surface alignments. Which one of these it does will depend on the true level of commitment to surface public transport held by the community which it serves. It has to be said that current trends run towards the latter alternative, which implies seizing the surface for people and public transport rather than yielding it helplessly to private transport.

LIGHT RAIL CHARACTERISTICS

Embracing and fully understanding the light rail concept really implies discarding preconceived notions about railed transport rather than taking on board any particular set of engineering rules. To start with, light rail can be thought of as a free-range railway, a railway unrestrained by fixed ideas, unconfined by fences, domesticated and able to run sociably at will amongst its patrons in their own environment – something like, in effect, a respected actor stepping down off a stage and mingling with the audience.

True LRVs have special characteristics which distinguish them from other rail vehicles. A tram is neither a train in the street nor a bus on rails; it is a distinct mode of transport in its own right. Fundamentally, trams are light enough and have sufficiently powerful brakes to stop fast in emergencies and to avoid collisions rather than being heavy enough to survive them without deformation. A tram, then, is a rail vehicle with some of the characteristics of a road vehicle.

Traditional railways generally rely on rigorous segregation from people and from other vehicles because the train's combination of speed and weight coupled with lack of emergency braking mean that its movement must generally be protected and constrained by formalised signalling systems. Light rail vehicles, conversely, can run on sight like road vehicles when circumstances permit and this is what permits them to do their unique job.

Light rail vehicles impose less axle load on track and bridges than do some heavy trains, and this means that new structures can be fashioned less substantially, more inexpensively and perhaps with more built-in stylishness and delicacy as well.

CONVENTIONAL RAIL

For fast journeys between centres of population and for moving heavy flows of passengers around in big densely-peopled conurbations, conventional railway technology will always have an unchallenged edge over all other forms of land transport.

Where short conventional rail journeys are concerned, though, the access times at each end of the ride can represent a high proportion of the total door-to-door travel time. Conventional railways do not always penetrate suburbs well, but the Altrincham line where it passes through Sale was a notable exception. They often also suffer from being raised out of reach on viaducts or hidden from view in cuttings or tunnels.

People who wish to use conventional railways sometimes have to negotiate tortuous accesses from the street to get on to the correct station platform. In the city centre, conventional railways either stop short of offices and shops or decant their passengers deep underground in the bowels of the city. Some of the walks through passages and up and down stairs on the London Underground seem as long as the station spacings themselves, and that's before you start your onward walk on the surface to wherever you're going.

BUSES

Another horse for another course is the bus. Nothing penetrates suburbia like the bus, but it is less comfortable and much slower-moving than the train on long runs in from the suburbs to the city centre. When they reach the city buses do take folk pretty close to their final destinations and in doing so make their availability known to others by being seen displaying their destinations and opening their doors in crowded public places. Endowed with penalty-free transfer facilites, buses might be made even more user-friendly and effective. The bus does not however enjoy a glamorous image and has comparatively little ability to attract car users onto public transport.

THE PANORAMIC METRO

It is a known fact that people enjoy watching their fellow human beings. On a conventional city train all they have to look at from the window are the ugly backs of buildings with perhaps an occasional glimpse of a street below as the train makes its way round the perimeter of the city centre. An even duller view is afforded from a train (or a tram) in a tunnel. Conversely, on a light rail vehicle the passenger is conveyed through city streets buzzing with human activity. There are shop window displays and attractive gardens to admire as you swan cleanly and quietly by on what could justifiably be labelled a "panoramic metro".

THE GOLDFISH BOWL EFFECT

The modern tram's large windows and in-street operation make it easy for passers-by and police patrols to see what's happening on board. This security is a two-way affair; well-used trams mean lots of pairs of passengers' eyes looking outwards and observing what is going on in the street. A clear view right through the interior of a light rail vehicle adds to passengers' feeling of confidence, as does the driver's ability to look round and see into the passenger area as well as forward into the street scene.

A WINNING COMBINATION

In an nutshell, then, thanks to its unrivalled alignment flexibility the modern tram compounds the speed of the train with the accessiblity of the bus and adds cleanliness, ambience and high marks on the ecological front for good measure.

2. THE LIGHT RAIL OPTION

1983 – THE RAIL STUDY GROUP'S FIRST REPORT

The Rail Study Group deliberated for six months before producing, in April 1983, an initial report "A Rail Strategy for Greater Manchester: The Options – First Report of the Rail Study Group". The report gave full coverage to all the alternative ways forward, which briefly were seen as:
1. Conventional rail solution, with East–West and North–South city-centre tunnels together with complementary work such as the possible reinstatement of the "Midland Curve" to allow the Calder Valley service to operate into or through Piccadilly Station
2. LRT operating on street across the city centre
3. LRT in tunnel across the city centre

4. Guided and/or conventional busway
It is important to understand how LRT came to be included in the Study Group's list of options at all. The idea that LRT technology might prove useful in Manchester was not something fished out of the blue during the relatively short period in which the Study Group deliberated. PTE planning staff, charged always with overviewing the development of public transport strategies in the County, had kept themselves informed about all available technologies. By 1980 no urban public transport professional could be unaware of what was being achieved around the world with light rail. Many surviving tramway systems were being progressively modernised and there was increasing talk of completely new systems on the drawing board in several countries.

▶ An attractive scene in Karlsruhe, one of the key places visited by Manchester's light rail planners when they were studying examples of LRT and street tramway practice in Europe. The need for reducing the visual impact of overhead wiring – note the complete absence of poles in this picture – was one of the lessons learned during those visits. In fairness, it should be emphasised that this view shows a mature tramway which may well have started life many years previously with a profusion of poles. In Manchester the removal of superflous poles has already started, so that the optimists amongst us can look forward to the PTE's vision of neat overhead equipment being realised one day. *Peter Fox*

▶ An important boost was given to Manchester's light rail proposals by the London's Docklands Light Railway, for a time intended to pioneer UK street light rail operation. Plans were changed, but not before the concept of modern street tramway operation had been given some welcome high-profile credibility. Now with third rail current collection and driverless operation, the DLR is unlikely ever to venture into the capital's streets. The railway was designed and built by GEC and Mowlem who are part of the consortium which has designed and built – and is now operating and maintaining – Manchester Metrolink Phase 1. This photograph shows DLR 04 at Island Gardens station on 26th March 1990
Peter Fox

LRT CREDIBILITY

Developments in light rail technology were gathering momentum and the existence of upgraded and new systems at no great distance from Manchester helped give trams a vital air of credibility. Stereotyped scepticism throwing back to the 1950s began to sound distinctly stagnant in the face of the tram's robust popularity in Amsterdam, Bonn, Zürich, Wien (Vienna), Melbourne, Boston and a whole host of other cities outside the British Isles. At home the Tyne and Wear Metro was beginning to demonstrate some aspects of the LRT concept and there was the bold prospect (sadly never to be realised) of some street running on the planned Docklands Light Railway in London. Talk of re-introducing trams in Sheffield, which in 1960 had been the last English city to do away with them, was raising eyebrows and hopes here and there.

Light Rail Vehicle manufacturers were turning out glossy brochures illustrating smart well-equipped new trams obviously capable of boosting civic pride, an important reward for investing in them. British firms were beginning to make known their ability and willingness to become involved with the burgeoning light rail industry both at home and abroad. All this was not lost on the politicians and county planners with whom the PTE planners began to discuss their findings. From one-to-one discussions over coffee, to small get-togethers in offices, to bigger and more formal meetings; from brief memoranda on bits of paper, to internal discussion documents, to more substantial reports — these were the ways in which the light rail idea gained ground in Manchester in the very early 'eighties.

SEIZING THE SURFACE

By 1983, circumstances in the city had altered very much in favour of seizing the surface for people rather than for cars. This contributed to establishing the right climate for LRT to be considered. Commitment to roads was becoming less extreme; prestigious City Council plans for expensive grade-separated highways — the City Centre Road and the Inner Ring Road — were replaced by the new GMC with the much more realistic ground level Inner Relief Route which we know today. Susequently, the Central Manchester Traffic Plan progressivley introduced bus and access-only routes across the centre. No longer was it necessary to think exclusively of tunnelling as the only possible way of taking railed vehicles to the heart (or, rather, the bowels) of a traffic-choked city.

Market Street's pedestrianisation, which took three months at the end of 1980, followed requests from retailers for improvement of the shopping environment. Market Street had been part of the main A6 route through Manchester as well as having the densest pedestrian flows in the city. In spite of fears of traffic chaos, there were no problems and other pedestrianisation schemes have followed Market Street's popular example. The scene was now set for LRT to penetrate the city centre on-street; the necessary transit corridors had been created and were just waiting to be identified, linked together and used to maximum effect as soon as possible.

Three separate Working Parties contributed to the First Report of the Rail Study Group, dealing respectively with conventional rail solutions, non-conventional solutions (including light rail) and with plans for new pedestrian access combined with potential light rail interchange facilities at Deansgate station in anticipation of nearby Central Station's conversion to a major exhibition centre (G-MEX, opened in 1986). The Report when published in May 1983 included annexes giving transcripts of two consultative seminars which had been held in February 1983 to discuss the Study Group's findings with GMC members and with District Councils and other bodies before submitting them to GMC Committees.

COMPARISON BETWEEN MODES

The criteria which any solution had to meet were:
- Flows in the range 1000−5000 passengers per hour with a maximum capability of 10000 passengers per hour over central sections.
- Maximum speed not less than 80 km/h with high acceleration/deceleration rates.
- Ability to operate over existing and proposed alignments without extensive engineering costs.
- High level of reliability.
- Acceptable environmental features.
- Capablity of expansion beyond the study network.

Buses, trolleybuses and trams on ordinary roads were ruled out on the basis that they could not meet the speed requirements. In addition, there were doubts about the capacity of buses and trolleybuses. Monorails and rubber-tyred metros were ruled out on cost grounds and in addition monorails were ruled out on environmental grounds. Various automatic guideway systems were also rejected generally on social and cost grounds, but also because certain of them were not 'tried and tested'.

Thus the choice was to be between a metro, light rail transit, a busway and a guided busway. The busway option was not rejected at the preliminary stage although doubts were expressed about the ability of such a system to meet the requirements above. It was considered that the requirement to operate at 80 km/h over converted railway alignments which include arched bridges and tunnels would not be feasible, particularly at the low minimum headways which would apply to the flows predicted above. For an articulated bus seating 64 and with 56 standees the headway would be 86 seconds for 5000 passengers/hour, but bunching would mean that actual headways would often be lower than this. In addition it is unrealistic to assume that every bus would operate at 100% load factor, and this would further reduce the peak headway. In addition poor weather would adversely affect the performance of the non-guided bus system to a much greater degree than either a guided bus system or a rail system.

Even if the objections raised above are not accepted as ruling out the idea of running non-guided buses down a railway track bed, the reduced speed of operation would mean that more vehicles were required than with the guided bus system thus putting up the capital cost of the vehicles. The system would also be less attractive to the passengers because of the increased journey time. Thus the guided bus system was seen as the main competitor to any rail-based system.

In theory a guided busway system should be able to provide a service rivalling that of a rail-based system, since the guided bus would not be subject to the constraints mentioned above for unguided buses enabling a high speed to be maintained even when vehicles are passing one another in confined spaces, e.g. tunnels. Thus the relative costs of the two systems need to be compared. However a note of caution was expressed since whilst the rail figures could be regarded as fairly accurate, the figures for guided busways were mainly based on manufacturer's claims regarding prices. which had the questionable assumption that the cost of the guidance system on the bus was small.

It was found that for the conversion of a double-track-km of existing non-electrified railway and for the frequency of service proposed that an LRT system worked out cheaper by £47,500 (expressed annually). Thus a busway would be more expensive despite the fact that there are doubts about its costs. The main reasons for this were twofold:
(1) To convert an already existing railway to a busway would cost £430 000 per double-track-km, whereas for an LRT system just the electrification cost (£75 000) is relevant.
(2) More buses and drivers were required than LRVs, and although buses were cheaper to build, the busway was still £3000 per double-track-km/annum more expensive.

The above assumed that a railway track existed and had to be removed in order to convert the railway into a busway. If no track existed then the capital cost of a km of busway would be decreased by £100 000 and that of a railway increased by £280 000. This would still mean that the railway was £9500 cheaper than the busway.

It was also considered that the soft nature of suspension of a road vehicle is not conducive to the carrying of standing passengers in large numbers at high speed. If the number of standees allowed per articulated bus (56) had to be reduced then the economics would make the rail option even more favourable. It was also by no means certain that passengers who would use a rail system would necessarily use a bus system. In Heidelberg when tram services were temporarily replaced by bus services during the construction of an underground section, patronage fell by 30%.

In the centre of Manchester, there could be no guided bus system without total segregation, since the guidance system stands up from the road bed, whereas a tramway is of course compatible with the normal road and footway system. The guided busway was therefore not considered further and the recommended system was therefore a light rail transit system with driving "on sight" in the street, but with railway-type signalling on the segregated sections.

TECHNICAL CONSIDERATIONS

The drawing and specifications of a light rail vehicle appended to the report were based on the Duewag Stadtbahn B 6-axle design which closely reflected the type of vehicle envisaged for Manchester's light rail system. All subsequent LRV illustrations, references and engineering designs were based on the same 6-axle configuration, which in practice turned out to be the configuration of the vehicles ultimately ordered for Metrolink.

During the early stages, of assessing LRT for Manchester, much information-gathering and evaluation was done by PTE officers looking at such matters as the dimensions of continental tram-only precincts, noise levels and environmental impact. However, no PTE retains in-house all the expertise or manpower necessary to pursue a wide-ranging project single-handed. To provide assistance with evaluating the various alternative options, the PTE engaged consultants to assist with detailed examination from engineering, environmental, economic, financial, general feasibility and development points of view.

Special attention was given to the light rail option which was already showing distinct promise. This thorough appraisal of all options was essential bearing in mind the undoubted magnitude of any emerging scheme, not to mention the coming need to present the Department of Transport with a watertight case seeking support. The resulting wide-ranging studies culminated in the production in 1983 and 1984 of at least fourteen special reports detailing the consultants' findings for the PTE.

LIGHT RAIL GAINS GROUND

Following publication of the Rail Study Group's First Report, the PTE proceeded to ask District Councils, adjoining local authorities and other organisations for their further views so that they could be taken into account before positively selecting a way forward. At the same time, consultation took place on County Structure Plan amendments related to the Rail Study Group's work.

Consultation of this kind had become second nature to Manchester's transport decision makers, perhaps more so than in any other part of the country. Herein lay one of the real secrets of success in bringing light rail to UK streets; politicians, businesses and interested members of the public were kept informed at every possible stage. They were wholeheartedly invited to question and criticise the proposals. That, perhaps more than anything else, is how such a trailblazing scheme ever got off the ground in the early days.

PUBLIC APATHY

It should not be thought for one moment that everyone who heard of the PTE's light rail proposals was instantly over the moon at the prospect of the tram's return. The truth was that the Manchester public had been fed on a bitter diet of failed public transport initiatives for at least two decades; to the average person in the street this was just another of them. A few years earlier, Picc-Vic had come so close to realisation that citygoers had started to become quite excited about it. They had felt badly let down when pro-road and cash-strapped Westminster deflated them by killing the scheme.

When, not very long afterwards, the idea of actually bringing rail vehicles into the streets was propogated by the Rail Study Group it wasn't surprising that most people didn't even bother to give it a second thought. What was the use? It was all pie-in-the-sky anyway, like the last time. This fortuitous lack of faith must surely have been a big factor in allowing the light rail proposals ever to reach three-dimensional reality substantially unopposed. After all, it's easy to vaguely enthuse about an idea when you don't remotely foresee your enthusiasm ever being tested by reality. Even as the rails went down in the streets the penny did not drop entirely in many minds; many people just didn't have a clue what was being introduced to their streets and only started to show a real interest as the poles and paving went in towards the conclusion of the on-street works.

Another and more positive factor which favoured light rail took the form of an emerging ecological awareness which, coupled with the success of pedestrianisation schemes in Market Street and St Ann's Square, generated desires for more progress in the same direction. Winning space from cars could obviously work, and light rail was the mode to do it like no other. These must have been the sort of ideas in decision-makers' minds when they were learning more about light rail and what it could mean to Manchester.

HORSES FOR COURSES

Metrolink's conception was conditioned by one crucial element — "Horses for Courses" — worth keeping foremost in the minds of all those charged with urban transport planning. In plain terms this meant that in order to justify choosing a particular solution, there had first of all to be a significant problem to which that solution was the best response. That is why so much care was taken by the Rail Study Group, in addressing the known problem, to examine all possible ways forward with the local rail system, including "do nothing".

A good analogy to the task facing the planners is that of a jigsaw with a missing piece. Light rail can be compared to a uniquely pliable medium able to fill many different gaps, but needing at the same time much more skill and hard work to accomplish the job neatly than would be the case with a more conventional or proprietary solution. It follows, of course, that there must exist a substantial enough hole in the jigsaw in the first place.

THE 1983 EUROPEAN STUDY VISIT

To give key people the chance to see light rail in action, the PTE organised a study tour to several continental light rail and tramway systems in the summer of 1983. The systems visited were Rotterdam, Utrecht, Köln, Düsseldorf, Essen, Karlsruhe, Rastatt, Freiburg and Zürich; it was felt that those places represented the best examples of various light rail practices within easy reach of the UK. The party, 19 strong, included representatives from the Rail Study Group as well as other GMC and City of Manchester Councillors and Officers together with an Under Secretary from the Department of Transport. A detailed 60-page report on the European study visit was published in September 1983.

Modes of operation looked at included street running, segregated and semi-segregated operation, pedestrianised areas and tunnels. The report covered every relevant aspect of operation, environmental intrusion, vehicles, safety, fares and ticketing, traffic control and interfacing, performance and financing, accessibility, implications for cyclists and so on. Undoubtedly the European Study Visit represented a major step forward by bringing back from the continent proof of light rail's credentials as well as lessons about how best to tackle related issues in Manchester. Useful by-products of this and later study visits were the photographs brought back by participants; some of these were used in later publicity brochures or for showing to interested parties to illustrate different facets of light rail operation or engineering.

Significant observations were made concerning operation in pedestrian areas; in Freiburg only three slight injuries had been recorded in over five years of operation, all involving pedestrians walking into the sides of stationary trams. Injuries due to pedestrians walking in front of moving trams were typically sustained by standing passengers on board emergency-stopping trams rather than by the errant pedestrians themselves.

In Utrecht the study tour participants saw the light rail system's new Swiss-built light rail vehicles. These vehicles were of the same configuration as those proposed for Manchester and they also happened to carry an uncannily similar orange livery to the one then envisaged for Manchester's LRVs. It was not surprising, then, that the Manchester party took a special interest in them and that subsequent artist's impressions bore a strong resemblance to the Utrecht vehicles.

1984 — THE RAIL STUDY GROUP'S SECOND REPORT

The Second Report of the Rail Study Group was published in January 1984 and was subtitled "Interim Report on the Preferred Strategy". There was no doubt about what the preferred strategy would be, for right there on the front cover was the now-familiar artist's impression of an LRV negotiating Market Street corner. The introduction to the Second Report explained that the findings of the Study Group, as published in the First Report, had been welcomed by the Department of Transport and widely endorsed locally.

The decision to further pursue the light rail option had been made by British Rail, the Greater Manchester Council and Greater Manchester PTE. One important attraction was the short construction period required by light rail when compared to other options. Other attributes were the high level of benefits coupled with relatively low capital costs and the ability to be progressively upgraded when necessary.

A group of City and County planners was set up to look at the development effects of LRT and published in December 1984 a report "LRT — The Development Effects". At the same time, Roger Tym and Partners were pursuing work on the attitudes of the business community to LRT as well as the potential effects in terms of improved shopping turnover.

RAIL NETWORK EXPANSION

Time has highlighted one singularly great additional benefit of the light rail option. This was that alignment-flexible LRT of the kind proposed by the Study Group would give the region an expanding local rail network physically able to keep pace with, and even influence, structural and economic developments in the county. By way

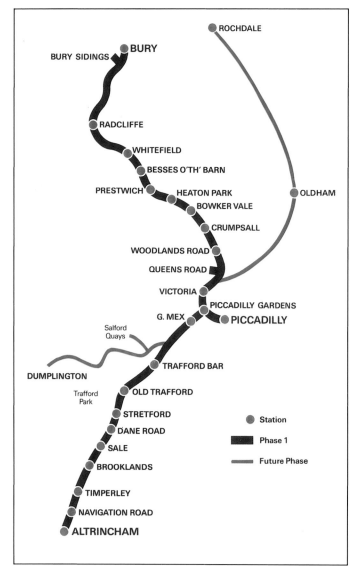

Map of Metrolink Phase 1 showing future extension plans.

of contrast, no one would seriously maintain that heavy rail passenger services could ever have been appropriate for the reinvigorated Trafford Park or Salford Quays, though it must be said that the Docks did in days gone by have a single passenger station to take patrons to the old Manchester Racecourse; the shallow tunnel which fed both the station and the Docks has since been obliterated.

Both Trafford Park and Salford Quays have now, as they enter new periods of vitality, the prospect of being well served by Metrolink. Similarly, Rochdale and Oldham could entertain no remote hope of ever securing heavy rail penetration into their town centres, yet both now have their sights set on street penetration by Metrolink rail vehicles in the not too distant future.

Meanwhile back in September 1983 further evaluation work was authorised to confirm light rail's cost/benefit superiority. Other continuing work would be the further investigation of possible tunnel routes so that they could be safeguarded if necessary, together with completion of preliminary planning for an LRT system. This further planning work would include settling details of alignments, deciding on the appropriate form of organization to run the system, and deciding on the powers and financial arrangements required to construct it.

CONSULTATION

The Second Report of the Rail Study Group included an important section detailing responses to the consultative exercises which had followed publication of the First Report and of the County Structure Plan Amendments. Although some respondents were plainly reluctant to let go of the Picc-Vic concept, the LRT option did receive majority support. Interestingly, it was in these responses to consultation that one saw the beginnings of moves to secure disabled access to the new system; initially there was no intention to provide it, even though the Tyne and Wear Metro already featured full accessibility and the Docklands Light Railway was shortly going to adopt it.

1984 – THE TRANSATLANTIC STUDY TOUR

Moving on to July 1984, GMC and GMPTE jointly published a report on a conference and associated study tour undertaken by GMC's Transportation Adviser to public transport undertakings in the USA and Canada. The report was entitled "Urban Public Transport in North America – an Expanding Public Social Service" – words which must have conjured visions of a public transport man's Mecca, of which more later. North America and Canada obviously merited further study.

Without further ado, a visit to the USA and Canada was organised in the Autumn of 1984 to build on the previous year's European study visit; the 7-day September/October study tour was undertaken by the Chairmen of the GMC Transportation Strategy and Passenger Transport Committees, GMC's Principal Transportation Adviser and Senior Transportation Planner and GMPTE's Director of Finance. The five participants visited Vancouver, Portland, Calgary, Edmonton, Toronto and Buffalo to study and compare issues as varied as transportation and financial policies, choice of transit system, rolling stock (including development and manufacture), network integration, fares and ticketing and – significantly – facilities for the disabled.

DISABLED ACCESS FACILITIES

Although clear signs were emerging that disabled friendliness was becoming obligatory on all new urban transport systems, the Study Group was still not entirely committed to it. The report of the transatlantic study tour, titled "Light Rail in Canada" and published in October 1984, concluded with the assertion that "For those who are confined to wheelchairs, the provision of a purpose designed midibus system as in the case of Toronto would seem to offer some significant advantages. The prevalence of this viewpoint at that time is not surprising when one reflects that even today there are those who steadfastly maintain that mass transit system design should not include access for people in wheelchairs. Nevertheless, the study tour report did include careful observations on LRT disabled access where the group had come across it.

One clear lesson learned was that dedicated disabled facilities like wayside or on-board wheelchair lifts were certainly not a good idea; apart from obstructing other passengers and being embarrassing to use, they seemed far too prone to failure and exposure to the weather as well as delaying the service. In Buffalo the study tour members had found something better in the form of new short high platforms for providing wheelchair access only to the leading entrance of LRVs. A year earlier, in Utrecht, the European study tour participants had observed LRT operation with full-length high platforms having small additional ramps to give roll-on roll-off access to the leading entrance only. The first glimmerings of Metrolink's novel profiled platforms were beginning to be implanted in decision-makers' minds.

ESSENTIAL INGREDIENTS FOR LRT SUCCESS

The public transport men from Manchester must have felt quite envious in the USA and Canada when they saw at first hand that admirable fiscal commitment to urban public transport prevalent abroad yet unknown in these islands, at least in recent times. This meant that the proportion of operating costs expected to be met from fares in the USA and Canada was as low as 42%; the report quoted for contrast the UK's typical fares ratio of 70% or more. How surprised the Manchester men would have been if they could at that time have foreseen the spectre of over 100% of Metrolink's Phase 1 operating costs being looked for from fares!

Other attributes of public transport policy noted in American and Canadian conurbations were: 100% public funding of capital costs, modal integration, through ticketing, parity fares regardless of mode, imaginative marketing, timed transfers and consistent long-term planning free of political oscillations. It will be interesting to observe to what extent, and when, these various desirable or essential features establish themselves in British cities as we approach the 21st Century.

The study tour participants noted that there had been few problems resulting from the reintroduction of rail operation to streets in North American and Canadian cities despite absences of many years. This augured well for Manchester because similar circumstances would apply there in due course. Contractual arrangements for bringing about system construction were also looked at, though nowhere was there to be found an example of the design, build, operate and maintain format later adopted in Manchester. However, one relevant point brought out in the study tour report was the need for strong project management during implementation.

▲ One extremely significant light rail development occurred during 1981 in the automobile-obessed USA, when a new system opened in San Diego, California. This view shows one of the Duewag cars operating along an attractive transit mall; the overhead wiring on this new system was commendably neat from the beginning. *Steve Palmer*

▶ Light rail in action; Amsterdam's Reguliersbreestraat, connecting Muntplein with Rembrandtsplein, is a pleasant place to be and it's an easy place to reach thanks to the three busy tram routes which operate along it amid contented pedestrians and cyclists. An important ingredient for success in these conditions is the use of the traditional tramway gong as the audible warning of approach. *Author*

▼ Newcastle's Tyne and Wear Metro, inaugurated in 1980, was the UK's first cautious venture into the world of light rail transit; this scene shows a Metro train at Whitley Bay. Compared with Manchester's Metrolink, Newcastle's Metro looks decidedly on the heavy side of the spectrum but its great success helped establish some of the principles on which Metrolink was founded, including mildly-subsidised public-sector operation and a high degree of organised integration with bus services. Deregulation was later to deny Manchester these important attributes. *The late Terrence Goulding*

3. THE PARLIAMENTARY BILLS

In this chapter we will look at events from 1984 onwards, including deposit of Manchester's first Light Rapid Transit Parliamentary Bills.

1984 – DEPOSIT OF THE FIRST BILL

A milestone was reached in November 1984 when GMPTE deposited in Parliament the UK's first modern Parliamentary Bill promoting on-street rail operation. A tramway is regarded at Common Law as a nuisance and it is therefore necessary to obtain the approval of Parliament to construct, maintain and operate one, in effect a very carefully-prescribed overriding of Common Law for one specific and localised purpose, itself just as carefully defined.

The Private Bill, entitled "The Greater Manchester (Light Rapid Transit System) Bill", sought powers for "the Greater Manchester Passenger Transport Executive to construct works and to acquire lands; to confer further powers on the Executive; and for other purposes". It was necessary to seek Parliamentary authority for various reasons, one of which was that the formal nature of the Parliamentary Private Bill procedure would give legitimately interested property owners and other parties due opportunity to register objections and to obtain amendment of the works or, alternatively, to be compensated for any loss resulting from the proposed measures.

Much of the Bill's content was concerned with giving precise details of the proposed city-centre alignments, referred to as tramroads off-highway and tramways on. Parliamentary plans were prepared to show the positions of the proposed alignments relative to streets, footways and structures. The limits of deviation on these plans were shown wide enough to include all affected properties and land; for the purposes of obtaining Parliamentary powers it was not necessary precisely to define track positions, which in any case had not been finally determined at that stage.

THE BILL'S CITY-CENTRE ALIGNMENTS

The chosen alignment through the city-centre was a compromise. There was a trade-off to be made between shoehorning the tracks into existing streets, with consequent sharp corners, or opting for gentler alignments requiring more property-take. An example is Market Street. By acquiring and demolishing properties adjacent to Tib Street, the light rail tracks could have been taken on a straight course out of Piccadilly Gardens towards Church Street to make a bee line onwards to Victoria by means of further demolition.

This is pure speculation, but there can be no doubt that the penalty of seeking to demolish a substantial number of buildings may well have been the complete loss of the Bill in Parliament. The end product, if ever there could have been one, would have been technically better in terms of providing a faster and less dynamically eventful ride, but the PTE had to practice the "art of the possible" and to go for the achievable but more contorted alternative, taking full advantage of LRT's pliability.

Another option would have been to use a short shallow tunnel to burrow beneath the environmentally sensitive, congested and busy Piccadilly Gardens and Parker Street bus station area. While being feasible technically, this would have cost more and could have required a longer and more disruptive implementation period than the adopted surface layout. Selective city-centre tunnelling does, however, remain an option for future consideration should it be thought necessary.

Also deposited in Parliament with the Bill was the Book of Reference, giving details of ownership and tenancies of all properties and lands affected by the proposals. Individual notices were issued to every person or organisation named in the Book of Reference to make sure that they had the opportunity to petition Parliament and register an objection to the Bill's provisions. Public notices were affixed to lamp posts along the alignment as well as being published in the local Press. Anyone interested enough was invited to inspect or purchase a copy of the Bill and to inspect the Parliamentary Plans and Book of Reference at the Town Hall or PTE offices.

THE BREADTH OF THE BILL

The Parliamentary Bill was comprehensive in its provisions, some of which referred to other relevant legislation such as the Tramways Act 1870, the Town and Country Planning Act 1971, the Public Health Act 1961, the Telecommunications Act 1984, the Public Passenger Vehicles Act 1981, the Road Traffic Regulation Act 1984, the Local Government Act 1974, the General Rate Act 1967, the Compulsory Purchase Act 1965, the Acquisition of Land Act 1981, the Lands Clauses Consolidation Act 1845 and the Transport Acts 1962 and 1968. These Acts have been quoted here to show what a minefield British legislation is to tramway promoters; all of them have some relevance to light rail in the street.

As far as the Tramways Act 1870 itself was concerned, Manchester's Bill sought to modify or disapply certain of the more anachronistic of the Act's provisions, though the ensuing Act actually gave the PTE the requisite powers under Section 1 of the Public Utilities and Street Works Act 1950 rather than under the Tramways Act. As an example of one of the pieces of legislation referred to in the Bill yet seeming unlikely at first to have much to do with tramways, the Public Health Act 1961 deals in Section 45 with "the affixing of apparatus to buildings for the purposes of street lighting"; Manchester's LRT Bill sought to widen that provision so as to include affixing "brackets, cables, wires and other apparatus required for the purpose of operating the light rapid transit system to any building or structure". In traditional tramway parlance this meant wall rosettes for overhead wire support, though today the fixings are made using less cumbersome devices.

THE THIRD REPORT OF THE RAIL STUDY GROUP

Once the Bill had been deposited in November 1984 the PTE and its Parliamentary Agents had anxiously to wait for objectors to petition Parliament. Meanwhile the Rail Study Group's Third Report "The Case for the Light Rapid Transit System" was published in November 1984, clearly showing the direction in which the studies were leading. Light Rail was gaining ground rapidly, and pressure was building up from the Districts for future extensions additional

---

Greater Manchester (Light Rapid Transit System)

ARRANGEMENT OF SECTIONS

PART I

PRELIMINARY

Section
1. Citation.
2. Interpretation.
3. Application of Part I of Compulsory Purchase Act 1965.

PART II

LIGHT RAPID TRANSIT SYSTEM

4. Power to make works.
5. Further works and powers.
6. Gauge of Works Nos. 1 to 10.
7. Power to deviate.
8. Subsidiary works for light rapid transit system.
9. Power to cross certain streets on the level.
10. Approval of Secretary of State.
11. Tramroads to be deemed tramways.
12. Application of Tramways Act 1870.
13. Temporary works may be made where necessary.
14. Alteration of works.
15. Works to be kept on level of surface of street.
16. Distance between passing vehicles when used on light rapid transit system.

to the proposed basic six-line network.

Penetrations of both Rochdale and Oldham town centres were proposed at this time, as well as extensions to New Mills and into Trafford Park. It must have been gratifying for GMC and GMPTE to receive so many requests for additional light rail services; certainly this indicated substantial endorsement of the Study Group's work so far.

The Third Report contained much evidence of the increasingly detailed work being done by the PTE and its consultants to maintain and accelerate progress. Evaluations reported on in the Third Report included demand forecasting for the various options, from which LRT emerged as the potentially most well-patronised non-tunnelled mode. Further planning and development evaluation had taken place as well as consideration of the assistance which an LRT scheme might bring to industry and employment. Detailed financial work was undertaken to quantify costs, savings and benefits of the options and to demonstrate to the Department of Transport that further expenditure on computer modelling, planning studies, financial evaluations and other scheme development work was justified.

FINE-TUNING THE ALIGNMENTS

The difficult city-centre section was the subject of careful attention, with special emphasis on the detailed planning of alignments especially where the LRT tracks would run adjacent to G-MEX from Lower Mosley Street up onto the railway viaducts taking them towards Cornbrook and Altrincham. It was at this stage that the conclusion was reached that it would not be necessary to safeguard any LRT tunnel alignments through the city centre because, if at some future date they were found necessary, the tunnelling work could be done without affecting properties.

Fine-tuning of surface track positions was possible within the limits of deviation embodied in the Parliamentary plans, but at the same time deposit of the plans had frozen the light rail route within those limits regardless of any better alignment opportunities which might arise before the implementation stage.

The Third Report of the Rail Study Group also set out the PTE's future programme, aimed at opening by 1989 of the first stage to Bury and Altrincham including the city-centre section. Before that a second Bill was to be deposited in November 1985, dealing with Phase 1 works outside the regional centre, and the Government would have to be approached for grant aid. Specifications and designs would be developed and it was envisaged that initial orders for rolling stock would be placed in Autumn 1986 for delivery from 1988 onwards, and that civil engineering contracts for works in Central Manchester and on the Altrincham line would be placed in 1987.

GATHERING MOMENTUM

The reader might be forgiven for wondering by what process light rail had gained ground so strongly in Manchester. First of all there was firm and unswerving cross-party support for the retention of local railways; their loss was foreseen as a certain blow if nothing was done to avert it. At the same time, LRT was being seen as a way of breaking out of the shackles of seemingly uncontrollable Section 20 local railway support expenditure.

In addressing the problems, the Rail Study Group had been seen to be meticulous in examining all options before recommending surface-operating light rail, a decision which received strong county-wide support in a succession of council resolutions which reflected widespread acceptance of the Study Group's findings. The light rail proposals were being borne along by this support and it was the duty of GMC and the PTE to respond positively in the way they did, by pursuing light rail as the preferred way forward.

Even when it was becoming clear that light rail implementation was going to be an uphill struggle, decision-makers persevered with it. Faced with strong signs that Westminster-imposed conditions and constraints might adulterate Phase 1 (Bury—Altrincham) to some extent, they took the pragmatic view that without the initial phase there would be no future phases, better-executed or not.

Even if Phase 1 should turn out in the short term to be a poisoned chalice, the chalice itself was worth coveting for future use even if its contents might for a time put local public transport out of sorts and cause a few temporary grimaces. At least the chalice itself could one day be polished up and used in a better way.

LIGHT RAIL'S LONG TERM PROMISE

Light rail technology had a unique long-term ability to fulfil Manchester's special requirements and this gave it a sure edge over the other options. The light rail proposals were further strengthened and complemented by "Centreplan", a GMC-inspired scheme which had its origins in the Inner Relief Road Working Group (IRRWIG, pronounced "earwig") back in the mid-70s, followed by the Central Manchester Traffic Plan. After Market Street's pedestrianisation in 1980, further progress was made with pedestrianisation, bus priorities and the reduction and channelling of through traffic in the city centre. These initiatives are important because they set the scene for light rail installation in the improved city centre.

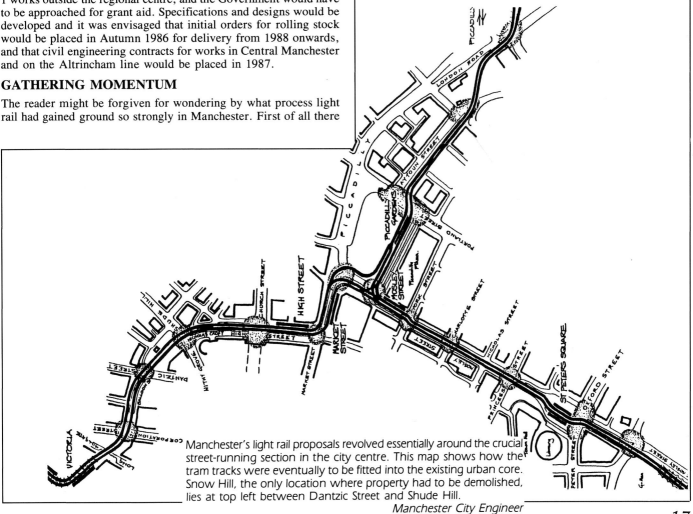

Manchester's light rail proposals revolved essentially around the crucial street-running section in the city centre. This map shows how the tram tracks were eventually to be fitted into the existing urban core. Snow Hill, the only location where property had to be demolished, lies at top left between Dantzic Street and Shude Hill.

Manchester City Engineer

Other factors were beginning to strengthen commitment to light rail as the best alternative to the grim "do nothing" option. Whatever the system would do in direct terms for labour force mobility, economic activity and so on, there was an increasing recognition of the good that it could do to Manchester's image as a modern, ecological, vibrant and pleasant place in which to work, shop, stay, live or be entertained. This was one of the aspects the study tour participants couldn't help noticing when visiting overseas cities served by light rail.

Another important attribute of light rail noted on the study tours was its outstanding disabled-friendliness, which accorded well with Manchester's increasing commitment to the needs of mobility-impaired people. To round off its eligibility, light rail would bring all this to reality sooner than other options because of the speed of implementation characteristically associated with it.

THE END OF THE SALAD DAYS

And so ended the salad days of Manchester's light rail transit proposals. Now the real hard work was about to begin. A trailblazing light rail Bill would have to be nursed through Parliament, and exhaustive supplications made to the Government for Section 56 funds. Many hurdles would be erected and would have to be cleared, and to cap it all the dark storm cloud of bus deregulation was looming on the horizon in late 1984, along with the prospect of abolition of the Metropolitan Counties, including GMC.

PETITIONERS AGAINST THE FIRST BILL

As 1984 gave way to 1985 all eyes were on Westminster, anxiously waiting to see how many petitioners would be objecting to the on-street light rail Bill, published on December 4th 1984. In the event, four objectors lodged petitions against the Bill in the House of Lords, where it was introduced on 16th January 1985. Three of them were property owners. In addition, Second House Undertakings were given to a further three objectors; these are referred to later.

This remarkably low incidence of objections to what was after all a new on-street city-centre rail system is a tribute to the quality of work done by the PTE, its engineering consultants (Mott, Hay and Anderson, now Mott Macdonald) and its Parliamentary Agents (Dyson Bell & Co) and, it has to be said, an indication of some lack of faith amongst the public that the proposals would ever come to anything. Parliamentary powers wouldn't guarantee construction; after all, an Act of Parliament had been obtained to construct and operate Picc − Vic and then the Castlefield Curve not so very long before, and had not altered the face of the city very much. The position is summed up delightfully well by a misprint in a report which said that the first Bill "had remarkably little opposition and achieved almost *anonymous* public support".

The PTE duly compensated the three property-owning petitioners sufficiently for them to withdraw their objections, preferring this course rather than risking any further lengthening of the time taken

◄ This May 1989 view shows the row of small businesses occupying the Shude Hill frontages of the only group of buildings demolished specifically for Metrolink. The remaining properties in this area, many of them in poor condition, are now threatened by the massive new Shude Hill Development; this is destined to be served by a station on Snow Hill, named after a tiny street which emerged onto Shude Hill through an archway to the right of this picture. The loss of traditional premises like these began with the Arndale Centre's construction in the early '70s. Today's tramway alignment passes roughly through the site of the amusement arcade (right of centre). *Author*

◄ Perhaps the most sensitive site affected by the light rail proposals was that occupied by the Cenotaph in St Peter's Square. It can be argued that a public transport system accessible to everyone is not a morally inappropriate neighbour for a war memorial, but not everyone saw things in that light. This scene shows the 1991 British Legion Service of Remembrance, the last held there before Metrolink arrived on the scene shortly afterwards. The 1992 Remembrance Service established modified arrangements wherein the parades are concentrated on the far side of the memorial site away from the neatly-installed profiled platforms, which do duty for the occasion as band platforms. *Author*

for the Bill to pass through Parliament. The fourth objection came from a the Greater Manchester Transport Action Group, a local transport pressure group affiliated to 'TRANSPORT 2000' whose members, while not objecting to light rail in principle, lamented the loss of Picc – Vic to such an extent that to disrupt the Parliamentary progress of its railed public transport successor seemed to them a legitimate course of action. This group held that proper consultation had not taken place before drawing up and depositing of the Bill, and that the Parliamentary Bill procedure itself did not in isolation give local people adequate opportunity to make representations.

In its petition the group picked out various details of the Bill and challenged them as well as calling into question the whole feasibility of street operation, which had already been approved in principle by bodies as august as the Railway Inspectorate of the Department of Transport and the local highway authority. To some this petition must have seemed like a rancorous boat-rocking exercise.

The group persisted until May 1986 when it was made clear to them that, not having property or rights affected by the proposals, they quite simply did not have locus standi (in other words a legitimate right) to petition against it in the first place. This denial of the right to make a representation did perhaps form the real substance of the group's protest, but GMPTE had to work within existing law and procedures and at the same time resist any further expensive lengthening of the already drawn-out Parliamentary process.

1986 – THE SECOND BILL CATCHES UP WITH THE FIRST

Eventual withdrawal of the last of the petitions allowed the Bill to reach the unopposed Committee stage on 15th May 1986, coincident with the arrival at that stage of the second Bill, dealing with work on the Bury and Altrincham lines. This Bill had been deposited in November 1985, a year later than the first Bill; the reason for its quicker progress was that it had attracted no petitions at all. The wisdom of the PTE and its advisors in depositing the pioneering first Bill a year earlier than the simpler second one had been neatly proven in practice.

MORE PETITIONS

Unfortunately though, all was not over on the objections front. When the interesting first Bill went to the Commons for its second reading, three more petitions were lodged against it. These three were from the objectors who had been given Second House Undertakings by the PTE when the Bill was in the Lords, and they were not as straightforward as the original three. One of the petitions was from the owners of property on London Road past which the light rail tracks would be installed; this particular objection was met by the PTE's agreeing to provide alternative access to the premises.

Another objection was jointly lodged on behalf of the owners of the Midland Hotel (now the Holiday Inn Crowne Plaza Midland Hotel) and the owners of G-MEX; this expressed concern about questions both of access and of possible noise from trams. The owners of G-MEX insisted on retaining the use at all times of one or other of their two Lower Mosley Street underground car park accesses during construction of the light rail ramp; they were subsequently satisfied with an appropriate guarantee from GMPTE.

The Midland Hotel's owners for their part were concerned about light rail's permanent effect on access for deliveries to their kitchens from Lower Mosley Street. Their objection was resolved when the PTE undertook to contribute half the costs of tranferring the kitchen access facilities to the other side of the building. As far as worries about noise were concerned, reassurances were given that the street tracks would be embedded in a polymer material with proven noise-reducing properties, and also that it was intended to include noise-reducing techniques in the G-MEX ramped viaduct structure.

The third petition was from the owners of the Snow Hill site, through which the tracks leading to Victoria station would pass; the most positive of the lot, this petition sought an additional stopping place within the site, which was scheduled for redevelopment. Naturally the PTE was anxious to accede to such an overture, and the Snow Hill tracks have been constructed so as to allow for a future station; hence the sharp hump at the Dantzic Street end of the site. In September 1991 plans were revealed for a futuristic £100 million shopping precinct, mall, leisure and office development on the site. There will also be a galleria and internal gardens plus an impressive dome. Metrolink will pass right through the middle of the development and there will be a station serving the whole complex.

Meanwhile, further towards the city centre on High Street, there was a building adjacent to Bridgewater Place, 20 – 22 High Street, which while not being directly in the way of the light rail alignment did have a rearward section protruding into a back street needed for department store delivery access when Bridgewater Place itself at its junction with High Street subsequently became blocked off by a light rail platform.

The PTE's Property Services department purchased the building, initially with the idea of knocking it down. However, the building lay within a conservation area and the City Planning Department would not allow it to be demolished. Happily, though, it has since proved possible to remove the obstructing rear five metres of the structure while retaining the main building with its attractive stone facade. Now the basement of the building will be used as an equipment room for Metrolink's adjacent High Street station; the ground floor reverted in August 1991 to occupancy by its former tenants – an amusement caterer.

During the passage of the Bills through Parliament, a number of Undertakings were given by the PTE to statutory bodies (British Telecom, North West Gas, North West Electricity and so on) owning buried plant in the streets and to other interested parties including BR, the GMC, and the City of Manchester. These formal Undertakings were put in place to protect the interests of the bodies concerned. An assurance was given by GMPTE to Mr Andrew Bennett MP in respect of his concern, relating to the No 2 Bill, that several measures would be put in place relating to the cessation of conventional train services on the Altrincham line.

1988 – ROYAL ASSENT

Both the first and second Bills received Royal Assent, and went onto the Statute Book as Acts of Parliament, on 9th February 1988. The first Bill had taken over three precious years to plod through the machinery of Parliament, longer even than the PTE must have anticipated. The rewards made all the waiting, negotiating and compensating worthwhile, for now the PTE had powers to construct, maintain, and operate its own light rail system. Empowering a public body to be a transport owner and operator must have badly choked the champions of bus deregulation but not to worry, that irritation could be sorted out by means of strings to the capital grant aid which the PTE would have to ask for in order to build the system.

THE AUTHOR

David Holt has taken an active supporting interest in Manchester's Metrolink scheme since its inception over nine years ago, having been particularly anxious to see that important lessons from the past and from elsewhere would not be ignored or overlooked especially with regard to safety in the city centre. To this end and he has taken part in the work of formally-constituted consultative committees and he has often written about the scheme either in a reporting or campaigning capacity. His own practical experience with tramways stretches back over thirty years with particular emphasis on tramway tracklaying at the National Tramway Museum, Crich, on which tramway he has held a full driving licence for the past 25 years. His first paid job on leaving school was as a tram driver on the seafront Eastbourne tramway, which he afterwards helped to reinstate at Seaton in Devon. His is married and has two children. His long-term employment as a British Telecom engineer based in the centre of Manchester has enabled him to closely observe Metrolink's construction, commissioning and operational phases and he joins with the Published in warmly welcoming the return of the tram to Britain's city streets and in wishing Metrolink every success. He has been the Light Rail Transit Association's Honorary Development Officer since 1986.

4. GRANT APPLICATION

MAKING A CASE FOR GOVERNMENT GRANT

Section 56 of the Transport Act 1968 provides for the making of grants by the Department of Transport towards the capital costs of new public transport infrastructure projects. Examples of Section 56 grants made before Manchester's July 1985 application were those which had gone towards construction of the Tyne and Wear Metro and the creation of Liverpool's Merseyrail system.

Rules governing eligibility for Section 56 grant are applied and kept under review by the Department of Transport; generally they mean that half the eligible cost of a qualifying scheme is met directly by central government and the other half is channelled from central government through local budgets subject always to a sufficient level of funds from the exchequer being made available by the Treasury to the Department of Transport. This latter is a point at which national politics and transport professionalism crucially interface with each other.

To be eligible for Section 56 grant aid, projects have to represent a substantial addition or improvement to local public transport facilities and need to be significant enough regionally and nationally for it to be reasonable to spread the cost beyond local sources. The most that Manchester could look for from Central Government under the prevailing rules was half the eligible cost of its scheme.

The PTE's application of July 1985 was for Section 56 funds to assist with the £42.5m projected capital cost of Phase 1 of the light rail scheme, the Bury and Altrincham lines having been found to represent the strongest case for early LRT conversion. The funds applied for were to go towards the cost of the following works:
- Conversion to LRT of the Bury and Altrincham lines.
- Construction of new track and overhead line between Cornbrook Junction and G-MEX.
- Construction of an underpass at Cornbrook.
- Renovation of structures, especially the Cornbrook to G-MEX viaduct.
- Preliminary diversion of statutory undertakers' services in the city centre.
- Various enabling works off the line of route in the city centre including traffic management and minor highway schemes.
- Modification to the computerised traffic control system.
- Construction of new track, overhead and seven stations in the city centre both on and off street.
- Installation of a 750 V d.c. power supply and distribution system covering the entirety of the Phase 1 routes.
- Provision of an adequate number of light rail vehicles to operate the Phase 1 system.
- Provision of all communications, signalling, fare collection and surveillance equipment.
- Construction of an operational centre and maintenance depot.

Some very detailed work had had to be done to put together the grant application. At the time of the evaluation, Section 56 was not the mechanism actually in use for applying government grants; the setting up of the County Councils in 1974 had featured the establishment of a system of block grants and supplementary grants serving the same purpose in a slightly different way.

THE ECONOMIC APPRAISAL

The criteria for securing these grants were based on proven and objective evaluation techniques. Manchester's economic appraisal had therefore consisted of a relatively straightforward social cost/benefit analysis exercise looking at the totality of the local public transport scene with and without the projected six-line light rail network. This comprehensive approach was possible because at the time the PTE still had the ability to directly manage county-wide bus and local rail services so as to make the best use of them for the community's benefit. Deregulation changed all that.

The economic appraisal was done by W.J. Tyson, the PTE's consultant transport economist, using the Greater Manchester countywide transportation model. This used a set of known parameters against which a range of theories, hypotheses and options could be analysed and tested using computer technology; it had been built up and refined over the years in the light of changing statistics, observed trends and known effects of previous influences.

Using the model, the effects of widely-differing policies could be predicted; thus the likely consequences of such diverse scenarios as complete loss of the local rail system or total implementation of all conceivable light rail routes might be foreseen in the most accurate terms possible. Further refining of the parameters during modelling enabled more accurate results to be obtained, resulting as it happened in higher benefits being identified than would have been revealed by the unimproved model. Throughout the evaluation processes there was continual dialogue with the Department of Transport aimed at maximising mutual understanding.

The analysis took into account the benefits of light rail implementation for users of converted rail services, the benefits to users transferring from other forms of personal and public transport (modal shift), the benefits and disbenefits to users remaining on other modes, and light rail's known ability to stimulate completely new journeys (generated traffic). Stated preference analysis techniques were used to find out in what way users would choose between two example journeys having different characteristics in terms of riding times, walking times, waiting times, interchanges, fares and so on. Different fare levels could be tested in this way to establish, for example, projected resistance to high fares. The benefits of light rail implementation were thus quantified not by guesswork or wishful thinking but by the use of sophisticated and accurate techniques.

On the other side of the coin, the disbenefits of retaining unchanged or of closing existing local railways were looked at against the lower cost of those unattractive options. Later on, life after closure was amply demonstrated to the public during protracted changeover shutdown periods on both the Bury and Altrincham lines. One of the principal yardsticks used in studies was the value of individuals' time; as a result of research work done by the Department of Transport, the monetary value of travelling time was increased by 25% during the evaluation process. This again improved the performance prospects of the light rail option, one of the special strengths of which was the speeding-up of net door-to-door journey times.

THE PTE'S APPLICATION FOR GRANT AID

The PTE's Section 56 application document set out the background to the rail strategy study and the results of the PTE's evaluations, research and surveys into the different options. Projected timescales for light rail implementation were given, suggesting 1989 as a target for opening Phase 1. There was a section dealing with possible corporate structures based on work done by consultants Kleinwort Benson, recommending that an LRT operating company should be wholly owned by the PTE; subsequently, the Government denied Manchester this option but let South Yorkshire adopt it for their Supertram scheme.

Further sections of the application dealt with the projected business and development impact, and there were relevant maps and other appendices listing reports and documents and giving technical information about the light rail proposals. It is interesting to note that the brief description of the vehicles mentioned the possibility of adopting low floors or varying platform heights to minimise boarding step heights.

Another appendix set out the overwhelmingly-supportive views of district councils, BR and other bodies, and full coverage was given to individual groups' feelings about the selected light rail option. Some groups gave their support conditionally; thus the Light Rail Transit Association supported the scheme in principle and expressed a desire for continuing dialogue during its development.

Recognising that "there's many a slip 'twixt cup and lip", members of the Association with wide experience of light rail and tramway systems knew only too well how dependent any UK light rail revival was going to be on experiences with the pioneering Manchester scheme. From the LRTA's point of view it was imperative for it to be implemented as a centre of British light rail excellence.

▶ Bury Interchange was constructed by GMPTE as part of the Picc-Vic scheme, and now forms the northernmost terminus of Metrolink; Altrincham Interchange, at the other end of the system, gained its adjoining bus station facilities in the same way, as did Whitefield, Piccadilly Gardens, at the centre of the system, features established interchange facilities on a much larger scale. The deregulating Transport Act 1985 and the consequent loss of opportunities for planned integration and (so far) through ticketting now deprives Mancunians of the full benefits offered by these past initiatives. This view taken from the East Lancashire Railway's new Heywood line overbridge, shows Metrolink Car No 1005 negotiating the scissors crossover at Bury Interchange on 6th April 1992; the bus station is in the background. *P. Renard*

SUMMARY OF THE SECTION 56 SUBMISSION

Because the Section 56 submission marked such an important milestone and condensed such a lot of work into one volume, it is worth quoting its conclusions in full:

(i) The local rail network represents a major transportation asset, but in its present form is expensive, underutilised, and has suffered from lack of investment.

(ii) A number of previous schemes to develop a coherent local rail network have failed to reach implementation, primarily because they would have required very large capital resources.

(iii) Recognising the need for positive action, the Rail Strategy Study was set up to evaluate a number of options ranging from major capital investment in conventional rail to closure of local lines.

(iv) An effective local rail network is an important element in achieving the five themes of the County's Structure Plan which are supported and endorsed by the Secretary of State for the Environment

(v) The need for economic regeneration of a substantial part of the County has been recognised in the creation of the Inner City Partnership and the Assisted Areas.

(vi) Planning of local rail options has been designed to complement BR Inter-City proposals, but not to be dependent on them. BR's commercial freight activities would not be inhibited.

(vii) Local rail development is consistent with PTE objectives for bus/rail integration to provide better service for passengers with more cost effective use of available resources.

(viii) Rail already accounts for a significant proportion of journeys to the Regional Centre. There is considerable potential to increase this proportion, and to attract other local or cross conurbation journeys.

(ix) This study has considered a wide range of possible public transport modes including Light Rapid Transit with tunnel or surface cross-city links, Busway, Guided Busway, Automated Rapid Transit and Conventional Rail.

(x) The detailed evaluation has compared the lowest capital cost option, LRT, against an existing rail base and a 'no-rail' all-bus base.

(xi) The financial evaluation shows that the lowest financial cost is achieved by the all-bus option, but that all LRT stages of the first phase assessed have lower operating deficits than existing rail. The first phase LRT would give a net financial gain to the PTE of £6.5 million, assuming 50% grant.

(xii) The economic evaluation of LRT (with surface cross-city links) shows that the first phase (Bury – Manchester City Centre – Altrincham) gives a positive net present value (NPV) and a good benefit to cost ratio compared to either the 'existing rail' base or the 'all bus' Base. For each intermediate stage, the NPV is still positive compared to the 'existing rail' base.

(xiii) Some environmental problems could arise with LRT surface operation but these should not be significant provided adequate ameliorating measures are taken.

(xiv) LRT would encourage development of a range of land uses, especially in the Regional Centre.

(xv) Surveys of businesses indicate strong support for LRT to attract both staff and customers.

(xvi) The LRT proposal is strongly supported by District Councils, and a wide range of other interested bodies.

(xvii) The project can be phased at a rate consistent with available resources. If Parliamentary Powers and Capital Grants were obtained by the end of 1985, the first phase could be operational by 1989 with a full network possibly in the early 1990s.

(xviii) The recommended structure for an LRT operating company is a wholly-owned subsidiary company of the PTE.

Finally the submission drew attention to the benefits which the development of LRT technology at home could bring to British industry, referring to the strong interest in the Manchester proposals demonstrated by civil, mechanical, electrical, rolling stock and traction equipment manufacturers, consultants and contractors.

SHIFTING THE GOALPOSTS

Until the two Parliamentary Bills relating to Phase 1 received Royal Assent and were enacted it was procedurally impossible for the Department of Transport to do anything other than scrutinise the Section 56 grant application and consider its implications. The reason for the application's mid-1985 timing was that the PTE needed to expedite matters in order to keep the project on target for early completion. It was hoped that the granting of Parliamentary Powers, then expected in the very near future, would be followed very soon afterwards by the final "go-ahead" in the form of the granting of the Section 56 application for funding assistance.

NEW OBSTACLES

Unfortunately things did not go quite in accordance with this optimistic plan. Coincident with enactment of the Transport Bill in October 1985 the Department of Transport issued, only three months after GMPTE had filed its grant application, a circular setting out new arrangements for making Section 56 grants. The circular ran over some unchanged basic rules for qualifying for grant, but set forth some demanding new ones. Applicants now had to show that their proposed scheme would be compatible with deregulation of bus services, scheduled to take effect in October 1986. Demand forecasts now had to take into account competing bus services and the fare levels likely to prevail under deregulation.

Until deregulation, the PTEs had used their executive power to integrate bus and rail services, thereby making the best use of each mode. This would no longer be possible after October 1986; the bus industry was to be thrown open to the free market. Loss of the professionally-structured approach to local transport provision which continues to characterise the most successful overseas systems threatened to remove one of the very cornerstones of the modern urban light rail concept – that of making the best use, by means of integration, of every technically useful urban transport mode.

The Transport Act 1985 effectively legislated against integration, co-ordination and co-operation; what effect would this have on Manchester's light rail proposals, based substantially as they were on experience of European and American systems clearly displaying all the best integrated urban transport principles?

◀ Ready for the "Off"; the reality of deregulation in High Street on 17th March 1992; Metrolink's car No 1004, seen here on driver training duties, lines up with a GM Buses "Centreline" and a Finglands bus, both of which compete with Metrolink in the city centre at less than half the tram's city-centre fare. For longer distances, Metrolink competes much more attractively, especially in terms of return and off-peak travel.   *Author*

Manchester's transport planners and their advisers and consultants had found it hard to believe that deregulation would be passed in all its raw extremity by Parliament. Now the stark reality of the new legislation meant that they had to begin all over again with their evaluation process, adapting their techniques to reflect post-deregulation conditions. Modelling was now concentrated on the Bury—Manchester—Altrincham Phase 1 corridor, widened to take in existing and likely future bus operations which might potentially feed the light rail routes.

Stated preference techniques were now used to analyse the effects of light rail fare levels pitched 20% above and below parity with bus fares; this new analysis showed that fares could go 15% above parity before passengers would start to migrate to competing bus services.

INTEGRATION — THE VITAL INGREDIENT

The deployment of bus services as suburban distributors for fast, dependable, comfortable, high-capacity rail "spine" routes has long been an essential feature of any truly efficient local transport system; the Tyne and Wear Metro was in the early '80s a fresh example of such a system, playing a key role in attracting no fewer than 70% of the population onto public transport at least once a week.

Plenty of fine examples of such integration were to be found overseas, notably in Utrecht where light rail inauguration had coincided with deliberate restructuring of bus routes to focus on outlying "Sneltram" stations rather than continuing to run inefficiently all the way from the suburbs to the city centre. Each mode was employed according to its abilities and the public responded by transferring in large numbers from private to public transport; when Utrecht's single-operator integrated light rail and bus system came on stream in December 1983 serving Nieuwegein and Ijsselstein it attracted 20% more passengers to public transport than the previous buses had been doing.

Whatever might have been said in favour of bus deregulation, it did not at first seem likely to foster cooperation between bus companies and a new light rail system. Competing for profit in a difficult marketplace, bus operators were going to have their work cut out even to survive independently for any length of time, let alone earn worthwhile surpluses. The publicly-capitalised establishment of light rail, a superior mode of transport which might attract people away from privatised buses, was hardly calculated to endear itself to those who had devised and implemented deregulation. It could even be projected that in the most uncompromisingly extreme deregulated environment it would be quite inappropriate to introduce light rail at all.

One conceivably bleak scenario was that private bus operators would embark on a ritual of cut-throat competition with light rail by introducing special bus routes parallelling and undercutting light rail services. GMPTE's projections and previous experience indicated, however, that bus operators would in reality find it impossible to compete effectively with rail and would be far more likely in time to restructure their routes to feed light rail in the suburbs. This was later borne out in Newcastle where, after three unsettled years of slugging competition, bus companies joined the Metro in a new joint through ticketing scheme in 1988.

The re-establishment in Newcastle of a degree of integration between privatised buses and a lightly-subsidised light rail system publicly owned and operated meant that while bus operating companies' costs remained substantially unchanged, their revenues went up. Buses were on the move earning money in the suburbs rather than crawling along wastefully in traffic jams in the city centre. Any increase in total public transport patronage due to integration was bound to benefit all astute operators of public transport services whether bus, rail or taxi.

This fundamental truth relating to the competitive reaction of bus companies came through in GMPTE's light rail evaluation process. Subsequently the PTE's findings about the public's preference for stable rail services was proved correct; local train patronage went up significantly when passengers turned away from flitting newly-deregulated buses. Coupled with increases in the cost of running the existing increasingly-unreliable subsidised rail network this gave the case for light rail a continuing robustness.

THE NANTES STUDY VISIT

Now that the Section 56 submission had been made and Parliamentary powers were being sought, the light rail proposals seemed to be gaining substance. Increasing attention had to be directed at the practicalities of bringing into service a new LRT system. To gain first hand knowledge and benefit from others' experiences, a group of Councillors and officers undertook a study visit in late 1985 to Nantes, where a completely new modern tramway had been opened the previous February.

The group paid special attention to all those features of the new system which related closely to the Manchester proposals, including: tramway alignment, traffic management, pedestrian safety, vehicle safety, traffic control, track and overhead, stations, fixed equipment, street furniture, rolling stock, depot facilities, design philosophy, public involvement, publicity and marketing, tram operations and signalling, tramway infrastructure maintenance, bus services, fares system and, finally, provision for the mobility impaired.

As in the European and North American study visits, special attention was paid to possible worries about unsightly overhead wiring equipment in the streets. The techniques and design work which had ensured minimal intrusion in Nantes were carefully noted for future reference. In common with the other study visits, the integrated fare collection system with parity fares across different modes was also noted.

At the time of the Nantes study visit it was known that the definitive French standard tram being developed for the Grenoble system was to be a low-floor development of the standard-floor-height Nantes vehicles. This trend towards catering on mass transit systems for less mobile customers had obvious implications for Manchester which were not lost on the study visit participants.

The Nantes Study Visit Report, published in December 1985, summarised the lessons learned for Greater Manchester as follows:
(a) Provided close attention is paid to environmental aspects and detailed design and traffic management a modern tramway can be introduced successfully within existing highway alignments.

The new Nantes tramway, visited by a Manchester study party in October 1985, demonstrated many of the features desired for Metrolink, with the notable exception of disabled accessibility. This scene, on 17th June 1985, shows one of the articulated trams calling at Souillarderie. Nantes is now in the process of fitting its cars with low-floor centre-sections.   *Bob Manders*

(b) Special attention should be paid to the needs of pedestrians, cyclists and the disabled.

(c) Junctions should be signalled with turning movements across the LRT track signalled separately and with the LRT linked into the Urban Traffic Control (UTC) system to maintain reliability.

(d) The public should be involved in the selection of livery, fixtures and fittings of the rolling stock to ensure the vehicles have the greatest possible acceptance in pedestrian areas and confined spaces.

(e) The public should be kept well informed about progress in the design and construction of the project, using high grade publicity material.

(f) Features of the light rail system, such as wayside ticket machines, should be tested in local use before introducing LRT, to gauge public attitudes and response to them.

(g) Co-ordination of bus and tram services can produce an attractive and rapid alternative to through bus services, even where tramway load factors are high.

(h) Revenue collection and accounting processes can be greatly simplified by adopting a simple transfer ticketing arrangement based on few fare values.

(i) Passenger flow and boarding times can be greatly improved if concessionary fares are purchased off-vehicle, through ticket machines or agencies.

(j) Successful conurbation-wide public transport provision can only be achieved through co-operation by all local authorities in the area.

In retrospect it is interesting to consider to what extent officers and members have been able to carry through the many fine ideas brought back from this and other study visits. What is clearly demonstrated by this and preceding reports is an optimistic resolve to do everything possible to secure for Manchester a high quality light rail system implemented in a manner which would secure its lasting popularity. Subsequently this resolve was to be frustrated in several respects; to give just one example, the very idea of emulating customary European and American practice by actually subsidising the operation as well as the building of a new and technologically-competitive means of transport was branded distinctly anti-market under the new deregulated regime.

GMC'S ABOLITION

As well as the deregulating Transport Act, another piece of unhelpful legislation which went onto the statute book in 1985 was the Local Government Act, which abolished the Metropolitan Counties. The Greater Manchester Council had developed the light rail proposals and brought the scheme to the Parliamentary approval and grant submission stage. Now GMC was set to be abolished in March 1986.

Abolition when it came disrupted progress with the light rail scheme for a short time while the transition took place to the new Passenger Transport Authority which was a joint board made up of 32 elected members — 3 from each of the ten districts with the exception of Manchester which as lead authority has 5 PTA members. One of the first resolutions made by the new PTA was to affirm unanimous support for the continuing development of the light rail proposals. The PTA has maintained this strong commitment to LRT through trying times ever since.

When the PTA took over responsibility for public transport policy in 1986, two Manchester light rail Bills were slowly passing through Parliament and a perfectly sound case for Section 56 support had been put to the Department of Transport. By all that is reasonable and honourable, everything should have come together shortly afterwards to ensure quick placing of implementation contracts. Instead, there now began an unpardonable two years' delay imposed on the scheme's promoters while they danced attendance on Westminster's cross-grained obsession with deregulation.

5. PUBLIC RELATIONS

The introduction of rail vehicles into the streets of a British city after 42 years' absence with no home precedents must rank as a big public relations challenge by any standards. Selling the light rail concept to decision-makers and to the Manchester public has been just one of the major tasks undertaken by GMPTA and GMPTE. Something of the way in which light rail for Manchester gained credibility and acceptance has already been mentioned; let us now have a look at some of the more concrete ways in which public endorsement has been cultivated.

PUBLICITY MATERIAL

As we saw in Chapter 2, the Passenger Transport Executive had taken care during the development of the light rail proposals to involve interested groups and bodies through consultation. With a pioneering city-centre street-based transport system — "trains in the street" to some — it was vital to ensure that nothing was being seen to be done behind closed doors.

At an early stage a light rail promotional film was commissioned by the PTE from Multivision Ltd, a local video production company. The film featured Tomorrow's World presenter William Woollard,

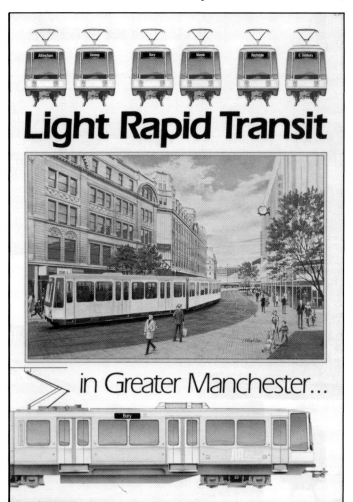

This attractive brochure was produced by GMPTE as the light rail proposals gathered momentum. The destination displays on the top six trams underline the fact that Phase 1 was always intended to provide the first two routes of a comprehensive network, though the system's growth may now be in other directions (see Chapter 15). The artist's impression, looking along Market Street from Piccadilly Gardens, shows orange-liveried articulated units passing under unobtrusive overhead wiring, with no buses in sight. The BR yellow-end treatment has been made unnecessary by the permanent use of headlights.   *GMPTE*

who was sent over to Holland at considerable expense with a camera crew to obtain Amsterdam and Utrecht tram footage. The editing of the film was excellent, answering in words and pictures many of the concerns felt about light rail by ordinary people. For example, one recurringly popular theme amongst the public at large is the prospect of cyclists' getting their wheels caught in the tram rails, or "lines" as they are always called in this context. The video showed Dutch cyclists happily weaving across double-grooved interlaced rails in Amsterdam's Leidsestraat, demonstrating that it is quite possible for cyclists to adapt to fixed features in streets. Exactly the same sort of sequence could be shot in Manchester's Market Street today.

Another shot showed trams almost brushing past pavement café tables where customers were obviously enjoying themselves next to a busy transport system quietly going about its business only inches away. Other scenes showed trams running amongst crowds of pedestrians, mingling with road traffic, running smoothly at high speed on segregated track or appearing in attractive profusion at city-centre focal points. Copies of the film were shown to all manner of interested parties including specialist user groups, MPs, District Councils, schools, exhibition visitors, conference delegates, local business people and many others.

Full-colour brochures and pamphlets echoing the content of the video were produced and distributed widely. Artist's impressions showing trams in the PTE's warm, high-visibility orange livery in key city centre locations were commissioned and used in publicity material including the video and brochures, and a 1/76th scale representation of the Market Street section was produced and exhibited at GMC, later PTE, offices. Subsequently the video was updated to include new artist's impressions and to reflect the substitution of Greater Manchester Passenger Transport Authority for Greater Manchester Council.

ENTERPRISE NORTH WEST

The first big public relations event to feature the light rail proposals took place at the Enterprise North West Exhibition, held from 5th — 16th March 1986 at the G-MEX Centre to commemorate its opening by Her Majesty the Queen. G-MEX, a major exhibition and conference centre is an exciting adaptation of the old Manchester Central Station.

PROJECT LIGHT RAIL

The first major public relations event featuring Manchester's light rail plans took place at Debdale Park, some three miles out from the city centre at Gorton. A somewhat similar event had taken place at Reims in France in the previous year when a Nantes tram had been demonstrated at an SNCF station. "Project Light Rail", as the Debdale Park event was billed to the press, was a joint venture between GMPTE (inspiration, publicity, promotions), British Rail (railway, power supply, general operational aspects, drivers), British Rail Engineering Ltd (project co-ordination), GEC Transportation Projects Ltd (vehicle provision, on-board staffing other than drivers), Balfour Beatty (overhead line equipment) and Fairclough Civil Engineering Ltd (lineside facilities, reception site).

In retrospect Project Light Rail must be seen as a triumph of co-operation between the public and the private sector, showing what can be done independently without interference from Westminster. Everything was accomplished in the short space of four months and there were many cost-saving initiatives which did not detract from the quality of the finished product. This in itself eloquently showed off light rail's engineering flexibility.

For instance, many of the structures used to support Balfour Beatty's overhead line equipment had been left in place since the line was used by electric locomotives and stock en route between the Woodhead/Glossop line and the Reddish maintenance facility. Other, specially-erected, overhead line supports were of a design recently used by Balfour Beatty for the Tuen Mun scheme; enquirers at the time were relieved when they were told that this equipment's typhoon-proof sturdiness would not be necessary for the Manchester scheme proper. The temporary station used for the demonstration was constructed from components eventually destined for a new railway station in the region, and the station shelter was in fact a bus shelter provided by Glasdon Ltd. And, finally, the borrowed vehicle used was the brand new Docklands Light Railway car No 11, on its way from its manufacturer in Germany to its home in London. Incidentally, this vehicle has now returned to Germany, as the whole of the class has been sold by the DLR to Essen for conversion to trams!

THE GUEST STAR – DLR NO 11

Though the DLR is an automatic railway with third rail current collection, No 11 was operated at Debdale Park in manually driven mode collecting its current from an overhead wire; a Brecknell Willis pantograph had been temporarily fitted to it for the purpose. The traction supply came from part of an electric multiple unit train parked some way away; this took power at 25 kV a.c. from the Glossop line, transformed and rectified it and then fed 750 V d.c. via a trackside cable to the temporary overhead contact wire instead of to its own d.c. traction motors.

The way in which a differently-destined light rail vehicle had been rolled onto unmodified British Rail track and operated successfully thereon closely echoed the nature of Manchester's alignment-flexible light rail proposals. The bi-directional single-articulated demonstration vehicle closely resembled the proposed Manchester tramcar in configuration and layout although its square ends contrasted with the tapered ends desirable for safety reasons at the rear end of a street-operating vehicle. All that was lacking at Debdale Park was a section of paved track for No 11 to run along, though a short display section of grooved street track was on show separately at the site, paved with Marshalls' block paviors just like parts of Metrolink's "real" street tramway today. There was, however, one facet of light rail's flexibility featured at Debdale Park which has not yet appeared on Metrolink and that is the cost-saving regular use by light and heavy rail traffic of the same piece of track.

TRACK SHARING

The demonstration project occupied for three weeks part of a railway then still in use for BR freight traffic. Although the line was double, one of the tracks had been blocked by temporary overhead line support masts cleverly bolted to the rails by Balfour Beatty. At the end of each demonstration day, therefore, the DLR vehicle would be run over a crossover onto a section of the mast-blocked track to be guarded by a security firm, leaving the through line clear for nocturnal freight train movements via Fallowfield and Chorlton. The most noteworthy feature was the way in which a close match between door sills and platform edge was achieved for the 2.65 m wide light rail vehicle while maintaining enough clearance for diesel-hauled heavy freight trains to pass through at reduced speed. Also proved was the compatability of the (nocturnally de-energised) light rail overhead wiring with full loading gauge heavy rail operation. During the day the line was blocked to heavy rail traffic for operational and safety reasons.

PROJECT LIGHT RAIL'S OPENING

Project Light Rail was opened by Mr David Mitchell, Minister of State for Transport on Tuesday 10th March 1987; the author apologises for being unable to give a first-hand account of this exciting day, having been invited to the event and then refused admission to the site because of a misunderstanding. Be that as it may, Mr Mitchell's ceremonial flagging off (not flogging off – that might come later) of the LRV set in motion nothing less than the departure of the first light rail vehicle to carry passengers publicly in Manchester as it set off on its mile and a quarter gently-downhill journey to a point just beyond the empty Reddish electric motive power depot before returning to the celebrations at the station site.

During the following three weeks, specific days were set aside for different groups of visitors who included local MPs and MEPs, councillors, trades union officials, special interest groups including representatives of disabled people, Chamber of Trade representatives, people from industry, the police, members of the House of Lords and of the House of Commons Select Committee on Transport, consultants, City and District planners and engineers and, last but not least, the Press and the media. Hospitality was provided and there was a lecture, film and video theatre on the site as well as reception facilities where representatives of the participating organisations could discuss light rail with guests and issue them with information packs. In addition, Balfour Beatty's rubber-tyred hospitality "tram" was in attendance helping to slake thirsts both for information and for liquid refreshment.

PROJECT LIGHT RAIL'S SIGNIFICANCE

As well as the local transport officials and councillors attending the event, there were visits from their counterparts in every other conurbation in the UK; it is true to say, in fact, that the professional interest the Debdale Park event generated was an accurate small-scale foretaste of the interest attracted today by its big brother, Manchester Metrolink. Project Light Rail admirably fulfilled its purposes as a shop window both for British industry's light rail manufacturing and equipping capacity and for Manchester's ability to promote its own light rail system. There can be no doubt that, at the same time, Project Light Rail gave an almighty boost to light rail's credibility at Westminster and around the country and was partly responsible for the flood of light rail proposals emerging since. It also, as we have already seen, showed what the public and private sectors could achieve in partnership in a cramped timescale.

Mr David Mitchell, Minister of State for Transport, ceremonially flags off Docklands Light Railway No 11 from the temporary Debdale Park light rail station and exhibition site on 10th March 1987 to signal the start of three weeks of demonstration runs for the general public, the Press and decision-makers from all over the country.   *GMPTE*

No 11 gave Mancunians their first opportunity to sample an LRT ride in their own city and was undoubtedly the main attraction at Debdale Park. Nevertheless, the accompanying exhibition formed an extremely important part of the event, helping to kick-start the boom in demand for light rail in UK   *GMPTE*

PUBLIC OPEN DAYS

The ordinary citizens of Manchester were not left out. During the weekends, members of the public were invited to attend the demonstration and to experience a ride on No 11. Special buses were laid on at no charge from the city centre and free tickets for the event could be obtained in advance from the PTE offices. In all, 7500 members of the public rode on the vehicle during the five open days and had the opportunity to see the promotional video, talk to PTE and company representatives about light rail and to collect brochures to take home and study.

Visitors were also asked to fill in questionnaire forms asking them to rate various aspects of the vehicle which, as we have already seen, closely resembled the type proposed for Manchester. The aspects addressed in the questionnaires were as follows: visibility, ease of boarding, outside appearance, inside appearance, vehicle layout, vehicle quality, comfort of ride, noise level, ease of opening doors, heating/ventilation, provision for wheelchairs, handrail positions, comfort of seating. Respondents were asked to give an overall score for each of the aspects. The responses were evaluated by allotting values to each score: very good = +2, good = +1, no opinion = 0, Poor = −1, very poor = −2.

Of the 7500 people (about 0.3% of Greater Manchester's population) who visited the demonstration, 593 took the trouble to fill in the forms and it seems fair to suppose that these folk were from the most interested and positive-thinking section of the public as far as rail transport is concerned; quite a few of them would have been out-and-out rail or bus enthusiasts. It is hardly surprising, therefore, that when the scores were averaged out they were wholly positive. The least positive score was for seating comfort, again hardly surprising because No 11's seats looked and felt solid to people who were used to softly upholstered bus and train seats.

USER GROUP VISITS

On the day set aside for user groups, several representatives of people with various mobility problems visited the demonstration. Tests were conducted to check ease of boarding and alighting for passengers in wheelchairs as well as the stability of braked wheelchairs during light rail journeys. Few problems were experienced, perhaps partly because the wheelchair users at the demonstration were well accustomed to testing access facilities and were relatively adept at manoeuvering in new situations. Also, the vehicle ran only on straight off-street track and had no magnetic track brakes; it could not therefore impose city dynamics on passengers.

As far as the future Metrolink was concerned the findings in respect of wheelchair carriage were of only limited value; after all, off-street and entirely high-platform light rail facilities had already been tested in service on the Tyne and Wear Metro. Manchester's planned light rail system would add to the cocktail sharp unsuperelevated curves, powerful magnetic track brakes, steep hills and profiled platforms.

In fact, that leads us to a fair concluding assessment of the Debdale Park event; it achieved its objectives and accurately reflected one and only one important element of the Metrolink strategy − the operation of a light rail vehicle on a traditional railway. This, however, was nothing new. What was going to be new and pioneering and important about Metrolink was its street operation, and Project Light Rail was unable to demonstrate that side of things. It has to be doubted, however, that many people present were particularly bothered by that omission; they were riding for nothing on a new passenger vehicle on an obscure freight railway and there was quite enough novelty in that for most folk.

Once the event was over, everything was dismantled − much to the dejection of those locals who had believed that this had been a trial for the Fallowfield line's reopening to passengers. The line saw some further use by freight trains until Autumn 1988 and is presently being dismantled from its Old Trafford end. No 11 was delivered, relieved of its temporary pantograph, to the Docklands Light Railway none the worse for its adventure, and the demonstration's overhead contact wire was re-erected at the Heaton Park Tramway in Manchester where it is now in use by tramcars on the lakeside extension, remarkably close to where Metrolink's newer trams rush under the park through Heaton Park Tunnel.

NAMES FIRST, VEHICLES LATER

During Project Light Rail, BBC Radio Manchester and the PTE got together to promote a competition to pick names for ten of Manchester's future trams. Visitors to Debdale Park were invited to take part in the "Name a Vehicle" competition and there were nearly a thousand entries. The ten winning names, announced on the air on Easter Monday 1987, nearly all commemorated people who in different ways had reflected credit on the city. They were: Sylvia Pankhurst, Sir Matt Busby, Ben Brierley, Lancashire Fusilier, Sir John Barbirolli, Pat Seed, John Greenwood, Squire Clark, Our Gracie and C.P. Scott.

Each competition winner was presented with a framed picture of DLR No 11 at Ardwick Goods Depot and a special information pack. Winners were assured of the competition organisers' will to ensure that the names would indeed be applied to the light rail vehicles as soon as they were available to carry them. They have not been.

THE BIRCHFIELDS ROAD MOCK-UP

While Project Light Rail was demonstrating operation of a light rail vehicle on a conventional railway, planning officers at GMPTE were grappling with the problem of the on-street stations where full-length railway-style high platforms could not be accommodated. Once the profiled platform idea (see Chapter 6) had been conceived, work was put in hand to produce a full-size mock-up to test the idea. A local firm of architects, EGS Design, was engaged to develop detailed profiled platform and associated designs in close co-operation with the PTE. In due course the full-size mock-up was constructed at the disus-

◄ Artist's impressions are effective promotional tools during the early days of major projects. GMPTE commissioned several of them showing different key locations, initially showing the trams in the PTE's own warm orange livery; we reproduce here one of the less well-known examples, showing a Metrolink-liveried car emerging from Piccadilly Undercroft into London Road.   GMPTE

ed Birchfields Road bus garage, originally built as a tram depot as recently as July 1928 and, sadly, the destination of Manchester's ceremonial "last" tram, number 1007 (a number now carried by one of Manchester's new trams) on 10th January 1949. Birchfields Road, apart from having enough historical associations to tie anyone up in knots, was a secure location for the mockup and there was plenty of space inside, though many buses rendered idle by deregulation were stored there.

The mockup profiled platform was stoutly constructed from timber and particle board and was complemented by a very skeletal mockup light rail vehicle built from the same materials. The main purpose of the Birchfields Road mockup was to test the passenger circulation and boarding/alighting aspects of a profiled platform interfaced at its highest level with the leading entrance of a conventional floor-height light rail vehicle. The few on-board seats, loaned by BR, were only intended to help people orientate themselves and perhaps to rest their legs by sitting down for a chat with officials; the seating layout itself was not, on this occasion, one of the topics for evaluation. Similarly, the borrowed locomotive controller fitted in the mockup's "cab" was only intended to show that that was where the driver would be on the real thing.

METROLINK'S PRESS LAUNCH

A secondary objective being pursued for GMPTE by EGS Design was the development of a system-wide corporate image for Metrolink, the name newly bestowed on the light rail project at a Press Re-Launch in June 1988 when the programme of statutory diversion works was also announced. Styling of architectural features such as railings, surfacings and canopies were examples of design details which could be made uniform across the system, enabling people to instantly recognise anything to do with light rail in Manchester. Since then, some of the initiatives have been absorbed in the establishment of GMML's own corporate image while others, such as the "designer" canopies, have been lost through shortage of funds.

The first consultative visit to the Birchfields Road mockup took place on 21st July 1988, almost before the job was finished but a neat sixty years after the depot was first opened to trams. For the next few months the mockup was visited by many different groups and was the scene of various testing sessions and much discussion. On two weekends in November 1988 the mockup display was expanded by the addition of working Manchester tramcar No 765, pausing en route between Blackpool and Manchester's "other" tramway at Heaton Park. The greater part of 765's restoration work had actually been done in Birchfields Road depot by volunteers several years

▲ Manchester's second public event promoting light rail took place at the Birchfields Road former tram depot (see the picture on Page 4). A representation of the proposed profiled platform and a vestigial light rail vehicle were constructed so that the design concept could be evaluated by officials, Councillors, representatives of people with various levels of personal mobility, the media and interested members of the public. On 21st July 1988, during the first consultative visit, Tony Young (Operational Planning Manager, GMPTE) is seen explaining the proposes arrangements to future passengers keenly committed to the quest for maximum access.   *Author*

earlier, so this was by way of a return visit for the car.

Other features of the open days included a GMPTE information stand, some vintage buses, a large-scale model tramway display featuring a Manchester-type LRV, a tea and bun stall, and Manchester Transport Museum Society (Heaton Park Tramway) and Light Rail Transit Association stands. The LRTA personnel answered questions relating to LRT generally; people asking specifically about Manchester's LRT plans were directed to PTE personnel for answers.

PUBLIC ATTENDANCE AT BIRCHFIELDS ROAD

Although free buses were laid on to bring people the three and a quarter miles from the city centre, attendance on the two public weekends was extremely disappointing. Staff shivered in near-zero temperatures waiting for the hordes who just didn't turn up; many of those who did beat a path to the event were familiar faces who already knew something about the light rail plans and may have wanted nothing more than a last chance to see the inside of Birchfields Road bus depot. One particularly welcome group was a small party of Frenchmen from Alsthom, builders of the Nantes high floor and Grenoble low floor trams.

A conversation overheard at Birchfields Road bears repeating here. A beaming senior official stood just inside the mockup's rudimentary door lobby watching a lady approaching with a baby buggy. As she wheeled it smoothly across the level gap between platform and vehicle the official pointed downwards and said "What d'you think of that then?" To which the perplexed lady replied "Well it's not bad — I got it from that pram shop in town." "No, not the buggy — the gap. You didn't have any problem with it did you?" said the official patiently. "Oh, that — I hadn't noticed it actually!" And therein lies a sobering lesson for all promoters of better access on public transport systems — the greatest pinnacle of success is reached when people just don't notice what's been done for them.

The Birchfields Road episode did confirm that the profiled platform idea was acceptable and practical enough to be incorporated into the design brief being worked up for Metrolink, though some representatives of the disabled saw the solution as a shortfall on their ideal of full disabled access to every part of every vehicle. Subsequently, the winning consortium modified the design so that the raised part of the platform served the two middlemost entrances of the leading unit of a coupled pair, instantly doubling the rate of easy access provision. Another modification involved substituting a cantilevered canopy instead of the type of shelter featured at Birchfields Road, the central stanchions of which had attracted adverse criticism for obstructing the platform area where wheelchairs and buggies would be manoeuvering near to the original easy-access doorway. Subsequently, Decaux "Murano" and "Standard" bus shelters have been substituted for the amended canopy design.

WINNING POPULAR SUPPORT

As the light rail proposals came nearer to implementation, public relations activites were stepped up a little. Overseas experience with street tramway construction had highlighted the need to win over public opinion at an early stage by keeping people well informed about intentions and activities. For example, in Grenoble prior to the start of comparable construction works, 400 delegates from the community were taken to Zürich to experience modern tramway operation there. The "Blue Fox" public information service was established, with a dedicated staff and city-centre shop premises used as a information point.

In Manchester, the two major public relations events (Debdale Park and Birchfields Road) had taken place remote from the city centre. The average citygoer still had only the cloudiest idea of what was proposed; after all, by no means everyone scrutinises the newspapers or watches the right television programmes at the right times − or, for that matter, believes what they read or hear when they do. GMPTE had an uphill struggle on its hands unless it grasped the nettle and took public relations out into the streets where the work would be done.

For a time there was talk of renting some city-centre shop premises and setting up a permanently-staffed Metrolink display and information point. In fact the PTE had acquired 20−22 High Street, ideally located half way along a city-centre profiled platform site − but not for that purpose. Another solution was adopted. In March 1989, work was starting on the diversion of statutory undertakers' plant in the city centre. This involved substantial relocation of bus stands in Piccadilly Gardens and of bus routings into and out of the city.

A PUNCH-DRUNK PUBLIC

The disruption itself did not seem to bother Manchester folk unduly. The city had been plagued for years with Victorian sewer renewals, not to mention pedestrianisation schemes, building work, stone-cleaning work, demolition work and so on. There can be little doubt that by the time the Metrolink activities started folk were already utterly punch-drunk from years of traffic diversions, scaffolded buildings, great big holes in the streets and all the clutter and mud associated therewith.

THE INFORMATION CABIN

Even so, Metrolink's effects on the buses were diverse enough to justify setting up a special enquiry point where people could ask how to find their bus home and could also discover what all the disruption was about anyway; accordingly a "Portakabin" type temporary building was set up close to the PTE's offices on a wide expanse of pavement at the corner of Piccadilly Gardens distant from the main bus station and future site of Piccadilly Gardens tram station. Prominent "Metrolink" name panels were fitted on top of the cabin and, following a suggestion received during a user group meeting, the cabin was made disabled-accessible like the future transport system to which it related.

Metrolink information was on display inside the cabin and leaflets were available. If questions couldn't be answered directly, the staff on duty could pass the enquiry on by internal PTE telephone to someone who could supply the information requested. About 500 enquiries were handled per week, around half of them being about Metrolink with the remainder being bus and miscellaneous enquiries. The information point was to have remained in position throughout the construction period, but only lasted until Christmas 1990; towards the end of its life it was often shut through a combination of staff shortages and a reluctance to work in it alone.

In the fortnight leading up to the start of the statutory diversion works, PTE staff made a point of telephoning or knocking on the

TRAM SIGNS

A GUIDE FOR DRIVERS AND PEDESTRIANS

Light Rapid Transit Systems (called "trams" in this leaflet) are returning to British streets. The first new system is in Manchester.

New types of sign have been devised for use where trams and other traffic mix.

This leaflet from the Department of Transport explains what these look like.

The Department of Transport also had to publicise the new tram signs. Unfortunately this has only been done locally, and therefore visitors to Manchester will probably be mystified by them.

doors of all 500 frontagers along the affected alignments in the city centre. They explained what was about to happen and asked for names to be contacted in emergency as well as advising business owners of their right to claim compensation if they were adversely affected. Many of the frontagers were pleasantly surprised to be contacted in this way and this must have helped reduce fears and secure support. The exercise was repeated by the PTE prior to the on-street construction works proper and again by GMML during trial running on-street. Apart from anything else, frontagers have thereby been able to explain in turn to their own business contacts and customers what was going on in the street outside.

THE PRESS AND METROLINK

Whenever any particularly newsworthy event has happened concerning Metrolink, such as the appointment of the consortium, a news conference has been called to supplement the usual press releases issued by the PTE. At these events, PTE officers and PTA members have given presentations to the assembled newsmen and have then made themselves available for interviews or to answer specific questions.

Throughout the development of the light rail proposals the press and media have assumed an objective supporting role and there has been none of the old hackneyed affectionate hostility to trams which used to permeate into every mention of them in the papers. Care has been taken by the PTE to keep the general public informed about impending works by means of regular Metrolink bulletins in local newspapers and on Greater Manchester Radio. Large signs were erected on all approach roads into the city centre explaining that the advanced works for Metrolink were in progress and at each work site small notices offered apologies for any inconvenience caused by Metrolink work.

From time to time the PTE has issued newsletters containing Metrolink update information and made them available at enquiry points. In response to demand from schools having children engaged in transport projects, the PTE has recognised the value of Metrolink as a self-contained topic for such work and has compiled study packs for both junior and senior school use as well as arranging for talks to be given on Metrolink. Part of the value of this community-conscious work is that the children are bound to pass on some of their interest and enthusiasm to parents and other relatives.

INVITATIONS TO SPEAK ABOUT METROLINK

Hard-pressed PTE and City Council officers have had no shortage of demands from various bodies asking for Metrolink presentations. Usually these have been dealt with by giving talks supplemented by suitable colour slides and by the distribution of leaflets, newsletters and brochures. Metrolink is becoming a popular theme for theses and students' projects, and this has been generating a steady succession of detailed enquiries to which PTE staff have tried to respond. In addition, many invitations to present papers at conferences and to write articles for publication have been met and have added to exceptional demands on already hard-pressed PTE staff. Another extra and not unpleasant burden came from the reception of official visitors having an involvement with the work or wishing to learn lessons from

Manchester. GMA and GMML have begun to inherit some of these workloads, which in time could help generate income through consultancy or vehicle hirings.

As the project slid into the construction phases, GMPTE continued to play the key part in the management of public affairs generally. One rather frustrating aspect of the work programming was the failure to finally finish off even a short section of track until as late as mid-April 1991 (Dantzic Street and Corporation Street crossings). The consequence has been to prolong and aggravate public concern and ignorance. Ideally, minor efforts should have been directed at reassuring the public by installing and attractively paving one very short piece of track in a prominent location as part of the reinstatement of the preliminary statutory diversion works. A notice could have been erected close to the demonstration length of track explaining that this was how neat and tidy the job would look when it was finished.

MARCH 90 – METROLINK'S "LOCKUP"

Part of the DBOM contract called for the supply of a prototype tram bodyshell for consultation and public relations purposes and to generally refine details of design; this had already been done in the case of the Docklands Light Railway, except that the DLR mockup had been much less substantial. After Italian customs delays, the 6.5 tonne body shell arrived by road from Naples in late March 1990. It had been constructed by Firema, the Italian firm with which GEC had placed the order for the 26 production vehicles for Metrolink.

The body shell, 14.5 m long and 2.65 m wide, was really half of

▼ The Metrolink Design, Build, Operate and Maintain (DBOM) contract required the successful consortium to provide a substantially complete pre-production bodyshell. Firema, vehicle supplier to the GMA consortium, accomplished this in record time, enabling the Italian-built pre-production prototype – or "mock-up" as it inaccurately became known – to be installed by GMPTE within a profiled platform in a railway arch near to Piccadilly Station, opened to the public in March 1990. The bodyshell, having served its purpose, now has been "retired" to the Transport Museum at Boyle Street (Queens Road)
GMPTE

a production tram without running or control equipment. An enormous internal mirror was cleverly fixed across the body shell's halfway "cut line" to give an impression inside of a full-length vehicle. By swivelling the semi-functional articulation, the mirror could be pivoted so as to give a realistic appearance of going round a corner.

The body shell was installed in archway number 97 in North Western Street, underneath the approach tracks to Piccadilly station − a location which was not, incidentally, anything to do with the Piccadilly Undercroft Metrolink station site. Once the body shell was in position a mockup profiled platform station was built around it, so that on the nearside of the body shell the highest part of the platform gave level access to the doorway nearest to the blanked-off articulation; this doorway and its neighbour in the missing other half of the vehicle would be the ones level-accessed at the production profiled platforms.

The mockup profiled platform sloped gently down towards the leading end of the body shell, providing an accurate representation of the single-stepped access to the forwardmost entrance of the tram. On the other side of the body shell, the mock-up platform was at a low level; this represented the situation which would prevail at all the doorways of the trailing vehicle of a coupled pair, assuming that at some time in the future there would be sufficient vehicles to allow the pairing option to be exercised. The low-level section let visitors test something else − how it would have felt to have had to board and alight from low on-street platforms if it had not been decided to make Metrolink disabled-friendly.

TICKET MACHINE EVALUATIONS

Following evaluation of the pre-production body shell and its relation to the mockup profiled platform, a working ticket machine, supplied by Thorn EMI Electronics Ltd, the Company which subsequently supplied all the ticketing equipment for Metrolink, was installed on the platform for consultation and demonstration purposes. The working machine allowed people to try purchasing various types of tickets. They weren't expected to pay for them, the tickets issued being only of the souvenir variety. A mockup ticket machine showing more closely the style and layout of the proposed Metrolink production ticket machine was placed next to the working version for comparison purposes.

Arch 97 was opened to consultation groups for ticket machine evaluation in June 1990 and to the general public for the same purpose on 1st July 1990. Visitors were asked to fill in Ticket Vending Machine (TVM) Questionnaires similar to the ones used for the tram body shell itself. Respondents were asked to say how they rated the ticket machine colour scheme, overall appearance, instructions for use, location of push buttons, height of coin slot, height of ticket/change tray, ease of use, ticket material and ticket information. As with the Debdale Park and body shell questionnaires, the responses were given a weighting of: very good = +2, good = +1, no opinion = 0, Poor = −1, very poor = −2.

Only sixty people responded to the TVM questionnaire, and the majority of them seemed pleased with it. Most of the comments dealt with the height of the coin slot and the lowness of the combined ticket and change tray. Wheelchair using respondents preferred both to be relatively low, but elderly or reasonably tall people were concerned about the awkwardness of reaching down to a low ticket/change tray. Unfortunately, the correct functioning of the coin slot, foreign body ejectors, coin selectors and detectors, coin receptacles, change dispensers and change tray dictated the extent of the height difference between the "in" and "out" parts of the whole process. Both could be moved up or down together but the gap between them couldn't be physically decreased.

Though a compromise height has had to be fixed, there were other options which were ruled out for different reasons. Metrolink's ticket machines are being made ultra user friendly in that they will give change, unlike for example the smaller and less expensive French and Swiss wayside machines which don't. Compact non-change giving TVMs could have been used on Metrolink, with adjacent coin-changing machines added if necessary. Or the TVMs could have been doubled in number and installed in pairs, one high and the other low. The possibilities are endless and it is idle to speculate further − suffice it to say that the solution adopted is one example of the sort of judicious compromise which designers have to make on our behalf all the time. It now appears that a second, lower coin input slot is offered by the TVM manufacturers for the use of passengers not requiring change; as with everything else, however, over-provision of facilities or excessive gadgetry risks confusing users.

As with the light rail vehicles themselves, more information about the TVMs is given in Chapter 14.

GMML'S ROLE

During the implementation period GMPTE has continued to shoulder the bulk of the PR burden, leaving GMML to concentrate on building, equipping, marketing and staffing the new transport system as well as preparing to operate it and give guidance to the public on how to use it. The high-street presence associated with a definitive street-penetrating light rail service will ensure that Metrolink markets itself without any special promotional effort though it will be essential for the operator to thoroughly understand the market and to explore every possible way of meeting the full potential of the investment made in the system. Presenting the Metrolink concept to the public in the right way is perhaps the major part of the marketing challenge taken on board by GMML.

Expecting a continuous barrage of questions from journalists, professionals and members of the public alike, GMA anticipated many of them by giving detailed information in a set of Topic Sheets which dealt with various aspects of the Company's operations. Each set, in an attractive presentation folder, covered Vehicles, Power Supply System, Signalling, Telecommunications, Fares & Ticketing System, Refurbishment of Cornbrook Viaduct, Stations, G-MEX Viaduct and City Centre Track and Alignment. Also supplied were maps of the projected light rail network and copies of the PTE's Metrolink brochure.

Though GMML's public relations role has tended to concentrate on marketing of the finished product, GMA did undertake a warm-hearted initiative in December 1990 when an illuminated Christmas tree was erected by staff adjacent to the track-laying works in High Street. Plans to place preserved Stockport open-top tramcar No 5 in front of Debenhams on the new segregated High Street track − it would have fitted perfectly well − one Saturday and collect money for the NSPCC were pursued as far as possible but finally had to be dropped.

SCHOOL VISITS PROGRAMME

When testing and driver training started on the Bury line it was time to make local children understand the full implications of playing about on or near the line, or of committing acts of vandalism. A small team of marketing and traffic staff from GMML toured a total of 60 schools in the vicinity of the Bury line, followed by schools on the Altrincham line, telling the boys and girls not to throw, touch or trespass.

ANOTHER NAMING COMPETITION

To coincide with the arrival of Metrolink's first tram in late August 1991, GMML and BBC Manchester jointly ran a "Nickname Metrolink" competition on the North West Tonight television programme. The idea was to find a snappy short name which people would use for the system; Chicago's elevated railways are affectionately called "The El" and London's underground is commonly referred to as "The Tube". What was wanted was a similar pet name for Metrolink.

Over 1000 entries were received from viewers. Many of them suggested names connected with Manchester's past association with the cotton industry, such as "The Thread", "The Shuttle" and "The Cotton Reel". One particularly imaginative viewer suggested "ABBA", for "Altrincham to Bury and Back Again". Even more appropriate was "TRAM", for "Travel Right Across Manchester"; but the genius who invented this brilliant acronym thought the name far too obvious to submit, otherwise it would surely have left all the other entries standing.

The winner was a lady who chose "The Met" (shouldn't it have been "The Med" in view of the trams' Italian origins?). This is being adopted by GMML with the intention of encouraging the public to refer to travelling by "The Met" rather than by tram. Before the war, London's Metropolitan Electric Tramways were affectionately known as "The Met" by tramway enthusiasts and employees, but the public stuck to "tram" unless they had to make a distinction between those belonging to the MET and those belonging to other operators. The same name and the same home truths apply in Melbourne today.

Any doubt about what the public will call the vehicles was dispelled by a conversation overheard at Victoria as the first one was taken into the streets for clearance tests. "Here comes the LRV" said a punctilious dad to his small son, who couldn't have been more than four years old. The little lad set his father on the right track towards a more homely appelation: "Why do you call it an LRV dad? It's a tram!".

6. QUESTIONS OF ACCESSIBILITY

WHY MAKE METROLINK DISABLED ACCESSIBLE?

Manchester's light rail planners had studied, both at home and abroad, many different access-improving light rail techniques. This encouraged them to respond to growing pressure from local groups and politicians to find ways of making new light rail systems accessible to all. Disabled people would not be the only ones to benefit from improvements; even though they had fought hardest for getting rid of obstacles to movement, which is what improved access is all about, it would be others who would enjoy equal or greater rewards.

OBSTACLES AWAY! – BUT WHO BENEFITS?

Amongst the other beneficiaries are: parents accompanying small children in or out of prams or pushchairs, elderly people, visually handicapped or blind people, pregnant women, temporarily disabled people, people with luggage or shopping and people with a whole range of invisible mobility-impairing complaints such as arthritis, vertigo, emphysema and angina. The most important thing to appreciate is that by no means all disability is visible and that to limit perceptions of mobility problems to people in wheelchairs exposes quite a gross level of ignorance.

It has been estimated that up to 20% of the population is affected in some way by mobility impairment, visibly or otherwise. When one considers that in the mid-'eighties, 17.9% of the population was of pensionable age (though not by any means all mobility impaired) and between 4% and 5% consisted of small children (every one of us is born mobility impaired and remains so for the first few years of life), it is easy to see the truth of that figure. Unfolded buggies and pushchairs may in fact pose serious on-board congestion problems.

▶ Whilst wheelchair users are often seen as the main beneficiaries of improved access, such is not really the case. Disabled people are certainly the ones who fight hardest for the removal of obstacles to movement, but parents with small children are amongst the many other types of passenger to benefit from level access. This lady is risking a slipped disc as she struggles to manhandle her laden, occupied buggy aboard a BR Pacer unit at Victoria station.   *Author*

By way of contrast, only 0.2% of the UK population habitually uses wheelchairs and it is only by glib convention that the wheelchair is seen as the key to improved access. Others benefit to a far greater extent; on the Tyne and Wear Metro a survey revealed that 30% of lift use was by parents with prams and pushchairs while only 2% was by wheelchair-using adults. The remaining usage was made up of people with no obvious impairment, many of whom were elderly. Yet it is people in wheelchairs who have fought hardest for the easier access facilities which the rest of us so easily take for granted.

LOW FLOORS FOR MANCHESTER?

The low floor concept had to be ruled out at an early stage. Thirty-five of the platform faces at which the Phase 1 vehicles would load and unload would be existing high platforms on the Bury and Altrincham lines directly inherited from British Rail. Six others would be new off-street platforms and a further seven would be new on-street platforms. The use of low floor vehicles would have meant either the lowering of a 60 m length of each of the 35 existing platform faces at the 18 stations directly inherited from BR (Navigation Road

◀ Contrast this extremely civilized scene with the chaotic one above. These ladies have walked easily aboard Metrolink Car No 1002 with their children and have chosen to remain together on board in comfortable security using the carefully-planned, caring facilities. The space occupied by the left-hand buggy is primarily intended for wheelchair users and has a passenger-to-drive call facility and intercom; the space occupied by the right-hand buggy was created after bodyshell consultation, by substituting a pull-down seat for a fixed seat.   *Peter Fox*

now has only one duo-directional platform), or raising the track through the stations the required amount which could with foresight have been done easily during the painfully prolonged Bury and Altrincham shutdown periods.

Perhaps a more compelling reason for keeping clear of the low floor concept was that the requisite high-capacity vehicle technology was not available in a sufficiently mature state of development. Just because a low-floor light rail vehicle works well on an urban tramway at moderate speeds there is no guarantee that it will survive the kind of heavily-loaded high-speed duty cycle imposed on it by high mileage on long uninterrupted stretches of track like G-MEX to Trafford Bar, Bury to Radcliffe or Stretford to Dane Road, even if the vehicle were capable of 80 km/h in the first place. Let us not forget that the decision had to be made back in the mid-'80s.

It is almost beside the point to observe that low floor vehicles tend to be more expensive than their conventional equivalents partly because of high development costs spread over small production runs, and that the expensiveness of all Western LRVs is one of light rail's greatest Achilles heels at the present time. Going for a low-floor vehicle would also restrict the choice of technology and supplier. Nevertheless, one tenderer did offer a low floor option for Manchester but this tender was not accepted.

HIGH FLOORS: ADAPTING THE STATIONS

The assumption that Manchester's light rail vehicle would be similar in configuration and size to Duewag's mature high-floored Stadtbahn B80 design prevailed; the question was, how to adapt the on-street stations to give level access to high-floor trams? Five of the on-street platforms were to be located where full-length high platforms were considered by the PTE to be unacceptable for reasons of pedestrian circulation or visual intrusion; these platforms were those intended for Market Street (outward), High Street (inward), St Peters Square (one for each direction) and Aytoun Street (outward).

The Aytoun Street platform has since been amalgamated with the nearby Parker Street (inward) platform to form the Piccadilly Gardens island platform, high level throughout its length. An additional outward profiled platform is located on Mosley Street adjacent to the Piccadilly Plaza complex. Many different options were explored for matching platform edge and door sill heights at the five sensitive sites before Manchester's pioneering profiled platform solution was developed.

One option explored was to drop the level of the track through the stations, enabling the platform height relative to its surroundings to be made correspondingly lower. First of all, however, this would have imposed the exact opposite of the energy-saving effects obtained in London by humping of Tube stations. Worse still, passengers would have been subjected to stronger braking and acceleration forces at stations, due to the addition of static downhill and uphill forces to the inevitable dynamic forces. Dropping the track substantially could also have created drainage and snow and litter accumulation problems. As a compromise, the track has generally been dropped 150 mm past on-street stations.

PROFILED PLATFORMS

Another way forward was to concentrate on providing system-wide level access at a proportion of doorways only. Buffalo's short high platforms, inspected by a Manchester delegation in 1984, serve either 12.5% or 25% cent (twin or single car respectively) of the available doorways and these proportions, in theory at least, physically reflect the proportion of mobility-impaired people likely to be using the system at peak and off-peak times. Cautiously assuming that every increase in the provision of level access makes for more efficient loading and unloading, it follows that wherever it is physically and environmentally possible, step-climbing should be altogether minimised at platform/vehicle interfaces.

Initially, the highest part of Manchester's profiled platform was to have given level access only to the leading doorway of the leading vehicle. Later the design was changed by the successful consortium to shift the level access facilities to the middle two doorways of the leading vehicle, doubling the rate of easy-access provision. Longitudinally the platforms slope gently away from the raised section, the apparent height of which is reduced by lateral sloping away from the track incorporated to ensure that wheelchairs and buggies tend to roll back from the platform edge rather than towards it. The high part of each platform is fenced at the back and equipped with a shelter and ticket machine.

Access to the leading and trailing doorways of the leading vehicle is from part way along the longitudinal slopes leading from the low parts up to the high part of each profiled platform. Passengers thus step from a sloping platform up to a level door sill and vice versa; this was not found to cause any problems in tests and in any case is a common enough feature of shop, house and office doorways sited on hills. When the time comes for the trams to run in coupled pairs, all of the trailing vehicle's four doorways will be accessed from the low-level portion of each profiled platform. All vehicles are equipped with steps which can slide out from beneath every door sill for this purpose.

▶ In the city centre the profiled platform design evaluated at Birchfields Road was adopted where it was impossible to insert full-length high platforms. This view shows how the then-unfurnished outbound platform at St Peter's Square adjoins the Cenotaph site and how the profiled platform interfaces with the tramcars. In passenger service, drivers stop so that the centremost doors of the leading car line up with the highest part of the profiled platform. This was the occasion of an official visit by HM Inspecting Officer of Railways on 24th January 1992. Number 1005 is leading No 1001. *Author*

◀ Grenoble is regarded as a centre of accessible light rail excellence, with its attractive – though expensive to buy – low-floor trams and general high-quality design. This is a Place Verdun in August 1990, showing the very low kerb-like platforms as well as the pleasing absence of visible traction poles. *Peter Fox*

▶ Accessibility improvements at Metrolink's 19 ex-BR stations have taken different forms depending on layout and topography. Ramps of varying length have been used for the most part, but lifts have been installed where it would have been difficult to install ramps. Here, on 23rd February 1992, are the pair of new hydraulic lift towers connecting Park Road with the platforms at Timperley Station. To the right is the Bridgewater Canal, while under the bridge can be seen a mobile gantry used by overhead line crews working on erection of the additional feeder cables used on the Altrincham line. *Author*

◀ One method of improving access which was ruled out for Manchester was the platform-to-vehicle lift. This view in Portland, Oregon, explains why. The driver is operating one of the wayside lifts, which temporarily renders this doorway unavailable to other passengers. Wheelchair users have understandable fears of being marooned on the vehicle by the failure of such mechanical devices and tend to prefer fixed, low-tech solutions like Metrolink's profiled platforms. No wonder this tram driver and his passengers look a bit glum. *Mike Ballinger*

HIGH PLATFORMS

Wherever possible, city-centre platforms are of the full-length high type to eliminate steps altogether. Metrolink's versatile trams can interface readily with either profiled platforms or conventional high platforms. The island platform in Parker Street is high throughout, and so are the new platforms constructed at G-MEX and at Victoria and Piccadilly railway stations. Outside the city centre the vertical dimension from rail to station platform was nominally 900 mm, though with conventional stepped-access trains it was not a dimension needing accurate maintenance. Platform heights varied quite a lot along their length, and the height of the track itself and its degree of superelevation through a station could also vary the height or tilt of the train standing on it.

One of the tasks facing Metrolink's civil engineers has therefore been to adjust the platform height and fix the track's position at all stations to achieve a close lateral and vertical match between door sill and platform edge over a length suffcient to span the middlemost two entrances of each leading tram; this is a contractual requirement.

There will in practice be a small remaining horizontal gap, necessary to allow for dynamic sideways movement of a tram running through without stopping; this gap is not expected to cause much trouble once passengers get used to it, though in Grenoble it has been found that total elimination of any gap promotes completely trouble-free boarding and alighting. The improved platform/vehicle interface at Metrolink trams' middle two entrances will help encourage passengers with a mobility problem to use the part of the vehicle which benefits from easy access on every part of the system; thus the chances of anyone being marooned on the vehicle at a city-centre stop are minimised.

Most existing railway platforms are normally accessed from adjacent streets by flights of steps. This has been one of the factors denying mobility-impaired people access to railways, apart that is from wheelchair-bound people for whom special arrangements can be made in advance by appointment. Parents with prams just have to make the best of it. To provide permanent easy access to Metrolink's stations where it did not previously exist, ramps connecting platforms to streets have been installed wherever possible.

Sometimes all that has been called for has been the knocking of a hole in awall or the construction of a short ramp. Ramps are being constructed to amandatory 1 in 20 gradient though paradoxically the gradient of the track, and therefore the slope of the vehicle floors, will sometimes be steeper than that. In some locations where a ramp would have been too steep or just could not be fitted in at all, hydraulic lifts have been installed. The improved access facilities will, as a spin-off benefit for the operator, help staff to move cleaning equipment around the stations.

ACCESSIBILITY AND INTEGRATION

A mass transit system open to everyone from chairbound person to champion gymnast will not only reflect credit on the society which promotes it, it will also enable the most effective use to be made of finite public transport resources. Dial-a-Ride accessible bus services can act as feeders and distributors to accessible mass transit services, achieving a microcosm of the public transport integration which should be a part of every light rail system's operating environment. It is of course essential for proper off-street transfer facilities to exist at suburban stations so that mobility-impaired interchange can be done without causing the kind of traffic hazards which would be created by, for example, loading and unloading feeder bus passengers on the brow of a narrow station overbridge adjacent to the top landing of a pavement-to-platform lift.

Greater Manchester Accessible Transport Ltd operates PTA-supported "Ring and Ride" services in Trafford, Bury and inner-city Manchester amongst other areas. The service is very much demand-led and GMATL looks forward to being asked by patrons to be taken to Metrolink stations so that they can continue their journeys by tram; once mobility-handicapped people fully appreciate multi-modal trip opportunities a whole new world will be opened to them - if GMATL and Metrolink respectively have the capacity to be able to encourage and hopefully sustain the extra demand thus created.

THE COMFORT FACTOR

When light rail transit is both disabled-friendly and street-compatible, engineers have to be exceptionally careful in designing and constructing it. The combination of high load factors, sharp curves and a high proportion of frail passengers means that ride comfort must be of the highest quality for success to be complete.

One way for planners and engineers to design severe dynamic disturbance out of new systems on the drawing board is by ensuring that all curves are of the largest possible radius; short sharp curves can impose short sharp shocks on passengers and equipment. Even more importantly, every curve should be properly transitioned at its entry and exit. This means that every bend or corner should merge with its neighbouring length of straight track through a short section gradually changing the radius, so that the tram always follows a path as laterally smooth as that of a steered vehicle.

Once they are laid and encapsulated in the roadway, the life of tram rails can be prolonged so much by wear reclamation that the geometry initially imparted to them during construction will endure for decades to come. Quite minor inattention during installation can inflict on passengers alifelong legacy of problems and stamp on the system an unwelcome negative image which no amount of public relations effort can overcome. Rework of track which proves geometrically troublesome will be so expensive and disruptive once the system is open that it is most unlikely to be done. The alternative is for trams to creep at something like walking speed over quirky trackwork, introducing an element of "quaintness" into the system's operation, possibly most so at its focal point where track contortions are at their most complicated.

Good quality engineering has wider benefits. The caring operator can benefit from the increased passenger tolerance of standing travel which is bound to result from a better quality, more dynamically-gentle ride. Most passengers, seated or not, will prefer to repeat a smooth ride rather than adynamically aggressive one. Standing at the back during light rail journeys instead of sitting "on the cushions" at the front is one very good way for off-duty drivers, managers and students of transport systems to increase their awareness of the journey quality being achieved on any system at home or abroad so that they can then do something about improving iit.

Emergency stops are another source of problems for standing passengers. Over-use of powerful magnetic track brakes can cause embarrassment, inconvenience, possible minor injury and, if repeated persistently enough, a resolve to stop using the service. Unless they are driven defensively at all times on-street and amongst pedestrians, light rail vehicles will have to make many emergency reductions of speed. In the great majority of cases, liberal use of the friendly and distinctive power gong not (yet) fitted to Manchester trams effectively minimises the need for emergency brake applications. One mark of success for the caring light rail engineer or operator must surely be to offer a ride so dynamically gentle that at all times a proportion of passengers will choose to travel standing even when seats are available.

ACCESS CONTROL

If there is any doubt about what articles passengers should be allowed to take on board a tram it is a good rule of thumb to limit access to everything likely to be put up with in a city-centre department store − and that, of course, immediately excludes bikes, garden rollers, Daleks and the like but emphatically includes wheelchairs, all forms of baby carriage including three-in-line-abreast and three-in-line-astern models with balloon tyres and shopping basket attachments as well as all manner of passengers' luggage and purchases.

In Manchester the tram drivers will have no fare-collection or revenue protection duties. Except in special circumstances when they might leave the driving position to attend to passenger problems, their job will not involve any direct supervision of passengers as they board and alight. That will mean, in theory at least, that anything which you see in the street which it is physically possible to do on board or to bring on board a tram, will be done or brought on board at some time notwithstanding the endeavours of travelling teams of customer service inspectors and transit police who will enforce observance of the Byelaws and Conditions of Carriage applicable to Metrolink.

The author well remembers being entertained by a sublimely good country and western busker on board a quiet but crowded Geneva tram and, on a busy Grenoble tram, attempting to converse in French with an electric wheelchair user travelling independently and equipped with, of all things, a saline drip. Moments like that elevate the tram-travelling experience considerably.

Enough has been said here on contention for on-board space and the design and layout of tram interiors to show how impossible it is to please all of the public all of the time. Reconciling multiple conflicting requirements to the satisfaction of most customers is, like it or not, the self-imposed goal of every disabled-friendly mass transit provider. Nowhere is this more acutely so than on a mass transit vehicle with a very high load factor which opens its doors bang slap in the middle of the most densely-thronged streets in the city centre, offering obstacle-free access to all and sundry.

ACCESSIBILITY'S REWARDS

Just what are the rewards of opening up the transit system to all comers? For a start, much motor-car usage is motivated by encumbrance; making it possible to bring awkward items, like a newly-bought continental quilt or a double designer buggy containing the twins easily aboard a public transport vehicle will help persuade people to shop in town by tram rather than by car and that must go a considerable way towards meeting the objectives of providing better public transport in the first place.

For the promoter and operator, one reward of opening up the system to everyone regardless of impairment will be to strengthen moral support for the scheme and to confound its critics, who may one day themselves be grateful for high-quality easy-access public transport. The moral high ground will be not be invulnerable, however; physical accessibility will have to be continuously matched by ride comfort and by financial accessibility. Undue raising of ordinary fares would risk destroying the caring image earned by making the system disabled-friendly.

The operator's commercial objectives should benefit in several ways from improved access when the system settles down. Once people have learned how to sort themselves and their accompaniments out on packed trams and on crowded stations, the high proportion of step-free doorways will help to speed boarding and alighting and to marginally reduce journey times. Tolerance of standing travel will be maximised by disabled-inspired riding comfort and this will have a positive effect on commercial viability. For the community at large, easy access will be the crowning glory of a showpiece public transport system, and if past experience is anything to go by the pride engendered will reflect itself in a reduced level of misbehaviour on and around the system.

THE USER'S PERSPECTIVE - NWTUCC

Users of British Rail services are represented by statutory Transport Users' Consultative Committees (TUCCs). Under GMPTE's No 2 Act − the one dealing with conversion to LRT of the Bury and Altrincham lines — the TUCC for North Western England (NWTUCC) has certain statutory powers relating to Metrolink. The Act also exempted BR from having to go through the closure procedure in respect of the Bury and Altrincham lines. Neither railway was being abandoned, though both would be shut down during changeover periods. NWTUCC secured agreement with GMPTE which in effect preserved the spirit of the TUCC's role in helping alleviate hardship caused by railway closure, albeit in this case temporary but rather prolonged.

Other representations made by the NWTUCC about Metrolink reflect the Committee's statutory obligations concerning services and facilities. While applauding the system's disabled friendliness, some concern was expressed about the loss of cycle carriage facilities with light rail substitution. The Committee has been invited along with other groups to have an input into the design details of the vehicles and stations. As the changeover took place, the Committee was concerned that Metrolink might not have enough capacity to attract more people to public tansport and that price might in time be used as a mechanism to restrain demand. NWTUCC would like to see more vehicles ordered, more car parking facilities provided at suburban stations and plenty of through ticketing to BR.

USER GROUP REPRESENTATION

Designing the system's facilities so that they best meet the aggregated needs of the public has been no easy matter. The process can be assisted from an early stage by consulting with representatives of potential users. The PTE was fortunate in that it had long ago welcomed the forging of a link with the community in the form of the Greater Manchester Transportation Consultative Committee (GMTCC), made up of representatives of over forty user groups each with an interest in local transport.

The Committee had been kept informed throughout the early development of the light rail proposals and had expressed majority support at all stages, at the same time putting forward the reservations held by a minority. GMTCC's light rail views were quoted in both the second report of the Rail Study Group and the PTE's Section 56 Submission. When the time came to start consulting on detailed aspects of the LRT proposals GMTCC and others formed a light rail consultative committee, which first met on 29th March 1988. At that first meeting, attended by representatives from the PTA and PTE as well as from GMTCC and other user groups, concern was expressed about the likelihood of the committee's views being lost in the turmoil of implementation; to some extent these fears have proved to be well-founded.

THE PTA'S SPECIAL NEEDS WORKING GROUPS

GMPTA in 1987 resolved to set up four special needs working groups so that the views of disabled people, elderly people, women and ethnic minorities with respect to public transport could be readily obtained. These groups have naturally included Metrolink within their remit and have been involved in advising the PTA and making representations to them throughout the implementation period. The PTA also supports four Passenger Transport Advisory Committees (North, South, East and West) which have maintained an interest in Metrolink's development inasmuch as it affects their own areas.

USERS' EUROPEAN STUDY TOUR

During the development of Manchester's LRT proposals, local disabled people's groups had organised their own study visits both to the Tyne and Wear Metro and to the Docklands Light Railway to learn more about improved mass transit access. GMTCC made the National Tramway Museum the venue for its annual summer outing in 1989 to witness the operation of rail vehicles in pedestrianised surroundings, while West Midlands and Avon had sent mixed groups to Grenoble in France to sample the new disabled-accessible tramway facilities there. In 1989, with light rail fast becoming a reality in Manchester, it was the right time for a party of user group representatives to undertake a study tour of appropriate transport systems across the Channel and to bring back their findings.

GMPTE and GMTCC jointly planned the itinerary and made the travel arrangements, and the trip was financially supported by GMPTA as part of the Metrolink consultation process. Two wheelchair users took part as well as the author and other GMTCC representatives. The group also included three PTA members and two professional officers, one from the PTE and one from Manchester City Council. Unfortunately, not all types of mobility impairment could be represented on the trip; for instance, the party did not include anyone currently using public transport accompanied by toddlers or babies.

Parents of young children just do not have enough spare time or personal freedom to engage in consultation processes or study tours. To compensate for their enforced lack of representation, it is necessary in consultative processes for everyone involved always to remember the needs of mothers with babies on public transport and to try to think of them at all times, so important a category of passenger are they. The same applies to other groups who may not be represented on committees and study tours for one reason or another, such as profoundly deaf people.

The study tour lasted six days. Starting in Utrecht, the 13-strong party went on to visit The Hague, Amsterdam, Lille (VAL), Grenoble and Geneva, where it was clear that homegoing commuters would cram themselves like sardines onto the trams until the doors would only just shut, in the full knowledge that an emptier one going to exactly the same place would be along in around two minutes flat.

After the exhausted party had returned to Manchester, delegates met for "de-briefing" sessions and agreed the text of a study tour report "Preparing for Metrolink" which was published in 1990 and is now out of print. Sadly, although the report was welcomed by the PTA, no official responses to its recommendations have been forthcoming. To some extent, then, the full value of the study tour has not been realised in that participants have not been able fully to bring their experiences to bear on the detailed implementation of Metrolink. The European study tour had been no idle jaunt for its disabled participants and their fellow delegates — it had been a gruelling few days spent energetically surmounting the many obstacles placed in the path of wheelchair occupants making an overland journey on the Continent. Using the disabled-accessible trams had been refreshingly easy in comparison with some of the trains and one of the aircraft used during the trip.

▶ In October 1989 GMPTA/E sponsored a study visit by a group of nine user group consultees, including the Author, to a selected range of Continental tramway and light rail systems so that they could evaluate the facilities and report back on their findings. Three PTA Members and two officers accompanied by the party on their gruelling odyssey through Holland, Belgium, and France to Switzerland. Here, at Nieuwegien Centrum on the Utrecht "Sneltram" system, the driver insisted on helping Brenda Trigance-Clarke aboard while Linda Evans, Derek Henshaw, Roger Tripp (GMPTE) and Cllr Winstone Ramsey (GMPTA) looked on.   *Author*

7. THE CONTRACT

Following all the work done by the PTE to re-evaluate the light rail proposals against the background of deregulation, a new submission for Section 56 grant was made in July 1987. Receipt of the submission at the Department of Transport was followed by an intensive series of meetings between Department officials and PTE representatives, during which the assumptions and evaluations were reviewed with a fine-tooth comb. At last, in January 1988, came acceptance in principle by the Department of Transport of the case for Section 56 funding of Phase 1 of Manchester's light rail scheme.

Good though this news was, it did not come without strings attached. What the Government was anxious to do with the Manchester scheme was to try taking away as much risk as possible from the public sector for the first decade or more of the system's life, thereby avoiding any perceived risk of saddling taxpayers with an ongoing revenue burden in the form of an operating subsidy. GMPTE and its advisers now had to embark on yet another costly bout of work to examine a range of options for involving private interests and transferring some or all of the commercial

risks of the scheme from the public to the private sector.

PUBLIC SECTOR PROMOTION

Today, schemes are promoted in the public sector because that is where the overview of local transport needs is maintained. While Passenger Transport Executive officers and local politicians can formulate plans and develop them, they cannot go out and construct bridges, lay track or build vehicles. Conventionally such work is put out to the private sector by way of contracts.

The "traditional" system is for the public sector, in partnership with its consultants and advisers, to put together a complete set of specifications and detailed designs for the required transport system. The private sector is then invited to bid for doing that part of the work which lies beyond the capacity of the public sector. Typically this would include major civil engineering works and vehicle supply but would leave operation and maintenance in the hands of the public sector.

Straightforwardly, separate supply contracts would be entered into with the most eligible tenderers in each field — principally

the ones offering to do each part of the work for the lowest price in compliance with the specifications. During the work, the public sector and its consultants would closely monitor progress and quality to ensure that the work met the contract specifications, designs and timings. Alternatively, in a 'design and build' form of contract like that used for the initial phase of the Docklands Light Railway, a single contractor or consortium would be invited to undertake detailed design as well as every aspect of the implementation work.

Of all the options, the cheapest and most cost-effective one would have been private sector construction followed by public ownership and operation; the Department of Transport accepted this fact. Even so, Manchester was forced into taking the 'design and build' process further towards complete privatisation. The options GMPTE had to examine bore a strong resemblance to those being put about in respect of British Rail privatisation, claimed by its proponents — perhaps with a degree of justification — to offer relief from problems blamed on public ownership and operation. This can be put in context, however, by arguing that the recent run-down of the railways towards privatisation has been responsible for more passenger distress than all the accumulated industrial action on the country's railways since their inception — but that's another story.

OPTIONS FOR PRIVATISATION

Let us be in no doubt that what was being looked at for Manchester was nothing other than the privatisation in some greater or lesser degree of two British Rail lines, Bury and Altrincham. Although it will be hotly argued that the project has not in today's conventionally-understood sense been privatised — for one thing it has not been floated on the stock market — there can be little doubt that from the Government's point of view one of the privatisation options for British Rail has been put into practice on Metrolink, the operation of which most assuredly has been put firmly into the hands of the private sector for the time being. By setting conditions on the release of Section 56 funds the Government was actually forcing GMPTE to implement for it a pilot railway privatisation scheme, like it or like it not. Any reader doubting this needs only to glance at the privatisation options which GMPTE had to look at in detail:

- Rolling stock ownership and operation.
- Complete system ownership and operation.
- Rolling stock ownership and operation plus infrastructure maintenance.
- Public sector constructed system sold on completion.
- Public sector constructed system franchised on completion.

At this stage, of course, GMPTA could have decided to go no further with the scheme but after much heart-searching no such

---

Light Rapid Transit System Greater Manchester

Applications are invited from suitably experienced companies interested in being included on a select list of tenderers for a contract to Design, Build, Operate and maintain this first phase of the proposed Light Rapid Transit (LRT) system.

The first phase of the LRT system extends from Altrincham to Bury and embraces both the existing rail network and a new City Centre link. In a total length of some 19 miles (31 km) the on-street trackwork to be laid in City streets amounts to 1.7 miles (2.7 km).

The works will, in addition to City Centre track works, include OHLE, signalling and controls, provision of LRT vehicles and civil works in connection with provision of one new viaduct and refurbishment of existing bridges, tunnels and embankments together with associated works of drainage, fencing and the construction of city centre LRT stations.

The value of the Phase I Capital Works including the provision of LRT rolling stock is anticipated to be in the order of £50m.

The operating concession granted to the successful tenderer will be for a fixed period of years with the ownership of the system, including the infrastructure and all the operating assets, remaining with the Passenger Transport Executive. The operating concession will include responsibility for maintaining these assets in accordance with standards laid down by the Passenger Transport Executive.

It is envisaged that the successful tenderer will be responsible for meeting the costs of operating and maintaining the LRT System and will receive all the operating revenues.

Tenderers will be required to specify the amount of public sector grant they would require. This will be based on the capital costs adjusted for the value attributed to the running of operations for the concession period.

A two stage tender procedure is to be adopted with Stage 1 tender documentation being available in October 1988 with a short listing of 2 or 3 tenders to be made following evaluation of Stage 1 submissions as presented in December 1988. Stage 2 tender documentation will be available by February 1989. The Stage 2 tender period to extend to May 1989.

Commencement of the work is scheduled for no later than September 1989.

The Stage 2 tenderers will be required to submit fixed price bids on the basis of a construction period extending over approximately two years.

The intention is that tendering should be restricted to tenderers of proven capacity and experience in the construction and operations of transport systems. It is unlikely that any one company will have all the requisite skills and therefore potential tenderers are advised to consider the formation of a consortium to undertake the project.

An application for tender documents will not automatically ensure inclusions on the Stage 1 tender list.

An information pack will be sent on request to all prospective tenderers.

This scheme has also been advertised through the medium of the Official Journal of the European Communities.

Application for consideration should be made by 30th June 1988 to:

I.E.M. Buttress, Director of Administration & Secretary, Greater Manchester Passenger Transport Executive, PO Box 429, 9 Portland Street, Piccadilly Gardens, Manchester M60 1HX. Tel: 061-228 6400

Greater Manchester Passenger Transport Executive

dog-in-the-manger stance was adopted. The project had come so far and had gained so much local cross-party and public support on its own merits that to throw it all away was unthinkable. The bitter pill was swallowed with many a grimace and in due course the first private sector option – private sector rolling stock ownership and operation – was found by the PTE to be the least uneconomic and the least unworkable way forward while still remaining within Government requirements – or so it was thought.

A GUINEA PIG PROJECT

The Department of Transport and the Treasury had other ideas, and imposed on the scheme an arrangement which became known as the "complete concession approach". This had been recommended by the DTp's merchant bankers and required that the private sector be invited to submit tenders for designing, building, operating and maintaining the system for a period subsequently set at 15 years. The words of the Secretary of State for Transport as he announced outline funding approval on January 18th 1988 were:

"I have concluded that, on the basis of the assessments which have been made, private sector participation in the construction and operation of this proposed system could bring useful benefits and could best be achieved by inviting bids from the private sector to build and operate the system on the basis of a public sector contribution towards the capital costs."

What the "complete concession approach" meant was that one single contract would cover the entire Phase 1 project from detailed design to the end of the operating concession period. No one company before or since could have undertaken such a wide-ranging contract alone, so it was expected that firms would form themselves into consortia to participate in a dauntingly-complicated tendering process. No-one could predict the eventual outcome several years in the future; in effect Manchester's light rail scheme was being used as a guinea-pig project to test out the Government's ideas about railway operation. It is perplexing, therefore, to observe that perverse constraints on the scheme have now denied the project sufficient vehicles to give private-sector operation a fair test.

The DBOM (Design, Build, Operate and Maintain) contract would have the following main features:

- ownership of all infrastructure, vehicles and assets to remain with the PTE
- an operating franchise or concession to be granted to the successful consortium for a period to be determined
- the successful consortium to maintain the infrastructure and vehicles throughout the concession period

TENDERING PROCESS PRINCIPLES

Once Royal Assent had been granted on 9th February 1988 to the two Acts of Parliament covering Phase 1, the Secretary of State's announcement enabled the PTE to set in motion the tendering process for the Government-approved DBOM form of contract. In essence two distinct financial assessments would have to be made by each bidding consortium, followed by a simple piece of arithmetic:
1. Determine the cost of building and equipping the system to meet the PTE's performance and other criteria.
2. Determine the estimated value of the operating franchise throughout the concession period.

By subtracting 2 from 1 the balance required from the public sector would be obtained. This public sector contribution would then be met 50% from Central Government (and as it turned out the European Regional Development Fund) in the form of a Section 56 grant, and 50% through the PTA in the form of authorised borrowings with full debt charge cover from Central Government (see later). The grant was paid to GMPTE to the contractor on a stage-by-stage basis.

In principle it would be the bidder offering to undertake the contract while making the lowest demand on the public purse who would be selected. Thus a consortium able to design, build and equip the system for £100 million and who was willing to put up £15 million for the operating rights (requiring only £85 million from the public purse) would be streets ahead of one wanting £120 million to build and equip and offering only £2 million for operating rights (requiring £118 million of public money).

In practice, the tendering process was not nearly so simple; the complexity and pioneering nature of the scheme saw to that. It was recognised from the start that the mere business of tendering for such a wide-ranging contract was going to cost each consortium a considerable amount of money, and that if ten consortia went right through the whole tendering process from start to finish, nine of them would have spent a great deal of money for nothing, and so would the PTE

This notice speaks for itself. Unfortunately the opening date proved rather over-optimistic.   *Author*

in assessing so many tenders. The tendering process had to be structured so that the amount of time and money expended by all concerned would be minimised.

THE TENDERING PROCESS BEGINS

In 1987 an LRT Project Group had been set up within the PTE to handle the implementation stages of the scheme. It was this group which now undertook, with advisers and consultants, the administration of the tendering process. The process started in April 1988 when a Press announcement was issued inviting applications from interested firms for inclusion on a selected list of tenderers. Announcements appeared in local and national newspapers, selected trade journals circulating both in the UK and overseas and in the Official Journal of the European Communities.

Some one hundred and twenty responses were received, many of them from small specialist concerns. At this stage all responses were expressions of interest only; no consortia had then been formed and details like tender price and so on would come much later in the process. Information packs were issued to all bona fide respondents and in due course twelve consortia came together and established themselves as likely candidates for placing on a list of tenderers to proceed to Stage 1 of a two stage tendering process.

Following discussions between GMPTE and the Department of Transport, it was decided to select eight consortia to go forward to Stage 1. The selection was undertaken using a scoring matrix which took into account various characteristics, both negative and positive, of each consortium. This placed the twelve consortia in graduated order of eligibility and it was the eight consortia with the highest scores which were in July 1988 invited by GMPTA on the recommendation of GMPTE to proceed to Stage 1 and take part in the tendering process proper.

Meanwhile in June 1988 the project had been re-launched with the title "Metrolink", a name designed to stick with the light rail scheme throughout its implementation, operation and growth periods. An embryonic operating company was set up – Greater Manchester Rapid Transit Company Ltd – which was intended to become in due course Metrolink's operating company. GMRT Co had a Managing Director (designate) appointed by the PTA. On 27th September 1988 the eight selected consortia were invited to attend a PTE presentation on the tendering process and to ask questions. On 26th October 1988 each of the eight consortia was issued with a complete set of Stage 1 tender documentation comprising some fifty volumes of non-contractual "data bank" information put together for advisory purposes and seven volumes of formal contractual documentation. All the tender documentation was commercially sensitive and had been prepared by engineers working in conjunction with lawyers.

Parts 1 and 2 of the Reference Specifications were the two principal documents against which the consortia were to prepare their bids. Part 1 contained the Operations Brief and Part 2 contained the Civil Engineering, Electrical and Mechanical, and Architectural and Building Works specifications. Consortia were free to amend any part or all of the Reference Specification but had to be prepared to justify to the PTE any changes and to reflect them in the bid price. Consortia were also at liberty to seek for themselves suitable sub-contractors at any time in the tendering or contract periods.

Thus a consortium might have had dialogue with more than one supplier of overhead line equipment and may have sought bids and product information from different ones. Similarly, individual suppliers may have been involved with more than one consortium. The main objective was to produce a working railway/tramway system; how consortia proposed to go about it was not an affair over which the PTE as public-sector client was allowed, in this case at any rate, to exert a great deal of influence.

All PTE dealings with tenderers had to be conducted formally, in confidence and in accordance with commercial protocol; any discussions and questions and answers between the PTE and individual consortia were properly logged and recorded to avoid misunderstandings. As part of the tendering process in December 1988 the tendering consortia were invited by the LRT Project Group to take part in a joint Sunday morning study visit to the Altrincham line to look at engineering features, morning condition and so on. In January 1989 a similar study visit took place to the Bury line; a diesel multiple unit was provided for the consortia representatives' use, the line being closed on Sundays. Other site visits not involving working railway lines took place on weekdays; examples were visits to the city centre and to the BR depot and train maintenance facility at Bury.

During the Stage 1 tender period three of the eight tendering consortia withdrew, leaving the following five consortia to submit their completed tenders to GMPTE on 31st January 1989:

CIE Consult
GMA Group (GEC/Mowlem/AMEC)
Trans-Man RT Systems (Simon Carves)
Trafalgar House/BREL
Norwest Holst/Hawker Siddeley

TENDER EVALUATION

The Metrolink Project Group now set about the task of evaluating the tenders. Each consortium was invited to make a formal full working day presentation to the PTE describing and explaining its tender submission. These "interview" sessions enabled the Project Group to learn more about each tenderer's eligibility than would have been evident from study of the submissions alone. They also permitted tenderers to explain any particular features of their submission. At this stage, for instance, more than one tenderer had decided that Bury BR depot, as it stood, would not be suitable for use as a light rail depot and maintenance facility mainly because of its less than ideal geographical position (at the far end of the system, involving excessive dead LRV mileage and staff travelling) but also because of the site and the building's condition and layout.

The Project Group brought in several different consultants to assist with the evaluation process, and there was liaison between the Project Group and GMPTA, the Department of Transport, Manchester City Engineer and Planners, British Rail and various statutory undertakers. Throughout the evaluation processes staff in the project office worked extremely long hours assessing the tender submissions, which they found to be of consistently high quality.

As with the initial selection process, a matrix method was used to place the tenderering consortia in a ranking order of eligibility. This time, however, the process was much more complex and instead of one matrix, four were used. Three of them reflected Financial, Operational and Technical assessments; the fourth merged the first three with a contractual assessment which took into account each consortium's proposed departures from the Stage 1 tender documentation. One noteworthy proposed departure featured the offer by one consortium of a low floor vehicle type. This interesting proposal could not, however, have been seized upon by the PTE in isolation; the nature of the evaluation process was developed to take into account all aspects of each bid as a package rather than looking at isolated initiatives. The fourth, or "overall", matrix gave the final aggregated ranking of the five consortia. At a meeting on March 14th 1989, GMPTA endorsed the PTE's appraisal by inviting each of the top three consortia in terms of overall matrix scores to proceed to Stage 2 of the tendering process. The three successful consortia were:

Norwest Holst/Hawker Siddeley
GMA (GEC/Mowlem/AMEC)
Trafalgar House/BREL

These three consortia were issued with updated and additional tender documentation and were asked to prepare detailed Stage 2 tenders, refining and developing their Stage 1 submissions. Again, there was much discussion between the PTE's LRT Project Group and individual consortia. Stage 1 of the tendering process had dealt thoroughly with the technical aspects and it was only necessary during Stage 2 to review certain technical features; for instance it was at this stage that the dual voltage concept (750 V d.c. on street and 1500 V d.c. off street) was dropped. Instead, 750 V d.c. has been adopted throughout.

THE SUCCESSFUL CONSORTIUM

During the Stage 2 tendering process there was much emphasis on matters such as capacity, the concession period's length, maintenance of assets, performance measures, risk transfer, network expansion and so on. In the final evaluation and selection process the Project Group looked at each consortium's total composite ability to fulfil the DBOM contract satisfactorily, with special emphasis on catering properly for disabled passengers. Finally, on 27th September an announcement was made that the contract was to be awarded to the GMA consortium led by GEC (electrical, signalling, telecommunications, vehicles, etc) and including John Mowlem & Co (civil engineering), AMEC (depot facilities) and Greater Manchester Buses Ltd.

The successful consortium then went away and commenced detailed design work, while GMPTE went to the Department of Transport with details of the successful bid and proposed contract. The reward for all the hard work and burning of midnight oil came on 24th October 1989 when Mr Michael Portillo, Minister of State for Transport, announced that Section 56 grant would be available for Phase 1 of the Metrolink project.

Even though work had started, putting together the contract documentation was no mean feat in itself and contract signing did not take place until 6th June 1990, exactly 89 years after the opening day of the city's first-generation tramway system. Further complications came from the intricacy of the funding arrangements, altogether the Section 56 eligible cost of the Phase 1 project was initially given as £90 million, broken down roughly into: 36% civil engineering, 30 per cent vehicles and 32% other work (signalling & telecommunications, depot & offices, overhead line equipment, ticket machines). The cost of facilities for the mobility impaired amounted to approximately 1.7% of the total capital cost of the scheme; this expenditure was eligible for Section 56 funding alongside other eligible scheme costs, in accordance with the Government's recognition of the wider benefits of improved access. The contribution from the consortium in respect of the operating franchise is believed to be £5 million. The final cost of the scheme has been about £135 million.

PUBLIC EXPENDITURE PROVISION

Overall, Public Expenditure Provision resurces of about £130 million were allocated for the Metrolink Project. These resources include a direct contribution of some £50 million made available by Central Governmemt through Section 56 Grant. In addition credit approvals were issued by the Department of Transport to the PTA authorising the borrowing of a further £70 million from the Public Works Loan Board; the Standard Spending Assessments (SSAs) of the ten member district Councils of GMPTA have been adjusted to take account if PTA's capital repayments and interest. The Government's contention is that the additional financing charges incurred as a result of Metrolink attract an increase in SSA and also in Revenue Support Grant for the ten District Councils and so have no effect on local tax payers.

The balance of expenditure of £10 million has come from initiatives by the PTE in seeking contributions towards the costs of the Project from third parties. In partnership with Manchester City Council the Urban Programme has been used for environmental enhancement of the Metrolink alignment in the City Centre (block paving, ornate fencing and so on). Central Manchester Development Corporation in turn resourced the enhancement of surface finishes and other works to provide a prestigious station in Piccadilly Undercroft. The final source of contribution towards Metrolink was the Eurpoean Commission through the European Regional Development Fund.

As the total level of Local Government capital spending is controlled by Central Government, the receipt of these contributions did not represent an increase in the PTA's level of capital expenditure. The main benefit the contributions bring is a reduction in the PTA borrowing requirement and consequently a reduction in debt service charges in future years.   Metrolink's £130 million public-sector cost can be compared with some current examples of private-sector spending. "Terminator 2", a recent feature film, cost around £120 million to make; the Shudehill property development in Manchester, for which a Metrolink station site has been reserved at Snow Hill, is expected to cost some £100 million; and the cost of buying a new Jumbo jet is £90 million.

The Government-imposed complete concession, or DBOM, approach would perhaps be better titled "SDBOM" (Specify, Design, Build, Operate and Maintain) because of the breadth of design freedom which GMPTE was forced to give to the tendering consortia and subsequently to the successful consortium. Thus, for example,

► On 31st January 1989 the Stage 1 tenders were opened at GMPTE headquarters. Taking part in this important event are Ian Buttress (then Director of Administration and Secretary to GMPTE), Cllr Larry Sullivan (GMPTA), Cllr Guy Harkin (GMPTA), the late David Graham (Director General, GMPTE), Cllr Winston Ramsey (GMPTA), Cllr Jack Flanagan (GMPTA) and Cllr Joe Clarke (GMPTA). Selection decisions were made by GMPTA with the advice of GMPTE. *GMPTE*

GMPTE was prevented by the Department of Transport from closely specifying the nature of the LRV on-street audible warning of approach, yet the Railway Inspectorate (then working within the same Department of Transport) looked to the PTEs collectively to secure standardisation of audible warnings across different LRT schemes in the UK.

The private sector has relatively little interest in standardisation bearing in mind that different competing contractors, consultants and suppliers are or will be engaged in different schemes around the country; conversely, the PTEs work together towards pooling knowledge and aiming for common standards through the PTE Light Rail Group. Such initiatives obviously come to nothing if the power to implement common standards is taken away. The result in the case of on-street warning devices is that Manchester is getting soft whistles specified by the contractor while Sheffield is getting air gongs specified by the client. Promoters of common light rail design "templates" face an uphill struggle in the UK.

The DBOM arrangement means that the consortium has accepted a wider range of risks than would have been the case within a less privatised implementation package. The successful consortium had had to assess all the risks by studying the reference specification and data bank information and making judgements thereon based on expertise within member firms and their consultants and advisers. As a consequence, several departures from the reference specification were proposed and, if judged reasonable by the PTE, accepted. In this way the winning consortia had been able, in agreement with the client (GMPTE/GMPTA), to moderate the risks within feasible limits.

THE RISK FACTOR

The following list of possible DBOM risks or contingencies is only intended to give an idea of their scope and nature. The list confines itself to matters concerning the LRVs and is by no means official. Some are design risks (d), some are build risks (b), some are operational risks (o) and some are maintenance risks (m), while others may be combinations of two or more categories of risk:
● Vehicle delivery delays (b)
● vehicle suitability for a system with such a wide-ranging mixture of alignments (d/o/m)
● Vehicle fleet size sufficiency (d/o)
● how slowly will the trams have to travel over city-centre trackwork? (d/o)
● will the track geometry meet required lateral jerk limits? (d)
● level of passenger tolerance of standee travel (o)
– these last three add up to: will maximum comfort/speed optimisation be realised on street, bearing in mind the system's admittance of disabled passengers? (d/o/m)
● how well will the on-board layout and station arrangements suit the mobility split of the clientele? (d/o)
● will there be any/many incidents involving serious damage to vehicles causing consequential loss through temporary fleet size reduction? (o)
● will the tram on-street whistle prove effective in clearing the way

and be sufficiently distinctive? (d/o)
The provision and use of a prototype vehicle bodyshell to refine detailed vehicle design will have helped minimise some of the design and operational risks of the trams, as also will earlier initiatives at Birchfields Road and Debdale Park and all the PTE's past consultative endeavours as well as user-group consultation pursued under the adverse conditions of the design/build period itself.

INSURING METROLINK

A distinction exists between risks which can and risks which cannot be covered by insurance. In the speculative list of risks given above, most are commercial risks accepted by the consortium; coverage of the insurable risks has been arranged separately by GMPTE in view of its ownership of all Metrolink's assets. The PTE interviewed several different insurance brokers with a view to putting in place insurance covering possible loss of or damage to those assets which include vehicles, infrastructure, station equipment, etc.

Jardine Insurance Brokers were duly appointed, and arranged for the PTE an owner controlled insurance programme ensuring that the PTE maintains close control of insurance cover, which otherwise could have spread itself out amongst consortium members with possible duplication of and/or gaps in the cover. Jardine's first jobs were to arrange contingent third party liability cover in respect of the pre-construction services diversion works, and insurance cover for the Arch 97 pre-production bodyshell display described in Chapter 5.

The Metrolink owner-controlled insurance cover encompasses both construction and operational phases. The policy covers public liability during construction and operation both in terms of third-party personal injury and of damage to third-party property. In a construction project like Metrolink, anything can happen; a crane might topple, a building might subside, a lady might have her jacket burnt by a spark from a Thermit welding process, a water main may be fractured and flood an important cable duct or close a department store for a day causing consequential loss, traffic surveillance cameras may be damaged by cable severance – the possiblities are endless, but they are all covered by the Owner Controlled Insurance Programme. Although there have been a number of minor claims it is to everyone's credit that there have been no major damage claims.

Premiums for the varied and comprehensive cover have had to be worked out from scratch with no real measure of the risks to use as a starting point, though Jardines already had an in-house public transport division with experience of bus and rail insurance on which to draw. The premium for the construction phase is funded, like the scheme's capital costs, as part of the expenditure eligible for Section 56 grant assistance. A provisional sum was included for the operational insurance premium, but if this amount is exceeded GMPTA/E (not GMML) will have to pay the additional premium from internal budgets. All insurance cover except employee liability is, then, publicly funded throughout the construction and 15-year concession periods.

The insurance includes fire cover, and along with the Fire Service Jardines have given advice on fire precautions and on the procedures to be followed in the event of fire breaking out. This has been especially relevant at Metrolink House, from where the Operations Centre controls the running of the entire system. The consequences of a fire in there have been fully evaluated, and adequate means of extinguishing any fires have been built in. Full disaster planning is being undertaken (see Chapter 14). Fortunately, light rail systems tend not to suffer catastrophic incidents thanks to the trams' powerful emergency brakes – but it's better to be sure that if such a thing did happen it would be dealt with efficiently. Staff are also being given First Aid training.

Because of the combination of various unknown elements making up the risks of running a disabled-friendly LRT system like Metrolink, there will be an annual review of the insurance cover. If necessary, independent auditors can be called in to give advice on risk reassessment and there will in any case be careful observation and investigation of all claims. The value of the owner controlled insurance cover is substantial enough for it to have been laid off around the world because no single insurer could take it on alone.

FORMALITIES

Apart from insurance, various mechanisms are built into the contract to protect against different risks and contingencies and to make sure that the consequences of any unforeseen circumstances are borne fairly. For example, the construction sector of the consortium will have to put right at their own expense any constructional faults, referred to as latent defects, which do not become apparent until the system is in operation.

The whole complicated abundance of contract documentation, Articles of Association, licences, deeds, guarantees and so on meant, as we have observed, that the work involved in setting up the contract and agreements went on well into the construction phase. The complicated and novel nature of the DBOM contract made the whole composite tendering, evaluation and documentation preparation exercise a little like building a precarious house of cards. It was vital to get all the documentation absolutely right because so many future arguments could hinge on it; in an ideal world, once prepared it would be locked away into a (large) cupboard and never referred to again.

A letter of intent was meanwhile issued to enable work to begin. Another task which got under way when the consortium was appointed was the formation of the new Metrolink company GMML (Greater Manchester Metro Limited) as supplier and operator; GMML was the new company set up by the consortium in preference to using GMRTCo. GMML had to be established as an incorporated company, the supplier party to the contract, before contract signing could take place. The client signatory was of course GMPTE.

GMML has as its shareholders GEC Alsthom (25.1%), John Mowlem PLC (25.1%), AMEC PLC (25.1%), GM Buses Limited (12.35%) and GMPTE (12.35%). Readers will note that GMPTE is both the client and a shareholder in GMML. Companies in the GMA group (GEC, Mowlem, AMEC, GM Buses) hold between them a total of 75.3% of the shares. Responsibility for the civil, electrical and mechanical engineering aspects is as follows: AMEC (Depot); Mowlem (Running line, structures, track); GECA (Rolling Stock, Power, Signals, Telecoms, Overhead Line Equipment, Fare Collection). It should be understood that GM Buses is emphatically not the operator of Metrolink; Greater Manchester Metro Ltd, in which GMBL is only one of several shareholders, is exclusively the system's operator.

A comprehensive set of Contracts and Agreements are embodied within the DBOM Contract. For instance, a Reversion Agreement ensures that the system's operation can continue on expiry of the 15-year concession period or if for any reason GMML defaults under the terms of the DBOM Contract, becomes insolvent or wishes voluntarily to relinquish the concession; this could happen, for example, in the event of unprofitability.

In contracting generally, the specifications and terms to which both parties are signatories are rigidly adhered to except when unforeseen variations have to be introduced. A completely hypothetical example might be an extra crossover somewhere on the system. The client, having decided during the construction phase to consider an extra crossover would ask the contractor to prepare a price for the work. The contractor's quantity surveyors would produce such a price, which would then be verified by the client's own quantity surveyors. If the client agreed the price, wished to go ahead with the extra work and could justify it financially then the work would be put in hand, covered by appropriate variation paperwork. This variation scenario could also apply between main contractor and sub-contractors.

Another type of eventuality which has to be provided for in contracting is the concession or waiver; in this context this means a per-

mission given to the contractor by the client to allow him to depart from the terms of the contract. Thus a contractor might want to change his supplier or even his sub-contractor during a contract. If this involved a departure from the specification the contractor would have to obtain an appropriate concession from the client, which under typical contract terms would "not be unreasonably withheld". These generalised background observations have been included only to show the great importance of contract paperwork and are not intended to relate specifically to Metrolink or to any other scheme.

PROJECT MANAGEMENT

It follows that the client must have adequate staffing resources to supervise and administer the contract and in effect to regulate the spending of public money, and that the more novel and complicated the project, the more staffing resources the client ought to allocate to guarantee complete success, minimise disruption and obtain value for money. The Metrolink contract has been handled from within GMPTE by the aforementioned Project Group consisting of a Project Executive with a dedicated staff which includes a Project Manager, a Project Engineer (civils), a Project Engineer (rail/M & E), a Legal Officer, a Project Accountant and an Administration Officer. This team has been assisted from time to time by specialists in different fields but has never enjoyed abundant staffing commensurate with the demands of the project. By way of comparison, some fourteen Engineers will form part of the thirty-strong Sheffield Supertram Design and Build project team acting for the client, backed up by Inspectors drawn either from Sheffield City staff or provided by the project management consultants.

In Manchester, the contract structure embodies a multitude of interfaces between contractors, sub-contractors and suppliers in addition to those with the operator and with many other agencies including British Rail, the City Engineer, HM Railway Inspector and so on. For example, Mowlem's sub-contracted permanent way work to Balfour Beatty and GECA sub-contracted overhead line work to the same group. Thus trackbeds and pole bases have been installed by one main contractor (Mowlem) and rails, poles and overhead wiring by sub-contractors (Balfour Beatty). More disparity, part of it inevitable, has been introduced by the varied origins of the equipment used; grooved tramway rail, tramway point switches, point motors and diamonds (crossings) have each come from a different supplier and have been married together on the city's streets. The vehicle itself embodies elements from a great many sources which have had to be initially proven and interfaced with the rest of the system in Manchester.

In Sheffield, where there is likely to be less dispersal of component supply, one single contractor is undertaking the civil engineering works, the permanent way installation work and the overhead line erection work; this is bound to make co-ordination, continuity, cohesion, communication and co-operation that much easier and to reduce the scope for error. Fewer detailed demands will be made on the project management team – which, paradoxically, as we have just noted, is far larger than Manchester's.

One of the tasks which fell to the Metrolink Project Group was the examination of critical path analyses projected by the three Stage 2 tendering consortia and the preparation of critical path charts in consultation with the successful consortium to assist with controlling the phasing of the work, especially in the city centre. Abundant interfaces with other bodies meant that there had to be a common timing reference to enable different activities to be dovetailed together into a coherent programme without conflicting with each other. The critical path analysis would also facilitate adherence to projected milestone dates and target completion dates for different aspects of the work, and hopefully enable remedial action to be put in hand to resolve problems when necessary and avoid delays. It would also be useful if at a later stage blame for delays had to be apportioned between contractors, sub-contractors, client and outside bodies.

THE STATUTORY DIVERSION WORKS

Knowing what an excessively demanding challenge the insertion of modern tramways into some of Manchester's main city centre streets was in itself, PTE planners and City engineers resolved to clear the way for the main job by arranging for the shifting and rationalisation of statutory undertakers' sub-surface plant and equipment. A similar programme of plant diversionary works had been undertaken in Grenoble, France in preparation for tramway installation.

A great deal of effort was put into identifying all currently-used underground telephone and electricity cables and gas, water, drainage and sewage pipes. Careful consultation with all the owning statutory bodies was undertaken to fully identify everything which might have to be altered or moved; although recently-installed plant was accurately recorded on drawings, charts and plans there was plenty more about which little was known.

There were other services which were no longer used, including high-pressure hydraulic mains which once powered lifts, capstans (including those used in Piccadilly Undercroft for shunting railway wagons), cranes and even the Town Hall clock; Mercury Communications Ltd has since bought the hydraulic mains network for cable distribution purposes. Also lying abandoned were pneumatic tubes which carried telegraph messages on paper from the Head Post Office in Spring Gardens to outlying sub-offices, the Stock and Corn Exchanges and the Docks.

To further verify the extent and nature of underground services which would have to be moved or modified, trial excavations across carriageways were made at ten or so locations along the route in June and July 1988. As well as ensuring that the street track installation work would proceed smoothly, the plant diversion strategy was directed at ensuring that, once constructed, the light rail tracks and trackbed would never have to be disturbed or tram services disrupted while statutory undertakers did work on their plant. Anyone who has seen how readily trams can continue to run in service on their skeletal rails over the top of stupendous holes and complex civil engineering operations will know that this exercise was not absolutely essential − but it would help to guarantee a trouble-free DBOM concession period to the light rail operator.

Basically, all cables and pipes were sleeved where they passed under the trackbed alignments so that future renewals and changes could be done from either side with the trams (and other traffic) still running through. New services alignments with manholes for access purposes were constructed away from the swept paths of the light rail vehicles; unfortunately this obstructed the very sites where traction poles ought to be put for best effect, as we shall see later. Sometimes, main services were diverted to run along back streets, as with gas mains which were relaid in George Street parallel to Mosley Street. An additional benefit of the diversion works was that the LRT construction contractors would experience minimum difficulty and delay

caused by encountering nasty subterranean surprises when excavating the streets for the trackbeds. The disadvantage for the city was that two separate periods of disruption would have to be endured.

The plant diversion works proper commenced on Monday 13th March 1989 with the complete closure of Mosley Street for 3 months. This street had been used in both directions by buses serving the south-western part of the conurbation; these services were diverted, mostly via the parallel-running Portland Street. Similar bus diversions took place in and around Parker Street (Piccadilly Gardens) bus station to accommodate preparatory works at the centre of the future light rail system.

De-regulation saw to it that diversion of a substantial proportion of city centre bus services was not a simple matter. Liaison with around 23 operators had to be undertaken, but as GMPTE owned and controlled the bus station facilities it was at least possible for some degree of control to be exercised. It is to the credit of the bus as a non-fixed mode of transport that termini and route alignments could be altered so readily, but that didn't make things any easier for a perplexed member of the public trying to find the new departure point of his bus home. Twenty-one bus stands have been permanently relocated. Bus service disruption has continued throughout the implementation period and has imposed unusually heavy workloads on the team of PTE staff responsible for bus station administration and customer liaison.

A PTE Community Liaison Supervisor with extensive working knowledge of bus services in the city centre was appointed and a Metrolink enquiry point was established in his charge on the edge of Piccadilly Gardens; this facility is described in more detail in Chapter 6. Weekly meetings were held in the PTE offices between all parties involved. During these Monday meetings the coming week's work would be discussed to maintain co-ordination. These meetings continued throughout the construction period; every Monday evening at 17.00 a PTE representative has been allocated airtime on Greater Manchester Radio to inform the public of the current "state of play" in the city. Regular notices have also appeared in the Manchester Evening News saying what city-centre roads would be affected in the coming days.

▶ This elevated view shows the course of part of the city-centre tram route during its construction. The cream-tiled Arndale Centre, complete with rooftop houses and gardens, fills the top right of the picture while the straight, level Snow Hill section of tramroad at bottom right is surrounded by the site of the proposed Shude Hill Development − which may one day may have its very own Metrolink station. Shude Hill is near to the centre of the picture, adjacent to the spiral car park ramp. The tramway continues along Nicholas Croft and High Street to "Debenhams Corner", where it turns left into Market Street to reach Piccadilly Gardens in the top left hand corner of the picture. Note the long tent on Nicholas Croft, erected to protect the rail-encapsulating polymer from the weather.   *Author*

▶ Tracklaying in progress on Snow Hill with grooved rails placed in position on top of the concrete trackbed. The tent which can be seen on the left hand track was used in the early stages of polymer pouring to protect the Sika polymer from the elements until it dried.
Peter Fox

8. THE VEHICLES

THE FIREMA CONSORTIUM

Metrolink's fleet of 26 articulated trams has been supplied by GEC-Alsthom and built by the Firema Consortium of Italy. The Firema Consortium was established in Milan in 1980, bringing together several Italian builders of railway rolling stock and public transport vehicles.

Firema's tender was accepted by GEC Alsthom, the GMA consortium member responsible for vehicle supply, because the Italian consortium was already an established supplier of vehicles which came close enough to the design required for Manchester. Firema had recently supplied Milan's "Jumbo" articulated trams — capable of handling depot curves down to 15 m radius — as well as articulated trams for Genoa and Naples and for Rome's ACOTRAL interurban service. Metrolink's vehicles bear a family likeness to the Firema trams in the latter three cities. Another factor in Firema's favour was the production capacity they offered, giving an obvious head start in meeting Metrolink's tight two-year design and build deadline for delivery of the 26 cars. The Italians were also quite capable of communicating in English with GEC-Alsthom. The relationship works both ways: GEC-Alsthom has recently supplied equipment to Firema for new suburban rail vehicles to be used on the Circumflegrea and Cumana railways.

Combining sleek Italian elegance with a smart UK-designed livery, Metrolink's trams make proud flagships of an exciting new dawn in British urban history. Conforming to the six-axle bi-directional conventional floor-height design always envisaged for Manchester, the vehicles can attain a top speed of 80 km/h (50 mph). They can negotiate curves down to 25 m radius and tackle gradients as steep as 6.5% (1 in 15), giving them a versatility which helps explain their £1m price tag.

THE PRE-PRODUCTION BODY SHELL

As required by the DBOM contract, a well-equipped mock-up body shell was constructed by Firema and installed by GEC Alsthom within a representation of an on-street profiled platform installed by the PTE near to Piccadilly station in Arch 97, North Western Street. Chapter 6 gives more information about the display itself, which was used to develop the detailed design and promote Metrolink's point of interface with its public — the light rail vehicle itself. The bodyshell is now part of the collection at Manchester's Museum of Transport to the rear of Queen's Road bus depot, close to the home of its 26 tram descendants at Metrolink's Queen's Road HQ. The preserva-tion of the body shell reflects its importance in helping determine the final design of Britain's first street-running light rail vehicles.

FLEET SIZE AND ROUTINE MAINTENANCE

Metrolink's production fleet of trams consists of 26 vehicles, 23 of which are needed to cope with peak services. The three remaining vehicles will be on standby or undergoing repair. Pedometers fitted to all vehicles will assist with equalizing vehicle mileages and with monitoring distance run between routine maintenance operations. All vehicles will normally be stored in the open on stabling tracks. Under the terms of the contract, each tram will be washed externally and cleaned internally every day. External washing is done by driving the vehicle slowly through the Queens Road washing plant, while internal cleaning is done on walkway-accessed stabling tracks by specialist cleaning contractors. Vehicles will also be swept out at the Bury and Altrincham termini.

To retain close control over vehicle condition, tram maintenance is carried out entirely in-house by Metrolink staff using equipment supplied for the most part by sub-contractors Brown & Root Limited. The extent and nature of the facilities and equipment and the level of staffing are all directly related to the size of the initial fleet of 26 vehicles though everything is expandable. All maintenance staff have been encouraged to train as drivers; this means that they will gain first-hand experience of how the trams "feel" in service, reaping dividends in terms of increased awareness of the conditions under which the equipment has to perform "out on the road".

Queens Road is well equipped with wheel lathe, wheel press, jacks, overhead crane, fitting shop, welding bay, electrical repair shop, battery room, bogie maintenance area and stores — everything, in fact, that is needed to carry out regular maintenance functions. It is envisaged that most work will be done during normal hours; only 14 vehicles are needed for the off-peak service, releasing several for interpeak attention. A certain amount of work will be done at night. Irregular work such as collision damage repair may be contracted out, perhaps involving sending the vehicles away.

CONSTRUCTION AND DELIVERY

The 26 vehicles were constructed in four major Firema plants; 4 at Officine di Cittadella (Padua), 8 at Casaralta (Bologna), 7 at Fiore

▼ This General Arrangement drawing shows the principal features and dimensions of Metrolink's fleet of Firema articulated tramcars.

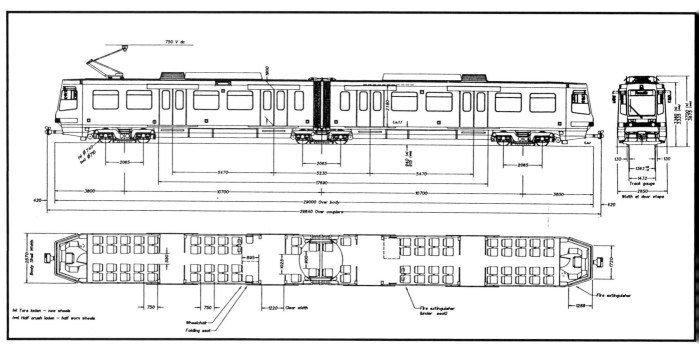

Car No 1011 is seen here on the main inspection pit at Queens Road on 13th January. This photograph shows detail of the visible under-parts.

Colin J Marsden

(Caserta, north of Naples) and 7 at Officine Casertane (also at Caserta). Design work was done jointly by GEC-Alsthom in Trafford Park, Manchester and by Firema in Milan. All the bogies, including a complete extra car set for maintenance rotation, were constructed at Officine Meccanica della Stanga (Padua) and then were transported to the other plants for association with car bodies.

Electrical equipment supplied by GEC-Alsthom from Trafford Park and Preston was shipped out to Italy and fitted to the trams, along with other non-Firema items. Approximately 60% of the tram content is of British origin; the ability to secure this degree of home participation was another important factor in selecting Firema.

Delivery began in August 1991 with car number 1001. This 30 m long 45 tonne tram was shipped complete by road as a "Convoi Exceptionnel" across Europe on a trailer featuring computer-controlled steering of every wheel. The journey was eventful and prolonged and was not completed until around 20.45 on 29th August 1991 when No 1001 was manoeuvred skillfully into Metrolink's Queens Road premises, to become next day the first street-running light rail vehicles to set wheel on UK rail.

An interval of one month elapsed before the next tram, No 1002, arrived in sections — two separated body halves and three bogies — by road on 28th September. Division of the trams into smaller loads greatly eased the transport problem and began to dash hopes that they would be glamorously shipped in pairs aboard a giant Russian Antonov freight jet. The third arrived in sections by road on 16th October, and soon after that deliveries settled down to one a week, each taking 3–4 days to cross Europe, with the last of the 26 vehicles expected in February.

On the first few vehicles a considerable amount of testing and commissioning work had to be done at Queens Road by GEC-Alsthom staff with the assistance of two Firema engineers. Soon, though, the vehicles began to arrive factory-tested, considerably reducing the amount of work needed before their release for test running. Here, GMML's driver training programme interacted with GEC-Alsthom's

test runs, with trainee Metrolink drivers acting as "chauffeurs" to the GEC-Alsthom engineers as they carried out some of their tests.

The tram livery, like the corporate design image it reflects, was developed for Greater Manchester Metro by Fitch RS and Design Triangle. The principal colour, a very pale shade of grey, is relieved by a darker shade of grey for the window surrounds and lower vehicle/skirt area. A thick stripe of aquamarine is superimposed all round on the lower half the waist panels. The use of headlights, marker lights and tail lights day and night means that the menacing and livery-disrupting yellow end treatment found on BR units is thankfully not necessary on Metrolink. The GMML logo, featuring an encircled geometric "M", appears over the leading bogie position and the whole effect is a great improvement over the rather bland colour scheme initially shown on the bodyshell.

BODYWORK

The bodywork consists of welded steel sections and sheets. The composite floor has a fireproof underside of stainless steel sheet, composite wood sheets in the middle for strength, and rubber covering on top for grip and abrasion resistance. Each tram consists of two separate almost identical halves united back-to-back by an articulation. One half — the one with the pantograph — is designated A, the other B. The articulation is the product of Firema's long experience in designing articulations. This began before World War Two with the Stanga-Urbanati type developed in cooperation with Signor Urbinati, Director of Rome Tramways at that time, by Officina Meccanica della Stanga — the company which, within the Firema Consortium, has constructed all of Metrolink's bogies.

Metrolink's tram articulations, as well as permitting movement in the usual lateral and vertical directions, also allow one body half to twist slightly in relation to the other. This feature comes into play when entering and leaving sharp superelevated curves or negotiating tight S-bends at any appreciable speed. Shear-tolerant bellows material was specially obtained from Germany. The top of the articulation arch is located by spring-loaded cross-arms linking the roof ends of the body halves while the lower part of the arch is supported on the bogie bolster beam.

PASSENGER ACCOMMODATION

With regard to the apportionment of on-board space, the Consortium's hands were tied by the PTA's performance specifications, which required that no passenger should have to stand for longer than 15 minutes outside the city centre. From this stipulation a seating capacity of 86 (82 fixed plus 4 fold-down) per articulated unit had been derived and would have to remain in force unless the PTA reviewed its vehicle capacity requirements in the light of experience. Metrolink's designed load factor (the ratio of standing to seated passengers) is generous compared with similar systems elsewhere, where $2+1$ or even $1+1$ seating arrangements release useful gangway width and provide more practical standee conditions. Metrolink's contrastingly seat-saturated layout is intended to reflect the load factor of the replaced trains and to help entice motorists out of their cars onto public transport. With a bigger fleet this strategy might make have made good sense.

Metrolink's Italian-made seats are upholstered in an aquamarine/dark grey lozenge-patterned moquette supplied by Firth's of Heckmondwike (now part of the Magna Moquette group). The $2+2$ seating arrangement is of the ranked airline-style pattern, there being no face-to-face seating. This enables the maximum number of seats to be fitted and was an arrangement for which women had expressed a preference. Each seating unit actually consists of a pair of adjacent single seats, a feature which will deter selfish (or broad) passengers from straddling double seats in the hope that no one will ask them to "move across please".

Mock-up body shell questionnaires had shown that a high proportion of people were prepared to stand, on average for 10 minutes. Perhaps this response was conditioned by the absolutely static bolted-to-the-ground steadiness of the body shell. Be that as it may, comments on the height of the body shell's ceiling-mounted longitudinal handrails resulted in their being lowered one and a half inches, moved inwards and increased in diameter. Good standee facilities in the aisles can serve a commercial purpose in drawing passengers away from door lobby areas, allowing more passengers to board. There are no vertical grab-poles in the seating aisles; passengers unable to reach the grab-rails will have to use the seat-back handles for support.

Each tram has two designated wheelchair spaces each equipped with a pull-down occasional seat for use when the space is not needed by a chairbound passenger. Metrolink looks like being the most dynamically-eventful disabled-friendly light rail system seen so far, yet wheelchair users visiting the extremely static bodyshell fortunately did not see any need for wheelchair-restraining clamps; their application and release would need staff assistance which, even if it were available, might give rise to delays embarrassing to the wheelchair user. No conclusion has in any case been reached as to whether chairbound passengers should be recommended to travel facing sideways, forward or backwards.

To answer requests for more general-purpose utility accommodation, space has been created opposite each wheelchair bay by substituting a pull-down seat for a fixed seating unit. Suitcase stowage can be a problem on intensive urban tranport systems, and passengers will always put their luggage where it is not wanted whatever is done otherwise; there is, for instance, space for small items of shopping and baggage underneath most of the seats. Unfortunately, some passengers will compensate for any shortage of obvious utility space by placing luggage on seats, consuming valuable seating space and defying anyone to ask them to remove it.

DOORS

Though the bodyshell's working door equipment received a great deal of attention, the secluded and static mock-up could nowhere near simulate the conditions prevailing "out there" on a working transport system. Nevertheless, some important lessons were learned; the SMC Pneumatics long-stroke belt-driven air-powered sliding type door equipment fitted to the production trams is basically the same as was fitted to the bodyshell.

British-made external sliding doors had been chosen because of their proven simplicity and reliability though they did incur slight sacrifice of body width. Swing plug doors would not have consumed body width but might have fouled platform edges in certain conditions, and internally swinging doors had proved too unpopular on the Docklands Light Railway for them to receive serious consideration for Manchester. One of the penalties of providing level access

on public transport is that it exposes door action to criticism; door movements occurring in stepwells, as on buses, attract little interest from the public.

The lightweight sandwich-construction doors have a closing action which diminishes in force as the doors approach each other. This reduces the likelihood of entrapment, though user-group consultees wanted auto-reopening of obstructed doors by so-called "sensitive edges" — an option offered by SMC Pneumatics but not taken up. Consortium officials pointed out that automatic re-opening would cause delays at crowded stations and that with the selected "stalling" action the doors would persistently exert a steady closing pressure on any obstruction so as to shorten dwell times. This was one example of passenger reassurance giving way to operational expediency in the real public transport world.

When a vehicle has stopped in a station, the driver presses a button to "prime" the doors on the appropriate side of the vehicle(s). This "enabling" of the doors is accompanied by a "ping" sound together with simultaneous illumination of the door opening buttons located on the inside and outside of the vehicle, inviting passengers to open the doors by pressing the handily-placed buttons; visually-handicapped users would have preferred a less flush-surfaced button type than has been provided. Wrong-side doors, not having been "primed" by the driver, will not open. The same-side external mirror swings out when the doors open and back again when they close.

The importance of the door/passenger interface on Metrolink can best be imagined by thinking of an tram moving off from, say, the busy Market Street stop into the area of teeming pedestrian activity at "Debenhams Corner", where drivers will certainly have plenty to occupy their attention. Closure of the doors is preceded by a loud "bleep" and departure cannot occur until the door-action limit switches interlocked with the control circuits confirm that all doors are closed. Dwell times of 20 seconds at suburban stations and 30 seconds in the city centre have been projected; recovery time built into the scheduling should allow these to be exceeded slightly in practice without causing undue service disruption.

Each entrance also has a sliding step which only emerges when the car forms the second car of a coupled pair, to give access from the trailing low portion of the on-street profiled platforms. Step mechanisms, to a Firema design, are interlocked like the doors with the door control and braking/traction circuits.

DRIVER'S CABS

There is a driver's cab at each end of the trams, separated from the passenger accommodation by a glazed partition having an unglazed door which swings into the cab so that it can still be opened even when standing passengers are crowded against it. The cab windows have been deepened and extended rearwards to improve the driver's range of view, though the pockets for the retracting mirrors still form partial blind spots at the sides. The side windows are arranged to open slightly to enable off-vehicle staff to talk with the driver at stations.

In his (a pronoun which is convenient but at the same time inadequate when used in the context of a system boasting drivers of both sexes) comfortable cab the Metrolink driver is surrounded by sophisticated controls and instruments well laid out to give him the high degree of control and management you'd expect on a vehicle costing a million pounds. Here it has to be pointed out that traction engineers have always had to strike a balance between the two extremes of providing completely foolproof "all-singing-all-dancing" control systems and, alternatively, relying on drivers' natural skill, discipline and resourcefulness to handle the vehicle properly. Control systems old and new have all represented some particular blend of gadgetry and simplicity. Simpler systems have always cost less to buy and maintain, but microprocessors are now allowing sophistication to be increased without undue technical or financial penalties.

PASSENGER/DRIVER COMMUNICATION

Passengers are able to see ahead from the forwardmost seats and, more importantly, they are aware that the driver is able to see them just by turning around. For the sake of on-board security at night, it is to be hoped that drivers don't feel compelled to draw down the anti-glare blinds fitted behind them — and that if the blinds do have to be lowered they are raised again on vacating the cab. Mirrors are fitted in the cabs to allow drivers to glance backwards into the saloons.

The cab doors, being solid and windowless and locked from the driver's side, have an emergency call point panel at head height by means of which passengers can communicate with the driver. Control at Queens Road is automatically alerted whenever it is used. At the wheelchair positions there are communication panels by means

The interior of the Metrolink articulation accommodates four single seats bracketted from the articulation arch. This isolates the seats from the turntable floor, which is hinged. The articulation arch structures cleverly accommodate emergency equipment. It is interesting to watch the performance of the articulation structures in motion both at speed off-street and in the city centre when negotiating sharp curves and changes of gradient.   *Colin J Marsden*

of which passengers with mobility difficulties can, for example, ask the driver for more time at an alighting point or ask him to travel more slowly through sharp corners. In the door lobby areas there are red emergency handles which can be rotated to release the doors so that they can be manually opened for escape purposes.

Drivers or controllers can speak to passengers through the PA system; normally every stop will be announced by the driver as the tram approaches it so that people can prepare to alight. This will reduce stop dwell times as well as assisting visually handicapped passengers. Apart from these interfaces, the driver will be as sealed off from his passengers as a train driver; only when customer services staff pay a visit to the vehicle will the passenger/staff isolation be relieved.

DRIVING CONTROLS

The first thing to say about Metrolink's tram controls is that the driver's feet are given nothing at all to do. British trams and trains have always featured hand-operated controls, so it is not surprising that Metrolink follows suit; on Manchester's trams the single Traction and Braking Controller (TBC) is operated by the driver's left hand. In electrical terms the TBC is a potentiometer operated by a T-handle looking something like an automatic car's selector lever. The top bar of the "T" is sprung to twist back anticlockwise to a fore/aft alignment when released and the stem is sprung to return rearwards to the full emergency brake position. The "driving hand" is given one additional job to do; a thumb-operated button located in the end of the TBC's cross-piece actuates the audible warning of approach.

The TBC is made active by means of an "ignition" – like key inserted in a panel to its left. The key-operated switch has three positions – "Off", "Shunt" and "Normal". In either "Shunt" or "Normal" modes, fore/aft movement of the adjacent TBC controls the vehicle's traction and braking circuits. In "Shunt" mode, the max-

imum speed is 12 mph, above which power is cut and the brakes come on; "Normal" mode permits running up to the full 50 mph maximum except on street when 30 mph is the maximum achievable speed.

The TBC has a mid-way "Coast" position in which the vehicle is neither motoring nor braking. In this economical freewheeling condition the axle speed is still being monitored so that the equipment will respond instantly and accurately to the driver's next movement of the TBC. When the TBC is moved forward of the mid-position power is applied to the motors; the further it is pushed the greater the acceleration will be and the faster the vehicle will go. Maximum acceleration rate is 1.3 m/sec ^{2}. Any wheelspin is taken care of by slip/slide detection equipment, which automatically equalises all the axles' speeds and which, if service experience requires it, can be modified to apply auto sand; no indication is given to the driver that wheelspin is being corrected, though as it usually occurs at the leading wheels where the slipperiest conditions are encountered he may hear or feel the wheels lose adhesion briefly.

Full power is harmful to d.c. motors when they are stationary or turning slowly. Traditional control systems protect the motors during acceleration by, in effect, "dumping" excess power as heat through resistances; the action of notching-up a classic tram controller cuts out resistance as the motors turn faster. Chopper control, a more sophisticated method of regulating the power fed to the motors, does the same job less wastefully. Instead of throwing away the excess power, the microprocessor-controlled chopper equipment fitted to Metrolink trams rapidly switches the current on and off so that the net power reaching the motors at any given speed of rotation is sufficient but not excessive.

This rapid switching of heavy currents to a highly inductive load is only practical with modern solid-state electronic components, principally the gate-turn-off (GTO) thyristor for control of armature current and the insulated gate bipolar transistor (IGBT) for field control. Chopping takes place at a constant frequency of 600 Hz; as the vehicle moves off from standstill the "on" period in each cycle is short and its amplitude is large. Conversely, at higher speeds the "on" period is longer and the amplitude smaller. When motoring at full speed there is no "off" period at all.

For any given motoring position of the TBC there is a "balancing speed" of the vehicle, up to the permitted maximum of 50 mph when the TBC is fully forward. Allowing the TBC to move backwards from the "coast" position sends a braking request condition to the electronic brake control equipment, again to a degree depending on how far it is allowed to move towards the fully-back position where a slight detent limits its normal service braking range; allowing it to come back further than the detent puts the vehicle into emergency braking mode.

BRAKING SYSTEMS

Metrolink trams have no fewer than five separate braking systems: air-applied spring-released disc service brake, spring-applied air-released disc parking brake, regenerative dynamic service brake, rheostatic dynamic service brake and totally independent battery-powered magnetic track emergency brakes. These systems work through three separate braking mediums − 8 (see later) axle-mounted disc brakes, 4 traction motors with dynamic braking capability, and 6 track brakes.

Exemplifying the diversity of suppliers contributing to the Metrolink trams, the wheel-brake systems embody parts supplied by three separate firms. The axle-mounted brake discs and outside-hung calipers are by Poli, an Italian company. The combined service and parking brake actuators on the powered axles and service-only actuators on the unpowered axles are by SAB WABCO, an international company, and the electro-pneumatic brake control equipment is by Davies and Metcalfe, a British firm based locally near Stockport.

The bogies are fitted with levelling valves which control the height of the secondary suspension air bags to maintain constant door sill height relative to platform edge height. The air bags in turn are pneumatically connected to "load cut-off valves" associated with the braking controllers. As the air pressure in the bags depends on the passenger load the tram is carrying, these valves act as load-weighing devices matching braking effort to tram load. Service braking is primarily regenerative; the motors are used as dynamos to generate current, and the load this places on them constitutes the braking effort. The power they generate is initially offered to the line via the pantograph. If the line is receptive − that is, if other trams are taking current from it − the regenerated power is absorbed by the motors of the other tram(s). The substations themselves cannot do anything with the regenerated current; what really happens during regenera-

POLI disc brake:
division which is strength!

The division of the crown into spaced sectors produces a disc brake based on totally new concepts and provides exceptional results.

Complete safety and reliability: since 1978 POLI has placed more then 26,000 disc brakes in railway service and none of them has ever failed, wholly confirming the results of studies carried out by Milan Polithecnic.

High performance is constantly proved in both railway (suburban operation, locomotives, Eurocity, rapid freight wagon, high speed) and metropolitan application (underground services, trams, light rail vehicles).
Research performed by Trieste University (Italy) proved, also theoretically, the much higher thermal load capacity due to the crown division into freely expansible sectors.

Replacement of the crown is always guaranteed without removing the wheel, because the flange hub is unalterable, the sector connection being fixed. The spare crown is identical to the original and therefore ensures continuing high performance.

Low cost/performance ratio: it is reduced by up to one-third thanks to
— long life of the crown which always reaches its wear limits
— low specific consumption of the special alloyed crown and braking pads
— perfect condition of the hub
— minimum maintenance and inspection costs.

Poli Officine Meccaniche S.p.A. - CO.MA.TRA S.p.A. - C.T.E. S.r.l.   supplies:

— complete disc brake equipment (cylinder, caliper, pad holders, pad, disc)
— complete wheelsets for traction units and trailers
— electromagnetic track brakes

— reduction gears
— axles
— air springs
— resilient wheels
— spare parts

POLI Officine Meccaniche S.p.A. - 26014 ROMANENGO (CR) ITALY - Tel. (0373) 270126 - Fax (0373) 729097 - Telex 320821 POLI I

tion is that less power is taken from the substation, in effect reducing the size of the electricity bill and, to a tiny extent, man's consumption of the world's energy resources.

If the line is not receptive — if for instance our tram is the only one out at the time — the line voltage will begin to rise as the tram tries to feed power back into it. The same happens if the pantograph is not in good contact with the wire for any reason. The control electronics instantly detect the rising line voltage and redirect the current to roof-mounted resistance units, which dissipate it as heat.

The braking controller monitors the braking effort being provided by the motors and supplements it with air-operated disc braking as necessary to provide the requested braking effort; hence the term "blended braking". To give the motorless centre bogie something worthwhile to do besides carrying the articulation, each of its axles is fitted with two disc brake units and the control equipment is configured to make more use of these disc brakes than of those on the motored axles. The maximum service braking rate is 1.3 m/sec^2. It must be emphasised that passengers will not notice the transitions between service braking modes and neither will the driver have to worry about the distribution of service braking effort; it is all done automatically.

The traction motors can only act as dynamos down to about 4 mph. Without any other braking the tram would drift on at around that speed until friction, an adverse gradient or a headwind brought it to a standstill. What actually happens is that the disc brakes automatically bring the vehicle to a final smooth and accurate standstill. Furthermore, the rotational speed of each axle is monitored continuously and if any pair of wheels begins to slide during braking, a condition which can put flats on the tyres, air is individually "dumped" until all axle speeds are again equal.

When the driver allows the TBC to come back beyond the detent and into the emergency braking position the effect is to cancel the anti-slide device and apply full air and dynamic — but not magnetic — brakes regardless of axle rotation. During training drivers had to learn not to allow the TBC to come all the way back past the deliberately mild detent during service braking, and this incurred a number of wheel flats during training sessions.

As well as embodying an air-applied spring-released service-brake mechanism, the single brake actuator on each powered axle also incorporates spring-applied air-released parking-brake mechanisms working independently. The spring brakes apply automatically as air leaks away from the service brake system. For hill starts, drivers are provided with a push-button which holds the air brake on while the TBC is moved forward into the initial motoring position; when the motors begin to "pull" the button can be released to allow the tram to move smoothly away from rest. The parking brake also acts as a fail safe feature in that it will be automatically applied by the intervention of a bogie-mounted pneumatic valve in the event of loss of pressure from the tram's air system.

The magnetic track brakes, of which there are six each rated at 60 kN, are extremely effective and are activated only when the driver strikes a red emergency stop button located in the upper middle of the control panel, when he releases the safety ("deadman") device incorporated in the TBC handle or when the Automatic Train Stop (ATS) is tripped. Full battery voltage is applied to all magnets, giving an emergency braking rate of 2.6 m/sec^2.

CONTROL PANELS

The main control panel in front of the driver features pantograph up and down buttons, flange lubricator button (7 of the cars only), sander button, fog lights switch, 2-speed windscreen wiper switch and washer button, directionally-adjustable air outlet nozzle, turn indicator switch and PA "talk" button. There is a speedometer and a brake pressure gauge with two needles, one showing main reservoir pressure and the other showing brake cylinder pressure. The radio keypad is located in the middle of the panel and above it there is an array of warning lights, next to which is the red emergency stop button.

To left and right of the driver there are further panels, controlling doors and mirrors on the left and right of the vehicle respectively. There is also a mirror de-ice button and emergency rear light switch. Step inhibit buttons allow the retractable steps on the trailing vehicle to be de-activated at the Piccadilly Gardens full-length high platform, in Piccadilly Undercroft (both platforms) and at Victoria and G-MEX (outbound platforms only). A separate panel gives control over saloon heating and ventilation and also houses the diagnostics panel showing information output by the programmable logic controller (see later). On the right is another panel; this one has various functions which include saloon lights on/off, emergency headlights switch,

hazard warning lights button, emergency step enable button, uncouple button and reverse button; this has to be held with the right hand while operating the TBC with the left. An audible reversing signal is given at the rear of the tram as long as the vehicle is reversing. The vehicle recognition system (VRS) keypad and its associated train ready to start (TRTS) button are also to be found on this panel; the driver uses the keypad to input service information at the start of each journey (see Chapter 12). Two important rotary selector switches are also located on this panel.

SELECTOR SWITCHES

The Running Selector Switch has three positions: "street", "street without steps" and "segregated". "Street" mode brings into play the following features: road traffic lighting (marker lights, tail lights, indicators, dipped headlights), soft air whistle, 30 mph speed limitation and steps. "Segregated" mode gives: railway lighting (tail lights and main beam headlights, no marker lights), time-lapsed auto door closing, loud air horn. The third position, "street without steps", is the normal street running position for single vehicles and has the same effect as the "street" setting with the exception that the retractable steps are not enabled.

The other rotary switch is the "train end switch"; this has two positions, "coupled" and "uncoupled". The former setting signifies to the control equipment that its commands are going to come from the leading vehicle to which it is coupled as part of a "train" of up to four units; normally it will of course be the second car of a coupled pair of trams. Amongst other functions, this setting de-activates the trailing vehicle's VRS and ATS systems. The coupling action itself happens automatically, on straight track at any rate, when the couplers meet; uncoupling is accomplished by pressing the "uncouple" button and moving away.

The protruding automatic coupler fitted for paired operation must, as well as remotely making all necessary control connections, be able to transmit strong buffing and tractive forces and to swing through wide arcs to allow for horizontal and vertical track curves. That is partly why no supplier offers suitable retracting couplers and why a protruding one has had to be adopted for Metrolink.

BOGIES

Each tram is mounted on three bogies, two motored and one unmotored. The unmotored centre bogie carries the articulation. The motored outer bogies carry pilot boards to displace obstructions from the path of the leading wheels. Bogie positioning is arranged so that, for improved traction, each motor bogie carries 70% of the weight of its body half, laden or unladen. This can be understood by imagining the power bogies located directly under the middle of each body half, where they would carry 100% of the weight, or positioned at the extreme outer ends where they would carry 50% of it, the rest being carried by the articulation bogie. The power bogie's actual position lies between these two hypothetical extremes.

All six axles are fitted with ventilated brake discs having renewable divided "crowns" or wearing surfaces, together with caliper-applied pads and dual-purpose actuators as already described. To take account of the reduced weight carried by the centre bogie, its brake actuators receive air at reduced pressure from a separate reservoir. All bogies are fitted with pairs of large magnetic rail brake units normally held slightly clear of the rails by springs. When energised, the electro-magnets are attracted to the steel running rails on which they exert their enormous drag via robust divided polefaces able to cut through rail-surface detritus. The extremely powerful braking force is transferred to the bogie frames and thence to the mass of the vehicle body and the unsuspecting passengers.

A bogie-mounted 105 kW separately-excited self-cooled d.c. traction motor (four per tram) drives each motored axle through double-reduction gearing. The entire weight of each motor is borne resiliently; in older electric traction practice, half the motor weight rested directly on the axle, contributing to a hammering effect at rail joints. Full traction motor suspension is one way in which modern trams gain their "pussy-footedness".

Unsprung dead weight on the steel tyres, which can add to noise and wear and tear, is further reduced by interposing rubber material in the structure of the wheels themselves; such composite wheel construction also permits tyres to be easily removed and replaced without resort to the gas heating apparatus traditionally associated with railway tyre renewal. Metrolink's resilient wheels are by Bochum. As the rubber material is an insulator, short braided copper "shunts" are fitted through some of the rubber blocks to carry the several hundred amps of return traction current from the wheel centres to the tyres and thence to the rails. Other hindrances to the return current's path, such as the axlebox roller bearings and the rubber suspension units, are shunted by earth return current units fitted at one end of each axle and by cables slung from body to bogie with the cables which feed current to the motors and brake magnets. Underneath the centre bogie are the pair of transponders for on-street signal interfacing and the magnetic equipment for the off-street auto train stop.

The bogies incorporate rubber primary suspension and hydraulically-damped airbag secondary suspension; most of this equipment can easily be seen from alongside the vehicle. The bogie frame and bolster consists of box-section welded steel. Air sander units are fitted to apply sand forward of the leading wheels; the sand boxes are visible on the bogies and contain dried quarry sand. Seven trams have flange lubrication equipment activated when the driver presses a button on his control desk; lubrication can also be applied automatically, for instance on a time-interval basis, and like so many other things this feature will be fine-tuned in the light of experience.

EQUIPMENT LOCATION

The high floor configuration allows most of the traction and auxiliary equipment to be carried under the body. There are no lifeguards in the traditional tramway sense. The retracting steps and their actuators, used at profiled platforms when the vehicle is the second car of a coupled pair, consume some of the available underfloor space, but enough is left to accommodate several air reservoirs (main, motor bogie brakes, centre bogie brakes, pantograph raising and door supply) as well as the rotary vane air compressor (Metcalfe/Hydrovane Type TB11), the air dryer and filter, static converters for auxiliary 110 V d.c. and 24 V d.c. supplies, Nickel-Cadmium batteries and battery isolator switches for 110 V d.c. back-up, electro-pneumatic (EP) brake controllers, line filter and motor series inductors, fan-cooled chopper equipment, Dellner autocouplers, bogie cable connection strips and finally the Davies and Metcalfe supplied whistles, horns and associated EP valves. The design of the whistles was adapted from an old steam locomotive type. Much of the under-floor equipment is mounted so that it can be withdrawn drawer-fashion from the side of the vehicle for inspection and attention.

Inside the vehicles some use is made of gaps under seats for equipment, though clear space has been left under the great majority of seats for passengers' luggage or shopping and for the accommodation of guide dogs. Thermostatically-controlled electric heating units are fitted out of the way at the sides for the full length at floor level, interrupted only by the doors. A saloon ventilating unit is provided in the ceiling in each body half. The saloon lighting is powered at 220 V a.c. through individual 110/220 V inverters. Each first pair of double seats in the end saloons accommodates equipment underneath; the programmable logic controller, the chopper control electronics, the VRS (Vehicle Recognition System) and ATS (Automatic Train Stop) units are accommodated in this way.

Ingenious use is made of the articulation arch structure to accommodate tall cupboards on either side of the saloon within the turntable area; the cupboards contain emergency detraining equipment. The four single seats carried within the turntable area are bracketted from the arch structure to isolate them from the independently-moving floors in the two body halves. Fire extinguishers are carried on all trams. Track short-circuiting clips for emergency use are kept in each cab.

On the roof of car A the Brecknell-Willis pantograph is mounted directly above the motor bogie; it is raised when air is admitted to a cylinder which tensions its spring. Also on the roof of car A we find the lightning arrester, fitted to protect the electrical equipment from surge voltages, and the braking resistor frames. The roof-mounted arms which locate the articulation arch have already been referred to.

Destination indicator blinds are fitted at front and rear and at the sides. The mechanisms are centrally controlled from either cab, and at present the displays include 19 out of a possible 25 indications: Bury, Bury Direct, Whitefield, Crumpsall, Woodlands Road, Victoria, Victoria Direct, Piccadilly Gardens, Piccadilly, G-MEX, G-MEX Direct, Old Trafford, Timperley, Timperley Direct, Altrincham, Altrincham Direct, Special, Sorry Not In Service and Driver Under Instruction. "Direct" implies that the service passes straight through the Delta junction without using the Piccadilly branch. Head, tail, stop, indicator and marker lights are provided and are worked from the 24 V d.c. battery-backed supply, as is the single windscreen wiper and washer fitted at each end. The saloon lighting is powered at 110 V d.c. through individual inverters. There is no on-board ticket issuing or validating equipment. The trams do not carry point irons;

these heavy steel implements might otherwise knock against panelling or, worse still, against passengers' shins and would not be suitable objects to have inside crowded vehicles. Instead, a point iron is kept in a padlocked container adjacent to each facing pair of street point switches for use by Customer Services Inspectors rather than by tram drivers.

To avoid the use of a number of control relays, a programmable logic controller (PLC) is provided. This takes care of many functions such as automatic time-lapsed door closing off-street to retain saloon heat. The PLC can supply systems status information to the driver or to an engineer through a display panel in each cab. The PLC can be interrogated by maintenance staff using a hand-held terminal.

SPONSORSHIP

"Theming" of trams, and indeed buses, for advertising purposes is commonplace these days. It is done with varying degrees of restraint, from downright tacky to heartily fun-loving. In Manchester the positive image being cultivated for LRT is sacrosanct and nothing is being done which could compromise it. Metrolink's tram theming thankfully avoids extremes and manages to convey messages subtly without being undignified. The corporate Metrolink name, livery and logo have been retained, complemented by roof boards and the application of discreet additional transfers.

Soon after its arrival, car No 1002 became the subject of the first "theming" initiative. 1002 has been named "Manchester Arndale Voyager", representing both the Arndale Centre — an important city-centre attractor, well served by Metrolink — and its integral "Voyager" restaurant. The flags the vehicle bears are those of P & O, owners of the Arndale Centre and sole holders of the sponsorship rights for 1002. Another 12 or so sponsorship deals are being negotiated, bringing additional income which will help keep fare levels down.

THE SPECIAL PURPOSE VEHICLE (SPV)

Every light rail undertaking has to have some means of fetching back failed vehicles from outlying parts of the network. A purpose-built recovery vehicle gathering cobwebs and rust between rare urgent sorties is a financial non-starter in more ways than one; far better to equip the recovery vehicle for a wide variety of other duties so that it earns its keep continuously instead of occasionally.

Brown & Root Vickers Ltd, charged by GMA with overseeing the maintenance requirements of the new transport system, identified the need for just such a versatile workhorse and engaged a British company, RFS Industries, to produce it. In effect Brown & Root Vickers set out to identify all possible requirements and asked RFS to meet them with one robust street-compatible vehicle. The resulting unit fills a gap in the market created by the growing number of LRT operators in the UK and overseas; it can be customised according to each individual client's needs and would also appeal to non light rail customers.

The finished product is designated the RFS "Mantis" 170 kW Diesel Hydraulic Rail Service Vehicle, or in Metrolink terms SPV — Special Purpose Vehicle. The SPV incorporates all the features of a diesel locomotive, mobile crane, overhead line inspection platform and a travelling workshop and store. It is based at the depot and will be used, along with a small fleet of road vehicles, to access all parts of the system to meet whatever operational requirements arise. The keynote of the SPV's design is its rugged simplicity. Adhesive weight and robustness are combined in a frame welded up from rolled steel sections and plate. The engine is a six cylinder Caterpillar 3306B turbocharged diesel unit with an intermittent rating of 170 kW (225 hp) at 2200 rpm, similar to engines used worldwide in excavators, farm machinery and other plant.

The transmission system is a heavy duty Caterpillar power shift unit mounted integrally with the engine and comprising single stage torque converter, planetary-type gearing and power shift clutches for forward, reverse and all speeds. Final drive is via cardan shafts to a double reduction gearbox on each of the two axles, which are fitted with rubber chevron primary axlebox suspension and monobloc wheels. The input shaft of each axledrive gearbox carries a ventilated disc acted on by the unit's straight air service brake system and air release/spring applied emergency and parking brakes. Pneumatic sanders are fitted.

The SPV's four-person cab is spacious and so well-equipped that it can even provide brewing facilities for work crews engaged on jobs at a distance from "civilization". The driver can choose a sitting or standing position at either side of the cab to operate the controls, which

Metrolink's Special Purpose Vehicle (SPV) is a customised version of RFS Engineering's "Mantis" design. It was built by RFS to the order of Brown Root, the sub-contractor responsible for supplying Metrolink's maintenance equipment. The SPV is kept in readiness for vehicle recovery but can earn its keep in a variety of other ways.
Colin J Marsden

are simple and permit actuation of towed tram brakes via compatibly-coded brake wire signals. Ever versatile, the SPV can also interface with railway rolling stock's continuous air brakes via standard brake hose connections.

A special quick-release mounting plate enables different couplers to be fitted according to need; Metrolink's SPV carries at one end a Dellner auto-coupler compatible with those fitted to the trams, and a plain coupling pocket at the other end; this can be used for attaching a general-purpose trailer supplied by RFS for use with the SPV. The SPV's couplers can be interchanged anywhere on the system by means of its integral hydraulic crane, which can also carry an insulated "cherry picker" man-elevating bucket for use when attending to the overhead line equipment or lineside structures. The SPV can provide hydraulic or air take-off power for tools, appliances or plant used in maintenance or recovery work as well as power for hand held worklights; portable electric power is in Metrolink's case provided by conventional equipment of a more portable nature. RFS can also supply a whole range of accessories for the SPV, including snowploughs and snow-blowers and track-cleaning equipment such as powerful vacuum suction cleaners and road-sweepers. A rather different RFS contract in 1991 featured the supply of new bogie frames to the National Tramway Museum for Liverpool tram 869.

PRINCIPAL STATISTICS OF METROLINK VEHICLES

	ARTICULATED LRV FIREMA TYPE T68	SPV RFS "MANTIS"
Tare Weight (tonnes)	48	22
Gross Weight (tonnes)	63.1	24
Motored axle load (laden) (tonnes)	11	12.5
Trailing axle load (laden) (tonnes)	9.5	n/a
Seating capacity	82 + 4 pull-down	4 (crew)
Wheelchair spaces	2	n/a
Standing capacity (4/sq m)	122	n/a
Length over body (m)	29	8 20
Overall width (m)	2.65	2.50
Overall height (m)	3.36	2.85
Contact wire height (minimum)	3.8	n/a
Contact wire height (maximum)	7.01	n/a
Bogie wheelbase (m)	2.065	n/a
Axle spacing (m)	n/a	3.4
Bogie spacing (centres) (m)	10.7	n/a
Minimum curve radius (m)	25	25
Maximum gradient (%)	6.5	6.5
Traction motor rating (kW)	4 x 105	n/a
Engine power (intermittent) (kW)	n/a	170 at 2200 rpm
Engine power (continuous) (kW)	n/a	125 at 2000 rpm
Wheel diameter (new) (mm)	740	840
Acceleration rate (m/sec$_2$)	1.3	n/a
Deceleration rate (service) (m/sec$_2$)	1.3	n/a
Deceleration rate (emergency) (m/sec$_2$)	2.6	n/a
Maximum speed (km/h)	80	40

n/a = not applicable, not relevant or not known

LRV for Manchester Metrolink

publiespo

Articulated Light Rail Vehicle Firema type T 68,
for the GMA Group - Manchester Metrolink
• Total capacity 201 passengers
• 2 areas for wheelchairs
• Access from low and high level platforms
• Propulsion equipment GTO Chopper
• Maximum speed 80 km/h

FIREMA - quality, experience, technology

FIREMA Consortium
Viale Edison, 120
20099 Sesto S. Giovanni (Milano) - Italy
Tel. (39) 02 2494396 - Fax (39) 02 26225380

This historic photograph shows Metrolink's first tramcar, No 1001, on 9th July 1991 when it was being initially assembled at Firema's Casaralta plant near Naples. The body halves are being lowered onto the bogies for the first time. *Firema Engineering*

▼▶ Metrolink's cab layout was designed by GEC Alsthom, the GMA Consortium member responsible for vehicle supply, power, signals, telecommunications, overheads lines and fare collection systems. The functions of the various driving controls are explained in the text.
Colin J Marsden

A motor bogie for one of the Metrolink fleet is seen here in the grounds of Firema's Officina Mecanica della Stanga (OMS) plant at Padua, where all the bogies were built. Traction motors, ventilated brake discs, pilot board, cables, suspension airbags and return traction current shunts are just a few of the items which can be seen in this picture. Over 60% of the content of the vehicles is of British origin.
Firema Engineering

▼▶ The differences between the motor bogie pictured above and this articulation or centre bogie can be seen by comparing the two photographs. The articulation bogie has two brake discs on each axle instead of one on each of the motored bogie's axles. Both these views show the way in which the backs of the steel tyres on the Bochum resilient wheels have been thickened to enable them to engage raised railway check rails (see page 80) without making the flanges themselves too thick for street-running on grooved rail.
Firema Engineering

9. FROM CHESHIRE PLAINS TO PENNINE SLOPES

Metrolink's two routes into Manchester could hardly be more different. The Altrincham line makes a level bee-line across the flat terrain surrounding the Bollin and Mersey valleys while the Bury line follows a more winding and undulating path as it crosses the valleys of the Irk and Irwell and the rising ground between. The two lines do, though, have one thing in common from an historical point of view and that is that they had both been electrified in response to tramway competition. The patterns of development along both routes were substantially influenced by both forms of railed transport for around a century, the trains and trams having jointly enabled people to live in the suburbs and work in the metropolis. It is, therefore, fitting that Metrolink should have joined together two formerly separate railway lines by merging two formerly competing railway technologies.

In this chapter we will be taking an imaginary ride from Altrincham (pronounced ''Olltring'am'') to Bury (pronounced to rhyme with ''Cherry''), looking at the two railways and their surroundings as well as at the various Metrolink works carried out off-street. Before we embark on our journey, which will be possible without changing only in the morning, we will have a general look at the work which has had to be done to convert both lines to light rail operation.

THE OFF-STREET WORKS

While the on-street work described in Chapter 10 was being carried out under the inquisitive gaze of the public, much was also happening in the traditionally secluded environs of railway territory. Details are:

- End-on links were established with the Bury line at Victoria and with the slewed Altrincham line at Cornbrook, the latter via a new underpass beneath the BR Manchester–Liverpool (via Warrington) railway.
- Cornbrook Viaduct had to be refurbished and tracked.
- A new viaduct had to be built at G-MEX to get the trams up from Lower Mosley Street onto the old Central Station throat.
- New Metrolink stations had to be constructed in Piccadilly Undercroft and at Deansgate (for G-MEX) and Victoria.
- A new operations and maintenance centre had to be built at Queens Road.
- Numerous bridges and viaducts had to be refurbished.
- 18 existing British Rail stations had to be adapted for disabled access and otherwise improved.
- Many kilometres of ex-BR track had to be attended to.
- Track remodelling had to be done at Altrincham to provide for separation of LRT and BR tracks.
- The Bury line had to be re-electrified at 750 V d.c. overhead instead of at 1200 V d.c. third rail.
- The Altrincham line had to be converted from 25 kV a.c. to 750 V d.c.
- Both lines had to be resignalled completely.

All the railway land and property over which Metrolink operates is still owned notionally by BR, but title and operating rights have been vested in GMML on behalf of GMPTE with the proviso that the title and rights apply only for as long as use for public transport continues. Metrolink operates under separate licence from BR between Altrincham and Deansgate Junction (see later), at Victoria East and in Piccadilly Undercroft.

OFF-STREET TRACK AND CIVIL ENGINEERING WORK

The track inherited from British Rail has been substantially retained, but a considerable amount of work has been needed to bring it up to the condition required under the terms of the contract. On the Bury line all the old side-contact third rail and its fittings were removed

for scrap soon after BR operation ceased. According to need, sections of both lines have been re-railed, re-ballasted, fully re-sleepered, spot re-sleepered (whereby every third or perhaps every sixth sleeper is replaced) or, completely relaid by BR before changeover. Considerable lengths of old jointed track remain. New track consists of continuously-welded 113 lbs/yd flat-bottomed rail on concrete sleepers. Heavy rail flangeway clearances are being maintained at points and crossings but the checkrails are being raised to engage the special tram wheel profiles which have a correspondingly thickened back at a slightly smaller diameter than the tread. This is explained further in Chapter 10.

Responsibility for a railway goes further than the track. All the existing bridges have been examined and repaired as needed, sometimes extensively. To deter the dropping of objects onto the line or the equally idiotic dangling of bare wires into contact with the live overhead, bridge parapets above the line have been increased in height. This feature, which sadly helps to hide the transport undertaking from the community it serves, has become a characteristic of both routes. Metrolink's corporate aquamarine and dark grey colour scheme has been applied to stuctures and fittings. Other remedial work has included putting drains in order, renewing or repairing fences and dealing with lineside vegetation.

OFF-STREET STATIONS WORK

All existing stations have been brought up to the same standard during Metrolink conversion, though no more money than is absolutely necessary has been spent. Existing steps linking streets to platforms have been retained but have been supplemented by well-lit 1 in 20 ramps – some of which seem inordinately long – or by hydraulic lifts or, in some cases, simply by making gaps in walls or fences to accommodate new footways. The lifts can be activated or deactivated remotely from Queens Road but are passenger-controlled.

Thanks to Metrolink's barrier-free open station concept, there is no limit on the number of accesses which can be set up between the public domain and the transport system. Regrettably though, many of the old station buildings survive as psychological deterrents to patronage; no one would deny that shop trade is stimulated by an attractive display of goods and an open door, so surely we should not hide attractive light rail services behind buildings with no remaining purpose. Woodlands Road on the Bury line and Old Trafford (formerly Warwick Road) on the Altrincham line provide us with good examples of true light rail stops. Contrastingly, at Altrincham, the station buildings perpetuate totally outdated bus/rail separation and do nothing at all to assist integration.

Every existing railway structure – however obsolete – has for the most part been retained on both lines. Some were already in use for non-railway purposes and it is conceivable that more will be rented, franchised or sold for use as restaurants, shops or pubs. Meanwhile many access routes onto the stations remain as before through old booking halls. Generally the Ticket Vending Machines (TVMs) are located on or adjacent to the platforms themselves. Other features provided on each platform are video surveillance cameras and passenger communication panels, both connected to Control at Queens Road; pressing the button on the panel immediately relays the image from the nearby camera onto one of the display screens so that the controller can see the calling passenger while dialogue takes place over the speech link.

To secure the close contractual door sill to platform edge tolerance opposite the second and third entrances of the leading unit, the track has been fixed laterally to station platforms by short timber ties and the platform edge slabs have been adjusted over the 8 m lengths concerned. Where the enhanced access zones do not line up with existing canopies, standard Decaux shelters have been provided opposite them,

Our Metrolink journey narrative starts at Altrincham Interchange, seen here from Moss Lane overbridge on 23rd February 1992. The whole section between here and Deansgate Junction (just beyond Navigation Road), including Altrincham station in its entirety, remains under BR control. Metrolink is allocated use of the two terminal platforms on the left while BR's Chester line services call at the two through platforms on the right. The adjoining bus station, as at Bury, is separated from the platforms by station buildings and is consequently not visible in this picture. The camera is pointing more or less due North, almost directly towards Bury, in fact.

Author

as they have also been at stations with no canopies or with unsuitable existing shelters. Stations have also been provided with prefabricated equipment rooms and with standardised signing and lighting inside and out.

THE ALTRINCHAM LINE

The Altrincham line has always been known as the MSJ&AR (Manchester, South Junction and Altrincham Railway) and this tells us a bit about its background. First conceived in 1839 as a cross-city link from the Liverpool and Manchester Railway at South Junction (near Liverpool Road) to the London & Birmingham Railway at London Road (now Piccadilly), the proposals by 1845 included, as an afterthought, a line all the way to Altrincham, a small market town in Cheshire. Both lines opened in 1849. Timperley, Sale, Stretford and Old Trafford are original stations; the rest were added later.

The Altrincham line, with which we are concerned here, was originally steam-worked, was electrified at 1500 V d.c. in 1931 and then re-electrified at 25 kV a.c. in 1971. During its life it also carried a "push & pull" steam service from Manchester to Liverpool via Broadheath and Lymm, branching off the MSJ&A at Timperley, and the semi-fast Cheshire Lines service from Manchester to Chester, initially steam and later DMU operated. The Chester trains, in the days when they started from Manchester Central, joined the MSJ&A at Cornbrook Junction much as the Metrolink trams do now, and left it end-on at Altrincham to continue through Hale towards Northwich and Chester. When Central closed, later to become G-MEX, these trains were diverted to Oxford Road. Recently they have again been rerouted, this time via Stockport.

The author leaves the reader to enjoy himself unravelling the tangled web of rich historical associations and ironic twists of fate surrounding the conversion of this line — and the Bury line — to light rail operation. Further study of Manchester's fascinating railway, tramway and general history in advance of a Metrolink journey will increase the rider's enjoyment considerably; not least in significance is the old wasteful rivalry between private railway operators. Today, going past successive stations and seeing the many open or redeveloped areas adjacent to the alignments, it is interesting to reflect on the vast amount of additional railway infrastructure which once existed next to the lines in the form of sidings, buildings, water towers, abandoned routes, coalyards and the like, which once provided direct and indirect employment for many local inhabitants.

ALTRINCHAM REMODELLED

We start our journey at Altrincham station, which forms part of a PTE bus/rail interchange set up under the auspices of the former Greater Manchester Council. Altrincham can be reached by BR from Chester and beyond or from Stockport, served by trains from London and many other places. Otherwise, some long distance coach services call at the interchange and there is a large free car park on the far side of the tracks. Metrolink's trams terminate in the nearer two station platforms, while the BR Manchester—Chester trains call at the two farther platforms. The whole Altrincham area, including the station and the lines as far as Deansgate Junction, remains under the control of BR. Altrincham station, level as it is with the adjoining bus station, is one of the few Metrolink stations where very little has had to be done to improve access.

Setting off from Altrincham, we find ourselves on the extreme left-hand track out of four. Passing under a new ramped-access footbridge, we can see on the right one of the two crossovers which link the light and heavy rail systems, the other being at Victoria; these cater for the delivery of stone ballast or other materials out-of-hours by heavy rail freight vehicles to the LRT lines. Not much further along from here, our double Metrolink tracks merge into single track just before Navigation Road level crossing, and we notice that the BR double track on the right does the same. For the short distance from here forward to Deansgate Junction there is only room for one pair of tracks. It was decided not to pursue light rail/heavy rail inter-running here as the cost of fitting all vehicles with automatic train protection would have been prohibitive for such a small stretch; the answer instead has been to re-designate the two tracks as separate single lines, one Metrolink and one BR. The alteration work was completed on Monday 22nd July 1991 after a fortnight's remodelling shutdown period.

Being located within the new paired single-track section, Navigation Road's platforms now "belong" to different operators. The platform on the right is now served by BR trains in both directions and the one on the left, with the easiest imaginable access from street to platform, is served by Metrolink trams in both directions. The pleasantly suburban and, in railway terms, almost claustrophobic section of track through here is one of two Metrolink locations where you might enjoy a "race" between a tram and a steam train, for steam-hauled specials pass along here from time to time.

Just after Navigation Road we come to Deansgate Lane level crossing, presided over by BR's Deansgate Lane signal cabin on the right. This box controls all BR and Metrolink movements on the shared alignment as far back as Altrincham. Deansgate Junction, located just after the box, used to be a conventional double junction but has been re-modelled as two single-to-double sets of points, one for Metrolink and one for BR, alongside each other. The doubled BR track swings right towards Skelton Junction, Northenden and Stockport and is used daily by ICI stone trains and other freight workings in addition to the Chester to Manchester trains diverted from the Altrincham line. The Metrolink tracks continue straight on under two railway overbridges, the first one belonging to the dismantled line to Warrington via Broadheath and Lymm and the second belonging to the just-surviving line to Shell Chemicals, which used to carry on over the Ship Canal to Glazebrook by way of Partington.

BESIDE THE BRIDGEWATER

Between the Metrolink tracks just beyond the second overbridge a turnback stub has been provided between the LRT tracks for use in case any future pattern of services should include short workings between, say, Timperley and Whitefield. The stub could also be used for overnight stabling, as could Altrincham station.

If we look to our left along here we will see the Bridgewater Canal joining us from the direction of Dunham and Lymm. From here to Stretford the Bridgewater accompanies us as it makes its lock-free way from Runcorn to Manchester via Cornbrook or to Worsley and Leigh via the remarkable Barton Swing Aqueduct over the Ship Canal, which will be accessible by tram when the extension to nearby Dumplington is built one day.

When the MSJ&A was first thought of in the late 1830s, one proposal was to convert this part of the canal to a railway; fortunately this never happened, and today we can enjoy from our tram the restful prospect of clean water, keen anglers, interesting artefacts, rowing "eights" now and again and, of course, pleasure boats both on the move and tied up. How many other lines so closely parallel a recreational waterway over such a long distance? As we drift under the Park Road overbridge and pull up at Timperley station with the canal immediately on our left, it is tempting to imagine future round trips by tram and canal with aquatic interchanges at Timperley and G-MEX. Pleasant thoughts.

If we look behind us at Timperley we will see that each platform is served directly from Park Road by a new hydraulic lift as well as by the old covered steps via the defunct booking hall. The line from here onwards passes through mature residential areas with many pre- and post-war semis in evidence. There is a long gap between Timperley and the next station, Brooklands, which lies just before Marsland Road overbridge. This station and the next two, Sale and Dane Road, all have similar layouts and access arrangements; the inbound platform has a new lift up to street level, while the outbound platform has level access to an adjacent station yard, though Dane Road outbound has a longer ramp to street level. All these stations, as well as Stretford and Trafford Bar, retain their MSJ&A covered steps access via disused booking-halls.

From Brooklands to Sale, two very closely spaced stops, the line takes on a roadside reservation character as it runs parallel to Hope Road immediately on the right. Along here we are reminded that the MSJ&A had vague tramway characteristics long before it was converted to Metrolink. Sale station serves a decent shopping centre as well as a pleasant residential area. From here all the way to Trafford Bar the MSJ&A used to be quadruple-tracked; it is still possible on our left to see empty trackbeds for much of the distance though in places the formation width has been irretrievably reduced.

Beyond Dane Road the line passes under the M63 motorway before traversing the Mersey Valley. As we cross the river itself, flowing in an unattractively deep channel to prevent flooding, we can see on the right the expanse of Sale Water Park with its water-skiers, windsurfers, anglers and dinghy sailors. Towards Stretford the line, assuming an interurban character, passes briefly through some delightfully rustic surroundings spoilt only by the distant pylons and a solitary block of flats. Alighting at either Dane Road or Stretford gives one access to miles of charming footpaths threading through the Mersey Valley, in the midst of which it is hard to realise how close one really is to suburbia.

After Stretford, which has a new direct access path to its inbound platform from the former station yard and to its outbound platform via a new ramp from Edge Lane, which passes over the railway here, another long stretch brings us to Old Trafford station, renamed from Warwick Road because of its proximity to Old Trafford cricket ground (on the left just before the station) and Old Trafford football ground (out of sight beyond the cricket ground). At this station, short ramps have been constructed to improve access from the adjacent streets and to give better access through the existing pedestrian subway beneath the tracks.

From Old Trafford onwards the line's surroundings become mainly industrial instead of residential. After a short run alongside Elsinore Road we cross over the former Midland main line — destined to become a Metrolink route to East Didsbury — to arrive in Trafford Bar station (where many sports fans used to alight by mistake when it was called Old Trafford). This is quite a good bus interchange point as well as having some useful specialist shops nearby. Access to the inbound platform is from the former station yard, while a new ramp connects the outbound platform to Elsinore Road. Moving off from here, we immediately enter the short Old Trafford Tunnel which takes us under an important road junction and into a cutting on the other side. Just after a small overbridge we swing left onto the alignment of the former tracks to Central Station, once used by the Chester trains. Ahead and to the right we can see the buffer stops truncating the former Altrincham line, now used as a turn-back stub for EMUs terminating at Oxford Road. The track severance and slewing were done on 5th January 1992. We pass the stub on our right as we descend to negotiate the newly-constructed Cornbrook underpass.

CORNBROOK UNDERPASS

In the days before Central Station was closed in 1968, Cornbrook was an important railway focal point. A vast area, much of it now developed or occupied by scrapyards, was covered with multiple railway tracks, junctions and carriage sidings. At one stage there was

a short-lived flyover to the Ship Canal construction railways and Salford Docks. Latterly the BR track layout has been whittled down to a high speed double junction between the aforementioned turnback stub and the Manchester–Liverpool (via Warrington) line, electrified at 25 kV a.c. as far as Trafford Park Containerbase; it is interesting to observe here that the heavy railway has tramway-type overhead while the new "tramroad" — to give it its Parliamentary title — has railway-type catenary.

To maintain Metrolink's physical separation from BR, the underpass had to be constructed to carry the light rail tracks under the heavy rail alignment; it cost £3.9 million out of a total Cornbrook contract price of some £5.5 million. As the future point of convergence of three routes — Altrincham, Trafford Park and Salford Quays — the site on the Manchester side is earmarked for a projected Cornbrook station which as well as being a useful interchange point would serve new developments taking place in the Hadfield Street Industrial Improvement area and in the former Pomona Docks area, both near by. We climb quickly out of the underpass, designated Bridge 222A by BR, to find ourselves lined up for a fast run into Manchester along Cornbrook Viaduct, built by the Cheshire Lines Committee back in the late 1870s.

At this moment we are passing from the Metropolitan Borough of Trafford into the City of Manchester, and we must have a very quick look round from our rapidly-moving tram if we are to miss nothing. On our left is the redeveloping Pomona Dock at the head of the Manchester Ship Canal, while beyond is Salford Quays — London Docklands on a human scale. If we glance behind us across the canal, we can glimpse the sparkling new glassed blocks of the World Trade Centre. The "launching ramp" pointing in that direction is an advance abutment for the bridge which will one day carry the Salford Quays/Trafford Park light rail tracks over the Bridgewater Canal, which waterway is keeping us company again immediately on our left; as accurately as any surveyor's instrument, it shows how level our route has been until now. This is the Manchester branch of the canal, and we cross over it as we run onto Cornbrook Viaduct after passing a concrete-producing plant on the left.

CORNBROOK VIADUCT

Central Station's main line and suburban railways used to approach the city by means of a varied succession of curving wrought iron lattice girder bridges and brick viaducts which carried the tracks over several roads, the Bridgewater Canal, Hulme Locks (linking the Bridgewater Canal with the River Irwell and the Ship Canal), sundry canal basins and last but not least the important railway line connecting Castlefield Junction with Ordsall Lane Junction (South Junction line from London Road). The elevated structures, known collectively as Cornbrook Viaduct, parallel the Oxford Road to Altrincham and Liverpool line as it gains height on an adjacent brick viaduct; as they accelerated powerfully up this gradient the old 1500 V d.c. Altrincham trains used to produce gear sounds which, echoing in full song off the brickwork, were enough to tingle the spine of any tramfan.

Stripped of its former five tracks, Cornbrook Viaduct had since 1968 been neglected but not entirely devoid of life if one thinks of the many small businesses still carried on underneath its arches. GMPTE planners identified the viaduct as an ideal way for the light rail tracks to approach the city from their link with the Altrincham line at Cornbrook. Part of the Phase 1 contract has therefore involved renovation of the structures followed by the installation of new double track and overhead line equipment. The Metrolink tracks generally occupy the side of the viaduct closest to the parallel BR line.

The work has included grit-blasting and painting of ironwork, repair of brickwork, freeing-up and repair of bridge bearings, re-decking of one of the bridges, and some re-plating and strengthening of weakened supports. Castlefield Bridge, which carries the LRT tracks across the main line railway, has been raised 75 mm as part of the work. This has been done to improve clearances underneath in preparation for Regional Railways electrification at 25 kV of the line from Manchester to Bolton, Preston and Blackpool.

As we approach the city along this succession of imposing structures, we can see many interesting sights on either side. The area through which we are passing used to have many industries served by the Ship Canal or the Bridgewater, and plenty of evidence remains of a completely different age. For example, in the granite-setted surface in front of the Bee Line bus depot part of a stone tramway survives; it once led to Pomona Docks and was used by horse-drawn carts. As we run swiftly along the viaduct the Ship Canal comes close to us and then vanishes from view on the left hand side to become

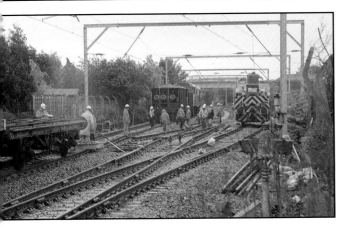

he River Irwell, which we will see again later in our journey. Here Hulme Lock, where the Bridgewater Canal joins the Ship Canal, nestles in a railway arch directly below us. In the distance to the right, beyond St George's Church, Hulme's acres of 1960s deck-access housing units can be seen; there has been some talk of a new light rail line to form part of this area's redevelopment.

Further along, over to the left again, we can see Liverpool Road, the world's first passenger railway station. At certain times a tank loco will be visible as it hustles short passenger trains along the internal railways of the Museum of Science and Industry which now occupies the station site as part of the Castlefield Conservation Area. Well worth at least a whole day's visit in itself especially when the annual boat rally or the Castlefield Carnival is taking place. The station to alight at for Castlefield, and for BR interchange, is straight ahead – G-MEX – so named because of the new conference and exhibition centre of that name based on the splendid former Central Station train shed now looming in front of us.

Some other features of the Manchester skyline visible from Cornbrook Viaduct are, from left to right, Sunlight House, Highland House, the Cathedral, the CIS tower block, the Town Hall clock tower with beyond it the cream-tiled Arndale Centre office block, the Sunley Building with its crown of microwave dishes, Piccadilly Plaza, Scottish Widows and, finally, the Refuge Building's russet-coloured clock tower. Immediately to the left of G-MEX can be seen the former Great Northern Railway Company's goods warehouse. On a clear day the Pennines can be seen in the distance to the north and east of the city.

G-MEX VIADUCT

Once Central Station had been closed and its tracks had been lifted,

the old station throat was surfaced over and used as a car park. A section of the car park has now been taken over for the Metrolink tracks and for the platforms of the new G-MEX light rail station, staggered partly because of the site's restricted width but mainly to provide safe at-grade crossing facilities. In effect a compulsory stop for the pedestrian crossing has been combined with a service and changeover stop. Pulling up at the inbound platform just before reaching the pedestrian crossing place, the driver carries out the changeover from off-street mode to on-street mode by rotating the selector switch to his right. Then, before setting off from a standstill, he can easily check that the crossing is clear. The same layout and reassuring procedure applies at Victoria.

Near to the crossing place a footbridge spans Whitworth Street West. Installed in connection with the opening of G-MEX, the covered bridge will provide easy interchange between Metrolink and the intensive local and long-distance BR services using the adjacent Deansgate BR station. The footbridge incorporates steps down to the street below. On the Castlefield side of the viaduct there is a lift giving direct access to the conservation area already mentioned.

The light rail tracks descend from here to street level by means of a long ramping viaduct sympathetically designed to tone in with the arched roof structure of the G-MEX building, formerly the main train shed of Central Station. Various possible ramp positions, layouts and gradients were looked at back in 1983 before selecting the present arrangement. All the precast concrete track slab units are separated from the bridge structures by elastomeric pads and the flat-bottomed rails themselves are encapsulated into slots in the slabs. These measures will minimise noise. The Metrolink tracks, incorporating a crossover, leave the existing elevated structure close to the site of the former Central Station turntable and immediately cross Trafford Street and Trumpet Street on reinforced concrete structures decorated with preformed brick-faced arch-shaped claddings with artificial stone embellishments.

We are now entering what is perhaps the most photographically rewarding section of Metrolink's routes, stretching from here to Princess Street. As we descend the ramp, G-MEX forms an impressive backdrop to the left, offset by the picturesque Briton's Protection and Tommy Duck's pubs on the right hand side. Between them, once the site of a long-distance bus station, is the projected site of a new concert hall for the city's Halle Orchestra, with beyond it an abandoned

Into the streets; Car 1004 bound to Victoria on 17th March 1992, passes G-MEX on a driver training trip. On a through journey from Altrincham the driver will already have rotated the selector switch at G-MEX station to put the vehicle into "street" mode and will have adapted his driving technique to suit the city centre's succession of sharp curves and to drive defensively in anticipation of the many sudden eventualities which can occur in busy streets and pedestrianised areas.
Peter Fox

arm of the Rochdale Canal destined for revival as a marina; this used to link in with the railway for goods interchange on its subterranean way under Central Station to the River Irwell down near Granada Studios, another Manchester attraction well worth a visit. Just after completing our descent to street level, observe at the junction with Windmill Street the way the inbound buses are now forced to perform an extraordinarily acute "S" manouevre through a chicane created by awkwardly-placed islands — the theory, as with tramways, seeming to be that if a vehicle can go round a sharp corner, make it do so whatever happens!

INTO THE CITY STREETS

As Lower Mosley Street is entered, one of Manchester's architectural splendours looms up on the left. Verbosely re-christened "The Holiday Inn Crowne Plaza Midland Hotel", the extravagantly ornate terracotta and red granite building will always be known to Mancunians as the "Midland" — the name gilded in terracotta 3D over its entrances — just as surely as the mouthful "Light Rail Vehicle" will never replace the simple word "tram", emblazoned as it is on roads and signs throughout the city centre. Be that as it may, the Midland Hotel oozes a special kind of easy opulence, just as you'd expect from the establishment where Rolls first met Royce in 1904. A carvery meal in the Trafford Room, with a table near the windows where the trams pass by, is highly recommended.

For information about the street tramways' construction, the preliminary works, the overhead line equipment and the traffic signalling arrangements, readers should refer to the appropriate chapters. Here we are just enjoying the tram ride, having a look at the immediate surroundings and perhaps sparing a thought for the previous generation of electric trams which were banished from these same streets over 40 years ago. The only city-centre Metrolink tracks which do not revive Manchester City Tramways alignments are those running from Shudehill down to Victoria.

Emerging from Lower Mosley Street we enter St Peter's Square, dominated by the Cenotaph erected on the site of the former church of St Peter, which is commemorated by the cross behind the Cenotaph. It was hereabouts in 1819 that the infamous Peterloo Massacre took place. The Free Trade Hall, which is the present home of the Halle Orchestra, can be glimpsed on the left down Peter Street. Immediately on our left as we pause at St Peter's Square profiled platform is the unusual drum-shaped Manchester Central Library and Library Theatre building, with next to it the Town Hall Extension and after that the back end of the Town Hall itself. The strange-looking small building just behind the sunken Peace Gardens forms part of a Town Hall creche. The notable Victorian Gothic exterior of the Town Hall is best appreciated from Albert Square, and its interior is well worth a visit.

After S-bending our way out of St Peter's Square and crossing the busy one-way Princess Street we enter Mosley Street, passing on the right the City Art Gallery where there are regular exhibitions and, further along, the Portico Library (now "The Bank" pub, enabling one to say truthfully "I'm just nipping to the bank" when going for a quick pint) — both have impressive Greek facades. If we look to the right along Nicholas Street immediately after the Art Gallery we might catch a glimpse of the Chinese Arch which is the focal point of the city's Chinatown area. Mosley Street is two way for trams but only one way (inbound) for buses. Though buses and trams inter-run here, there are no bus stops within the shared alignment and there is therefore no possibility of buses blocking trams except at traffic signals. After crossing York Street the buses acquire their own lane while both tram tracks swing onto a paved "trambaan" alignment, the site of the outbound Mosley Street profiled platform. Immediately behind this is the model railway shop where you might have bought this book; it must qualify as one of the closest such shops to "the prototype" to be found anywhere.

Facing us now is the set of points, its powered switches badly located in a busy bus lane, which lead either straight on to Victoria or to the right towards Piccadilly (BR). In continuing our journey straight on towards Victoria and Bury, we must not forget Metrolink's important Piccadilly branch which will be the destination of most services entering the city from either end of the system. The best way to include this arm is to re-start our imaginary journey from Piccadilly railway station. As a result of the Windsor Link, Piccadilly is very much the focus of the railways around Manchester. There are trains or connections from all over the country and in the near future this will be the arrival point for international travellers coming to Manchester from the Airport via the new rail link or from the Continent via the Channel Tunnel. It is therefore a very important Metrolink

station, and that is what has made the light rail promoters stick s tenaciously to the idea of locating their terminus conveniently in the Undercroft right beneath the main line station.

PICCADILLY UNDERCROFT

Various ways of taking the light rail tracks into or close to Piccadill station were looked at. The adopted solution is supremely elegan and looked most promising in terms of cost-effectiveness; the statio is elevated on a network of brick arches and, where it has been ex tended in bygone years, on a grid of cast iron columns. Between th columns there was sufficient open space for the light rail tracks an for platforms to be accommodated without moving any column.

Perhaps because it symbolised the imaginative and flexible approac towards transport provision which is characteristic of the light rai concept but still a little alien to these shores and not yet widely ap preciated, the Undercroft proposal attracted critical scrutiny. In 198 the Kings Cross tube-station fire took place and resulted in a lon hard look being taken at the Undercroft. It was not clear for a tim whether it was to be regarded as an underground station for the pur poses of fire risk.

At about the same time the Department of Transport instructe GMPTE to find ways of reducing the capital cost of the light rai scheme, including the idea of abandoning the resourceful Undercrof idea altogether and cutting services back to the opposite side of Lon don Road from the station. The loss of the strong interchange facilitie with BR did not seem to be taken into account at Westminster jus so long as the capital cost could be whittled down to satiate th Treasury.

GMPTA/E worked hard on plans for Metrolink to terminate o the opposite side of London Road but found that there was just no enough room for a safe terminus on the downhill-sloping site withou elevating everything onto a new viaduct. Such an elaborate structur would have cancelled out any cost saving besides eroding the benefit of locking the LRT services into a firm interchange with BR services

In the event, while the Undercroft has not been designated a underground station for fire precautions purposes (it is after all leve with adjacent streets and was previously used as a public car par and, before that, as a goods transhipment and storage area), anothe problem has been found. Increasingly sensitive about safety afte several accidents, British Rail engineers decided that they did not lik the idea of light rail vehicles running around in the space under thei main line station where they might in conceivable circumstances col lide with a cast iron column and cause partial collapse of the statio structure above; the columns are not spigoted or otherwise attache to the wrought iron beams above. At Cannon Street in London a train had run into the buffers at only 5 mph with surprisingly severe con sequences. British Rail Research determined that a "light" rail vehicle weighing 65 tonnes fully laden could crack or dislodge a column a only 12 mph, a speed which could conceivably be attained in the Undercroft. GMML has had to design the Undercroft facilities to satisfy BR's precautionary requirements, which could not be con tradicted.

To separate the trams from the columns they run within rectangular reinforced concrete single track tubes which also house the two separate station platforms, one arrival and one departure. The tubes will give 4 hours of fire protection to the cast iron columns and 2 hours to the roof structure, which gains no additional structural sup port from the Metrolink Undercroft works. Other tubes have been provided for pedestrian access from London Road and Fairfield Street. The Metrolink tracks finish in a double stub with a scissors crossover located within the existing brick cross-tunnel leading to Sheffield Street on the far side of the station. Eventually these truncated tracks may be extended to link up with Eastern Sector light rail routes.

The whole upgrading of the Undercroft is costing around £5 million and is delaying its completion until June 1992. British Rail, while maintaining a policy of welcoming light rail initiatives, considered the measures essential to discharge the "duty of care" responsibilities they hold towards customers and staff. GMML was understandably irked at the threat of being deprived of a major traffic generator for a few costly months though other delays have since put back Metrolink's inauguration to a time quite close to the Undercroft's projected completion. As far as safety is concerned, what has been created in the Undercroft is an intersecting labyrinth of tram and pedestrian tunnels and footways, possibly trading the risk of major incidents for the risk of frequent frights and minor incidents involving pedestrians and trams fitted not with distinctively clear-sounding gongs but with whistles which may be expected to sound in the tunnels exactly like echoing wheel-squeal.

The Undercroft platforms are linked by escalators and lifts to an intermediate mezzanine floor which could be provided with franchised retail outlets. The mezzanine floor is linked in turn by escalator and lift to the main concourse of Piccadilly Station. The Undercroft station is being seen as a major opportunity to enhance arriving visitors' first impressions of the city and is being upgraded visually with the help of the Central Manchester Development Corporation.

PICCADILLY TO VICTORIA

Having boarded the tram in what masquerades as an underground station, it is a surprise to roll straight out at street level and immediately swing right to join London Road on a "trambaan" alignment. Soon we cut diagonally across some vacant land to climb steeply onto Aytoun Street, joked about amongst Mancunians as the address of the main "unemployment" exchange, which establishment we pass on our right just after humping over the Rochdale Canal bridge. The tram now runs along an agreeable stretch of "trambaan" complete with centre poles and after passing the system's only city-centre crossover leaves Aytoun Street flanked by the buildings where the LRT proposals were conceived and then promoted; on our left is Westminster House, built originally to house the GMC, and on our right number 9 Portland Street, headquarters of the PTE.

Crossing Portland Street, we come out into the oasis of Piccadilly Gardens. This was the site of St Mary's Infirmary until its destruction by bombing in the war. Here the island-platformed Piccadilly Gardens station conveniently adjoins the busy Parker Street bus stands, beyond which rises the modern Piccadilly Plaza complex. Heading away from here we approach the Delta junction at which we turn right for Victoria, regaining our line of route from Altrincham to Bury. We turn immediately left out of the Piccadilly Gardens area into Market Street, noticing the high levels of pedestrian activity hereabouts. The next stop — Market Street, with a profiled platform — is located adjacent to the long canopy outside Lewis's department store and is well placed to serve the big stores, the Arndale Centre and the many smaller shops to be found nearby.

From Market Street we turn right into High Street to run alongside the Arndale Centre, noticing on the right the inbound equivalent to the Market Street stop, called High Street. This profiled platform adjoins Debenhams store. At the junction with Cannon Street we pass the summit of the city-centre section; from here onwards it is downhill all the way to Victoria. As we coast down Nicholas Croft and pass the spiral car park exit ramp on the left, we notice that the inbound track on our right can be shared with other traffic. This very short section is the only example of a fully mixed-traffic alignment on the entire system.

After crossing Shudehill we now enter a very straight and flat section called Snow Hill, destined one day to be swallowed up inside a massive new development. The alignment here has been designed to incorporate a new light rail station to serve the new complex. At the far end of the flat station site the track dips suddenly to cross Dantzic Street, from where we can see the CIS building towering above us on the right, and then descends Balloon Street, running alongside

the home of the Co-operative Wholesale Society. At the bottom of Balloon Street we cross Corporation Street to find ourselves rolling downhill across pedestrianised Long Millgate and into Victoria Station ready for our onward run to Bury.

THE BURY LINE

The line to Bury, along which we are about to travel, was quite a latecomer to that town. The first railway to reach Bury had been the East Lancs, which got there from Clifton Junction in 1846 en route to Ramsbottom, and we will run along this line where it survives as Metrolink from just north of Radcliffe to Bury loco junction. From Bury Bolton Street onwards this line has been re-born as the East Lancashire Railway, on which steam services are operated for tourists all the way to Rawtenstall (see the end of Chapter 15). A link is still usable from Metrolink at Bury Loco Junction through to Bolton Street and beyond.

The next railway to reach Bury was the East–West line from the Manchester & Leeds Railway at Heywood, recently reinstated as an ELR link to the BR network. Not until 1879 was the present Bury line opened by the Lancashire & Yorkshire Railway, joining up with the East Lancs at Radcliffe which in those days also had a line to Bolton and so, like Bury, was very well served by railways. Other original stations on the Bury line were Crumpsall, Heaton Park, Prestwich, and Whitefield; Woodlands Road, Bowker Vale and Besses o' th' Barn were later additions. Until they were diverted into the new Bury Interchange, the Bury electrics used to run into Bolton Street, from which another service, to Holcombe Brook, was started in 1882. Initially, at the Manchester end of the Bury line, the trains reached Victoria via Cheetham Hill Junction; it was not until 1904 that they were brought to the Long Millgate side of Victoria via Collyhurst Tunnel. The original link survived as the Queens Road loop until it was slewed and then obliterated during the construction of Metrolink's Queens Road headquarters.

VICTORIA

The new link at Victoria between the street tramways and the Bury line has been created on the site of the old platforms 6 and 7. Platforms 1 to 4 had already been wiped out in preparation for Picc–Vic and 5 was last used by the Bury BR trains before the line's shutdown. The Metrolink tracks enter the station after crossing Long Millgate and passing the far end of the yard used as a base by the contractors during the city-centre LRT construction work. A large hole was made in the side wall of the station to admit the double LRT tracks, which change from grooved rail to "DLR" 80lb flat-bottomed rail just before passing through the wall.

The entry hole has been substantially reinforced and protected by brick-faced reinforced concrete wing walls, as have other structural parts of the station. Once inside the station, the track continues roughly parallel to the concourse, passing an outbound Metrolink platform on the left. Here also the track passes over the River Irk which is hidden deep below in a large culvert. The Metrolink tracks split either side of a roof support column here and then swing sharply to the right

Car 1001 is seen here at Prestwich on driver training duties, 28th February 1992. *Peter Fox*

to straddle an island platform, the generous width of which contrasts strongly with the much narrower and potentially much busier Piccadilly Gardens island platform. It is worth watching tram pantographs at this corner as they follow the downward gradient in the contact wire where it descends from street height to railway height. On the outside of the outer curve here a brick-faced reinforced concrete wall has been built to physically segregate Metrolink from BR.

Having passed the island platform, we leave Victoria and pass under the Cheetham Hill Road bridge, the columns of which are protected from the trams by reinforced concrete "cutwater" barriers; the reason for the lack of similar structure protection adjacent to the tracks used by BR trains under the same bridge is that revised safety standards apply only to new work. Once through the bridge a facing crossover links the two new LRT tracks and another links the outbound LRT track with BR. An LRT siding connects at a trailing set of points with the inbound track. Miles Platting Bank, up which we are accelerating, is another Metrolink location where you might be lucky enough to run parallel with a steam special, this time slogging dramatically up the severe gradient en route to Altrincham and beyond via Ashton Moss. Part way up the bank, our tracks suddenly dive down into Collyhurst Tunnel, 390 m (426 yards) long, which carries us to the other side of the BR tracks and points us more towards Bury.

After traversing the Irk Valley on a succession of bridges and viaducts, we descend towards the bridge under Queens Road, having a good look to the left at Metrolink's Queens Road Operations and Maintenance Centre and at the trams stored outside.

Emerging from the tunnel we can see blocks of flats to the right and, to the left, an industrial panorama relieved only by the distant neatly-grassed area adjoining Metrolink's headquarters. The signal box at the foot of the landscaped rise is nothing to do with Metrolink; it is BR's Cheetham Hill Junction box. The railway passing it and then crossing underneath our track is the Manchester Loop, which now carries trains towards Oldham, Rochdale and Yorkshire. Another viaduct, bereft of tracks, curves downwards to the right from our line to join up with the Loop tracks. This link is earmarked for use as part of the future LRT route to Oldham and Rochdale.

ONWARDS TO BURY

Passing the small platforms of Queens Road staff halt, we dip under Queens Road bridge and begin the long climb out of the Irk Valley. Trailing through Queens Road Junction's pointwork we head up a deep cutting to arrive at Woodlands Road station, perched on a hillside amongst semi-detached houses. Here access to both platforms is by ramps, including a very short one linking the outbound side to Wigmore Road behind Woodlands Road substation.

From here the track, still climbing, enters the cutting which takes

The summit of the entire Metrolink Phase 1 system is to be found at Besses o' th' Barn bridge. This unusual inverted-T shaped structure crosses Bury Old Road and the M62 motorway; remedial work on it was one of the principal factors delaying conversion of the Bury line to light rail operation. Here No 1002 coasts into "Besses" station en route to Bury on Metrolink's first day of passenger service, 6th April 1992. The sign directing passers-by to the station can be seen on the left. *Peter Fox*

it to Crumpsall station. Located in a mature residential area close to the centre of Cheetham Hill, this station retains its old stairs which are supplemented by a new ramp on the outbound side and by the standard hydraulic lift on the inbound side. Just beyond Crumpsall is a trailing crossover, surviving from BR days. A little further on we emerge from the cutting to see quite a panoramic view to the right, including BT's distinctive microwave tower in Heaton Park. Bowker Vale, the next stop, is the place to alight for a brisk walk down Middleton Road to Heaton Park, where you can find Manchester's other operating electric tramway and perhaps ride on a first-generation Manchester tram. Bowker Vale station, elevated high on an embankment, has extremely long ramps connecting its platforms to the streets below.

The tracks now descend amongst suburban housing before entering Heaton Park Tunnel, 652 m (713 yards) long, which as it burrows shallowly beneath Heaton Park on a rising gradient has an exceedingly thin roof in places — though it is not true that dog-hairs stand on end when a tram passes underneath. Emerging briefly into a shallow cutting, the line passes under Bury Old Road to enter Heaton Park station with its two new hydraulic lifts, one to each platform. Situated in a shrub-covered cutting this is perhaps the line's pleasantest station and is another point to alight at if you want to visit the enormous Heaton Park or, indeed, to admire the slightly faded villagey atmosphere in the vicinity of the station and the park gates.

Climbing again we come out of the cutting and onto an embankment to reach Prestwich station, sited in a residential area overlooking a new shopping centre. Both platforms at Prestwich have new access ramps to supplement the existing steps and subway. Pressing onwards, still on embankment, we reach Metrolink's absolute summit at Besses o' th' Barn bridge, a reinforced concrete beam structure shaped in cross-section like an inverted "T". The bridge was installed when the M62 Motorway was built. It was this unusual structure's dose of concrete cancer which was one of the reasons given for the long delay in inaugurating Metrolink.

Immediately after the bridge we run into Besses o' th' Barn station (known for short as "Besses", like the brass band from which it took its name). This is an island-platformed station having a new hydraulic lift giving access down into the existing step-accessed subway and thence via new ramps to street level. Continuing on embankment running down more or less to ground level we arrive at Whitefield, which with plenty of trees close by is another of the line's more pleasantly-sited stations. Nearby there is a PTE bus interchange, and there is space not far from the inbound platform for car parking. Both platforms have new ramped accesses as well as retaining the former steps to street level. On the inbound side can be seen one of the large mirrors fixed at concave-curved platforms to improve the driver's view of his doorways.

The Bury-bound exit from Whitefield is via a short tunnel under Bury New Road, which brings us into a long, deep cutting which caused no end of engineering problems when the line was originally being built. Today, however, it is one of Metrolink's fastest stretches, taking us down into the Irwell Valley at Radcliffe. From here onwards we begin to obtain good views of the hills which lie behind

Bury. After crossing over the Irwell we arrive at Radcliffe station, once called Radcliffe Central to distinguish it from Radcliffe Bridge on the line to Clifton Junction. Radcliffe Central was a junction and you could change there for Bolton via Black Lane. Today the station has a massive Park and Ride (and, according to the surface markings, "Kiss and Ride") car park. There is ramped access to both platforms in addition to the old steps and subway.

After we have curved to the right away from Radcliffe station the Manchester, Bolton and Bury Navigation is intermittently visible on the left. This part of the defunct canal is being restored as a linear water park. Further along we come to Hagside level crossing, now controlled and overseen from Queens Road. After this we cross the Irwell again before paralleling both the river and the canal.

From here we can see Bury during our approach. On top of Holcombe Hill, behind the town, the monument we can see commemorates the achievements of Bury's most famous citizen, Sir Robert Peel. When Sir Robert was Prime Minister he was responsible for repealing the Corn Laws in 1846, and this is what truly set the Industrial Revolution rolling. He is best remembered, though, for originating the police force as we know it today. It was indeed Sir Robert who inspired the enduring nickname "Bobby" for the British policeman. This affectionate name is also, as a matter of interest, still sometimes applied to railway signalmen as a long throwback to the days when train movements were controlled by railway policemen. Another similarly-derived name for the police — "Peelers" — did not stick. What a splendid name "Sir Robert Peel" would have made for one of Greater Manchester's new trams.

This small excursion into the town's history brings us to Bury Loco Junction, not initially included in the Metrolink Signalling Plan because it was intended to have been removed. However, it was found expedient to use the surviving Bury BR depot, to which it leads, for supplier's modifications to Metrolink trams; the entire six-track depot fan has now been modified to accommodate both Metrolink and BR wheel profiles. As we bear right towards Bury Interchange we drop below the level of this track, which leads ultimately to the East Lancs Railway at Bolton Street. Our lower level position means that we cannot quite see Bury depot, with its two preserved Bury BR units standing outside, as we pass it on our left hand side.

We now begin the final climb through landscaped surroundings to Bury Interchange, passing under the new bridge built to carry the East Lancashire's rail link to BR at Heywood. The island-platformed terminus is entered via a scissors crossover and there is access by escalator or lift to the bustling centre of Bury and to the large adjoining bus station. From here it is well worth while, on days when the East Lancashire Railway is operating, to stroll round the corner to Bolton Street station and visit the railway museum or take a steam train ride to Rawtenstall. From Ramsbottom, an intermediate station, you may be able to catch a connecting bus to take you to Holcombe Hill and a working cotton mill. What is certain is that you will find the area much more pleasant than you could ever have hoped if you had believed the Lancashire clogs-and-shawl and mill-chimneyed images of the past.

◄ End of the line — all change for the East Lancs Railway! Through passengers for the ELR arriving by tram at Bury Interchange should ascend to surface level and bear left via Haymarket Street and Broad Street to join Silver Street before turning left onto Bolton Street, where the East Lancs Railway's present terminus will be found. Check ELR availability first. In this view, taken on Metrolink's opening day — 6th April 1992 — Car 1005 stands in passenger service at the left hand platform while another car, on driver training duties, waits at the right hand platform. *Peter Fox*

10. STREET TRAMWAY CONSTRUCTION

In this chapter the emphasis will be on the new and unfamiliar aspects of Metrolink's construction work, principally the installation of modern street tramways into a bustling British city centre.

On 5th April 1990, Metrolink's street track installation programme was inaugurated at a ground-breaking ceremony carried out by Jack Flanagan, Chair of the PTA's Metrolink Working Party. On 5th June, ceremonial installation of the first grooved rails was carried out by Minister for Public Transport Roger Freeman.

These ceremonies signified the start of the biggest construction project seen in the streets of Manchester since the original tram tracks were installed a century or so ago. On Monday 23rd July 1990 the first consignment of new grooved tram rail arrived from Luxembourg and the scene was set for some intense action.

TRAM TRACK LAYING SKILLS

John Mowlem Construction Plc are ultimately responsible for the management and execution of all Civil Engineering works in the city centre. Mowlem sub-contracted various specialist activities to sub-contractors, including W S. Atkins Consultants (engineering design), John Lloyd (road surfacing), Manchester City Council (street lighting and signing), Balfour Beatty Railway Engineering Ltd (rail laying) and Rotra Metro (rail grinding).

The art of tram track installation is so different from conventional railway tracklaying that it is really a separate skill in itself, developed initially over a period of almost one hundred years in the UK. On the demise of first-generation city tramways around 1960, accumulated expertise and equipment was passed on direct to tracklaying personnel at the National Tramway Museum, thus maintaining a scarce working link with past knowledge backed up by archived information. When the revival came, would-be practitioners with no tram track construction knowledge could look overseas or seek advice from Crich or from Blackpool. During the Metrolink tendering process advice was in fact given at Crich to the tracklaying sub-contractor in one of the tendering consortia seeking to supplement extensive railway tracklaying experience with some grass-roots tramway tracklaying knowledge. The consortium concerned was not selected.

The heavy railway approach to tracklaying can only be adapted to street tramways with the greatest care and commitment; Balfour Beatty Railway Engineering Ltd, the tracklaying sub-contractor appointed by John Mowlem & Co Plc, had undertaken street track construction in Tuen Mun (Hong Kong) and so had some in-house experience. Balfour Beatty Railway Engineering dealt only with the installation of the rails themselves; the concrete trackbase slabs were set out and installed by Mowlem engineers.

TRAM TRACK IMPERATIVES

An almost completely different set of imperatives applies to street tramway construction and operation than those which apply to railways. Railway track construction is done behind fences away from public places; relatively speaking it is an activity of significance only to railway users and railway staff and no-one else. Street tramway track construction, on the other hand, has to be done right under the noses of the general public and in very close proximity to heavy traffic. It is of much wider interest and significance to the community at large in the city centre and to various statutory bodies having buried pipes, cables and ducts under the streets.

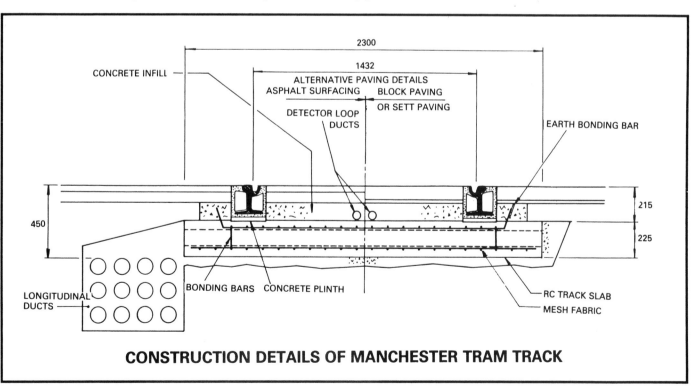

CONSTRUCTION DETAILS OF MANCHESTER TRAM TRACK

All of Metrolink's city-centre trackwork consists of Ri59 grooved rail secured in position and encapsulated using pourable polymer products. Two different polymers — Sika's KC330/UK and Edilon's "Corkelast" — were used, as described in the text. This cross-sectional drawing features Sika-encapsulated track, the rectangular ballast tubes of which are loaded with injected mortar grout. Edilon track differs from Sika in that the ballast tubes are of a round cross-section and are left empty, and continuous steel shuttering is interposed between the polymer and the surrounding road materials. It is the exposed top edge of this shuttering which enables Edilon track to be the most easily distinguished from Sika.

◀ Each of Metrolink's grooved-rail tracks is supported on a separate reinforced concrete slab. Double track has two individual slabs - as in this photograph taken in 1990 on Halliwell Street, adjacent to the sub-Post Office at Victoria Station. The left hand track is almost ready to receive concrete having been fitted with shuttering assemblies to form shallow channels on top of the slab for the rails. The two layers of reinforcing mesh can be seen; these are electrically connected to the substation pole (*not* earth) so as to reliably intercept any stray return traction current.
Author

◀ Metrolink's grooved rails were joined to each other throughout by the traditional Thermit welding process. This is a rapid and supremely elegant method of permanently uniting two rails in such a way that the finished joint will have the same properties as the rails themselves, so that the finished trackwork will wear evenly throughout. This Thermit reaction is taking place in Mosley Street near to the bus station. The passer-by might well look a little surprised — the reaction occurring so close to his feet is taking place at a temperature approaching 3,000 degree Centigrade. *Author*

▼ Manchester's tramway "special work" is concentrated at the heart of the system. The triangular (or "delta") junction has three facing and three trailing sets of points and three diamond crossings. Flange running, a conventional way of silencing tramcars' passage over grooved rail intersections, has not been used in Manchester. There is a trailing crossover in Aytoun Street. Here, assembly of the junction special work is seen in progress during June 1991. This work represented a triumph of the surveyor's and setting-out engineer's art when one bears in mind that the full layout had not previously been test-assembled in a manufacturer's yard and that its construction had to be done in separate segments to maintain bus movements.*Author*

► Tracks across critical intersections had to be installed at weekends with the roads closed. A case in point was Portland Street. Here Edilon polymer is being poured in around the rails on Sunday 12th May 1992 during a weekend occupation. Piccadilly Gardens island platform occupies the space between the two tracks where they straighten out in the background. *Author*

► Edilon shuttering for the triangular junction trackwork had to be fabricated on site; here it is being arc-welded in place amongst the diamond crossings. It should be emphasised that no arc-welding or flame-cutting was done on the rails themselves to avoid introducing localised metallurgical changes. To join the austenitic manganese steel crossing castings to plain rail, fishplates had to be used as no Thermit process exists which is capable of uniting the two dissimilar metals. For permanent security the fishplates were fixed into place with "Huckbolts", as seen here, rather than with conventional threaded bolts. *Author*

▼ Most of the city-centre trackwork is either asphalted or block-paved. The track along the upper part of Balloon Street has been smartly finished off with granite cubes especially imported from Portugal; this shows the start of the granite-paving process looking downhill towards Victoria, at Balloon Street's junction with Federation Street in May 1991.*Author*

There are other differences between railway track and tramway track. Stability is an important characteristic which has to be carefully built into railway track. Tram track achieves its stability by being held firmly in place in the road structure by various methods which must ensure that:

● Rail position and gauge are reliably maintained.

● A good watertight seal is maintained where the road surface meets the rails; no water must be able to enter the track/road structure.

● The rails do not move directly against the road material or supporting substructure; as well as permitting water entry, such movement could cause attrition and wearing away of the material under the rails.

● Corrugations (noisy undulations in the surface of the rails, a common and little-understood fault which can develop in street tramway and railway track) are prevented from forming.

● Return traction current cannot escape from the rails and find an alternative path back to the substation negative pole through earth or through statutory undertakers' underground pipes or cables.

● Minimal interference with the surface of the road is caused by the track's presence.

● All materials exposed to the surface will resist the weather and the passage of road vehicles.

Some of the requirements listed above are statutory; for instance, the avoidance of stray earth return currents. Even though modern tramway track is welded into continuous lengths which form good return paths, small stray currents could still conceivably find their way to underground metalwork such as pipes and cables which they would corrode by electrolysis at the point of exit of the current. Polymer encapsulation ensures that the return current is entirely confined to the rails.

POLYMER ENCAPSULATION

The grooved rails in Manchester have been embedded in pourable polymer products which cure to form an electrically insulating, resilient, tough rubbery material. The resilience of the polymers is also effective in preventing the transmission of ground-borne vibrations to adjacent structures and buildings. The method of installing the rails by means of polymers is called encapsulation.

In encapsulated track the rails are completely separated from the surrounding road materials by a flexible grout poured in around them while they are accurately held in position by temporary clamps, tiebars or anchor fixings. Initially Sika KC330/UK pourable polymer was used. The instructions issued to users of the product clearly state that the polymer grouting material must be mixed and applied in absolutely dry conditions, and for this reason Metrolink's first production grooved tracklaying, which was done on the Snow Hill off-street section and afterwards along High Street as far as Market Street, was successfully carried out under long tunnel-like plastic tents heated through when necessary by warm air blowers.

The Sika method was also used along Mosley Street from York Street to Princess Street and along Lower Mosley Street between Peter Street and Windmill Street. During the work on Mosley Street, Manchester lived up for once to its unkind reputation as a rainy place and it was found impossible to keep up the required rate of progress and at the same time maintain the absolutely dry conditions needed for the Sika polymer material to cure without becoming spongy and frangible. A mid-contract switch was therefore made to the Dutch Edilon system. In fairness it must be emphasised here that both the Sika and Edilon systems have been used elsewhere with great success for many years.

SLAB CONSTRUCTION

There is a separate track slab for each direction. The slabs are of similar dimensions for both the Sika method of encapsulation and the successor Edilon method. The first tracklaying operation in either case was to excavate a channel wide enough to accommodate the slab and the trackside nests of cable ducts, followed by compaction of the exposed surface. A thin "blinding" layer of concrete was then applied to the exposed surface to form a clean base on which to work. Two continuous layers of steel reinforcing mesh were then laid in place and supported one above the other by concrete pads. The mesh not only strengthens the slab physically, it is also bonded to the negative substation pole and therefore acts as a second-line defence against stray earth currents. Once the slab had been constructed, rail installation could begin.

THE WHEEL/RAIL INTERFACE

Railway rails are always laid leaning inwards so that their "table"

or top surface has an inward inclination of 1 in 20, helping the rails resist lateral loadings. The wheel profiles have a correspondingly sloping tread, or "coning", which helps make them roll in a true straight line during high-speed running. Tramway rails, on the other hand, derive adequate lateral support from the surrounding road structure or from tiebars and need no inward inclination. They must be laid perpendicular to the formation because to carry any inclination round sharp corners would require rail bending to be carried out in two planes, horizontal and vertical.

Tramway wheels generally have a tread slope of 1 in 40, and a matching inclination is rolled into the surface of standard grooved tramway rails. Metrolink trams will run for most of the time on railway track with the steeper 1 in 20 head inclination referred to above. It therefore made sense for the consortium, charged under the DBOM terms of the Metrolink contract with designing a suitable wheel profile for Manchester's LRVs, to go for a profile with a matching 1 in 20 "railway" tread slope; the selected profile is a modification of the BR standard P8 profile.

At first, attempts were made during initial grooved tracklaying work on Snow Hill to lay the tramway rails inclined inwards so as to match the railway wheel coning of the LRVs. After failed attempts to carry the inclination round the curves in Nicholas Croft and difficulties with setting them up on straight sections at an angle, all the tram rails were afterwards laid normal to the formation.

To achieve the desired 1 in 20 head inclination to match the wheels, the grooved rails have after installation been lightly ground by Rotra Metro, a specialist Italian sub-contractor engaged for the purpose by Mowlem. The two units of the small rail-grinding "train" became, on Monday 19th August 1991, the first self-propelled rail vehicles to run on the street tracks; the work was completed within a fortnight. Inspection of the lightly-ground rails shows that this has been a worthwhile process; the grinding has helped remove some surface iregularities from the rails and should ensure that the LRVs run more sweetly than they would have done on un-ground rails.

RAIL BENDING

Tramway rails, not particularly flexible by nature, have to be bent round sharp curves in the street. This is a laborious and exacting task traditionally done by the simple "jim crow" method. A "jim crow" rail bender grips the rail in two places and applies a powerful bending force midway between. When this is done at frequent intervals, it puts a smooth curve into the rail. The bending force is applied via blocks shaped to fit the rail section so that no twist is put into the rails. Modern rail benders apply the force by hand-pumped hydraulic rams, an advance on older ones which used a screw action actuated by a huge tommy-bar.

At first during Metrolink street tracklaying an impressive Geismar rail bending machine was used. Two pairs of feed rolls propelled the rail through a third pair of rolls which could be traversed to apply the bending force. Although this machine was efficient and enabled close quality control to be maintained, it was awkward to move about and required the rails to be lifted to its working height before they could be bent to predetermined data ensuring that they would fit accurately in their intended location. By the time Market Street corner had been reached, it had been found more convenient to allow individual platelaying gangs to use conventional Geismar hydraulic "jim crow" rail benders to manually bend the rails in position. This remained the normal method of bending the grooved rails throughout the rest of the contract.

It is interesting to note that ride quality measuring equipment supplied by Geismar can be used to assess the skill with which their railbending equipment has been used; the Macmeter, for instance, will amongst other things reveal curve geometry faults by recording lateral acceleration and lateral jerk levels.

Setting-out of track positions and alignments, followed by slab installation, was done exclusively by Mowlem to designs provided by W S Atkins. Initially — that is, on Snow Hill, Nicholas Croft, High Street, Mosley Street and Lower Mosley Street — the track slabs were given a flat surface. Balfour Beatty, as rail-laying sub-contractor, then had to bend the rails to fit the geometry of the slabs. The position of each track had been determined very closely with relation to buildings, platforms, adjacent tracks and bus lanes in close consultation with other bodies and it was considered so important to keep the tracks accurately aligned with the geometry determined by Atkins and executed by Mowlem that a change was made to the use of deep narrow grooves which closely defined the final line of the rails. It is important to remember that the position of the extremities of the tramcars' bodywork together with the need to build in good lateral

► The two pictures on this depict the start and finish of tram track installation for Metrolink. On 5th June 1990 Minister for Public Transport Roger Freeman ceremonially installed Manchester's (and the UK's) first grooved rail for a street-running light rail system. In the background is Victoria Station and a line-up of GMA, GMPTE. GMPTA and other personalities. Compare this photograph with the top of page 62, taken in the same location a few weeks afterwards. Tie-bars like the ones visible here were not used in the production track apart from on a localised temporary basis during assembly. *GMPTE*

► A length of rail forming part of the last section of grooved track to be laid for the city centre tramways is seen here being bent in situ by Balfour Beatty platelayers on 9th February 1992 using a hydraulically-operated "jim crow". The inner curve leading across London Road and into Piccadilly Undercroft is being shaped to fit the geometry already cast into the concrete track-base slab, set out and installed by Mowlem Civil Engineering, the GMA consortium member responsible for tracklaying, civil engineering and structures. Balfour Beatty Railway Engineering dealt only with the installation of the rails themselves to Mowlem's requirements. As with other important road crossings, the work across London Road had to be done during weekend occupations with road traffic and bus diversions in force. *Author*

dynamics which are the critical factors in determining rail position at any particular spot. Even so, some of the city-centre track geometry will look puzzling to observers unaware of all the factors contributing to its final form.

THERMIT WELDING

Manchester's Ri59 grooved tramway rail, weighing 59 kg/m, was delivered in standard 18 metre lengths. The first 300 lengths were stored in a fenced compound at the junction of Dantzic Street and Balloon Street, handy for the initial tracklaying operations. The second batch was stored on land adjacent to the alignment joining London Road with Aytoun Street. Rails were distributed as required from the stores to stacks adjacent to the on-street working sites, taking care to orientate half of them one way round and half of them the other way to save having to turn any on site. From then onwards all rail handling was done by means of special mobile gantries with traversing chain hoists, or by manhandling the rails along the formation on trunnioned rollers.

Once the rails were in position and bent to shape if needs be, they had to be welded together into one continuous length, fishplated joints being no longer used on street tramways except in special circumstances — of which more later. In Manchester's case all the on-street rail welding has been done by the German-produced Thermit process. Thermit welding was developed around the turn of the century and was in common use on first-generation tramways; the process has changed very little since those days.

In Manchester the rails were cut to length where necessary using rail saws or abrasive disc rail cutters. Neither oxy-acetylene nor oxy-propane was used at all to cut or make holes in the rails because the localised heat could have weakened them and could possibly have led to fractures in the future. In preparation for Thermit welding a measured gap is left between the ends of the rails to be joined, the gap being filled during the welding process with a measured quantity of molten steel which when cooled will have exactly the same properties as the rails themselves.

To prepare them for welding, the rail ends are clamped into a special jig which held them in accurate alignment horizontally and vertically. A pre-formed bonded sand mould is assembled around the joint. The Thermit crucible is then set up and charged with Thermit mixture. Using a powerful oxy-propane torch, the rail ends and sand mould are next heated to around 600−700*C to drive out all moisture before swinging the reaction crucible into position over the joint. Finally a sparkler-like Thermit igniter is placed into the charged crucible to start the reaction.

The Thermit mixture consists of finely divided iron oxide powder mixed with metallic aluminium and alloying agents; the purpose of the alloying agents is to give the weld metal the same properties as the rails themselves to make sure that the whole finished joint will wear evenly. Iron oxide and aluminium react with each other exothermically, i.e. the reaction gives out heat. Plenty of flames and smoke emanate from the top of the crucible and a white-hot stream of molten steel from the bottom.

The igniter starts the reaction, which is over in a few spectacular seconds; the tremendous heat of the molten steel automatically melts a fusible plug in the neck of the crucible allowing the molten steel to flow down into the pre-heated joint to unite indivisibly with the rail ends. Excess molten steel overflows from the top of the mould and runs off into special receptacles on either side. The reaction crucible is then removed, the moulds are broken away and red-hot excess metal is trimmed from the joint using air chisels frequently cooled in water.

For sheer drama in the city streets there can hardly be anything to equal the Thermit welding process. Some welds had to be carried out surprisingly close to crowds, providing an ever-popular spectacle; after all, it's not often that people have the opportunity to freely observe steel-founding at close quarters. Once the rails were welded into continuous lengths they could be set up ready for encapsulation, a process which is described below.

FISHPLATED JOINTS

The only exception to the use of Thermit welding has been the use of fishplates to join together the manganese steel castings used for the diamond crossings at the triangular junction and at Aytoun Street crossover, and to join the castings to the plain rails. No Thermit process exists which unites plain steel rails with manganese steel castings, though there is a special Thermit process (not used in Manchester) which can unite manganese castings with each other.

In view of the intended encapsulation of the rails, ordinary fishplate bolts were not considered appropriate for tightening the plates into the rail webs. Instead, "Huckbolt" high performance rail joint fastenings have been used. These are in regular use on railways and are applied with the aid of a powerful hydraulic tool. First of all the rail ends are drilled for the fastener pins. Then the fishplates are fitted in place and temporarily tightened up with ordinary bolts to check for correct fit. Next, if all is well, the Huckbolt pins are inserted in place of the conventional bolts.

A steel collar is slipped over the end of each pin and pushed against the plate with the installation tool. The pin has annular rings instead of the conventional bolt's screw thread; the installation tool grips the pin and pulls it, at the same time pushing on the collar. This combined action squeezes both plates very firmly indeed into position. At a predetermined tension the collar is swaged, or reduced in diameter, by the installation tool until it moulds itself fully and permanently into the annular rings. The final action is for the pin tail to snap off under tension at a neck located slightly outside of the collar position. The finished "Huckbolt" can then only be removed with the aid of a special collar-cutting tool; otherwise it will not budge during the entire life of the rails.

SIKA ENCAPSULATION

Once the rails have been bent if necessary, welded and positioned accurately to standard 1435 mm (4'8½'') gauge with a 25 mm gap between their bases and the surface of the concrete slab, encapsulation can begin. The Sika process involves three pours; the first, of pure KC330/UK liquid grout, runs in under the rails and over the edges of their bases, firmly and resiliently fixing the rails to the slabs. The second pour, bulked with sand, forms a 20 mm thick "wall" between temporary plastic shuttering and special rectangular PVC ballast tubes glued into the rail webs. This second polymer pour is carried up to the underside of the rail head.

During subsequent tarmac surfacing, the hot asphalt is rolled in over the top of the polymer "walls" and into contact with the rail head. The asphalt should then soon afterwards be cut neatly away from either side of the rails widely enough and deeply enough to expose the top surface of the polymer, after which a third pour of bulked polymer grout can be run into the resulting slots to form a permanent, watertight surface seal. Mortar grout is injected into the continuous rectangular ballast tubes, loading the rails and helping prevent them vibrating. The ballast tubes also save on the amount of costly grout needed for the encapsulation process.

Unfortunately on Mosley Street time caught up with the tracklaying team, by then working well behind schedule. By previous agreement with the City Engineer, the street had to be re-opened for Christmas traffic — mainly buses — by 15th November 1990. As the date drew near there was no time for the asphalt to be slotted out either side of the rails for the third pour, and so the street had to be opened to heavy bus traffic with thin fragile strips of asphalt, never intended to last long, either side of each rail. The buses made short work of loosening and breaking out the asphalt around the rails, leaving ragged linear holes of varying width either side of each rail

all the way up the street.

The contractors regained possession of Mosley Street on 15th January 1991 and then had to find a way of reinstating the broken road surface and completing the third pour. This was not finally accomplished until February 1992, with Mosley Street re-opening fully to buses on the 14th of that month. The remedial work was carried out without serious ill effects on city centre bus and traffic flows. Appropriately enough, the first vehicles to traverse the full length of the street with its partly finished track were rail vehicles. Metrolink's RFS recovery unit and LRV No 1001 passed both way along the street during the 15th September clearance trials. Further re-work took place on parts of Mosley Street during January 1992.

EDILON ENCAPSULATION

Because of the difficulty of maintaining the dry conditions essential for success with the Sika process, a switch was made to the Dutch "Edilon" process in early 1991. The polymer grout material used in this process is "Corkelast" which is not sensitive to damp during curing. The Edilon application technique is different from that used for Sika encapsulation, and the tracklaying team were shown how to carry it out by a team from Holland. In Manchester the Corkelast has been bulked with fine gravel to reduce costs.

In the Edilon process, the rails are lowered into the channels cast in the concrete track base slab and are clamped in place against cured Corkelast pads while liquid Corkelast grout is poured in and flows under the rails. Temporary tie bars were used to help keep the rail vertical, to gauge and in position during encapsulation; tie bars were also used temporarily from time to time during Sika encapsulation. With either polymer, any permanent tie bars would have to have been fully encapsulated to preserve the isolation of the track structure from the road structure; surface evidence of permanent tie bar encapsulation can be seen in the Edilon-encapsulated Delta pointwork.

The Edilon process features round ballast tubes which are fixed either side of the rails in the angle between the base and the web. The purpose of the ballast tubes is purely to save on the amount of costly grout used, without detracting from the quality of the finished product; Edilon ballast tubes, unlike the rectangular Sika tubes, are left empty.

Permanent vertical sheet steel shuttering fixed to the concrete slab either side of each rail enables the Corkelast to be poured right up to surface level, and at the same time acts as a strong, rigid interface between the polymer and the road surface. It is the visible top edge of this shuttering either side of each rail which, apart from colour differences (Sika polymer is black and Edilon tends to be greyish-beige) enables Edilon track to be easily distinguished from Sika track. Edilon produce a specially-rolled heavy steel interface strip but this has not been used in Manchester.

Once Edilon encapsulation had been completed, the track structure could be handed over completely to the surfacing contractors. During surfacing the permanent steel shuttering serves an additional useful purpose by protecting the resilient grout from surfacing contractors' heavy road rollers and other machinery.

Polymer encapsulation of tramway rails can complicate future maintenance operations. The material itself is adversely affected by the high temperatures involved in the reclamation of rail wear by metal-deposition; this is a technique used to build up new metal on rails in places where they have been worn away by the action of LRV wheels, particularly on sharp corners. Typically, new metal is deposited by a technique similar to arc welding. With encapsulated rails there are basically two methods of protecting the polymers from high welding temperatures; either the polymer material is first cut away from either or both sides of the rail head and replaced with new grout afterwards, or the welding is done in long "passes" with enough time allowed in between for the rail head to cool.

SPECIAL WORK — THE DELTA JUNCTION

In tramway terminology, "special work" is the name given to all trackwork which incorporates pointwork or crossings. Metrolink's tramway special work occurs for the most part in Piccadilly Gardens where the three sections of tramway meet at a triangular or delta junction expanded on advice given by engineers from the Portland light rail system in the USA. Preliminary work on the layout was done by the MVA Consultancy, while the detailed design was done by W.S. Atkins Consultancy working in close co-operation with GMPTE and the City Engineer (Highways Division). The Piccadilly Gardens area is already heavily used by buses, pedestrians and servicing traffic making deliveries to shops and it required some careful design work to fit the tramway junction into what was already a difficult area. The result is that considerably more space is now available for pedestrians' use.

Expansion of the junction has increased its LRV capacity by providing extended internal links where baulked trams can pause without obstructing other movements. In this way the junction's ultimate capacity has been increased to 24 movements per arm per direction per hour, though we will have to wait a few years before we see it performing under those busy conditions.

Metrolink's only other example of tramway special work is the emergency crossover in Aytoun Street, where trams will be able to turn short of Piccadilly Undercroft if necessary. This crossover has early use pending completion of the elaborate structural works demanded by BR in the Undercroft. The switches undercroft-end are set up for the time being as spring points.

Tramway special work is subjected to heavy wear and tear and is typically constructed entirely from austenitic manganese steel. This is an exceptionally tough material which work-hardens in use; it is commonly used for excavator jaws and stone-crusher teeth. Edgar Allen Engineering Ltd of Sheffield has been supplying complete tramway junction layouts cast throughout in manganese steel for over one hundred years; the firm has recently supplied the Toronto Transit Commission with tramway pointwork.

In railway practice, manganese steel is sometimes used for rail crossings (or "frogs") where traffic is heavy; manganese steel resists the hammering action of the wheels far better than rail steel. Railway point switches (the parts where the wheels are actually deflected) are, however, always built up from ordinary rail steel because their large radius protects them from particularly heavy attacks from wheels. It is because of tramway point switches' small radius and consequently heavier flange pressures that manganese steel has traditionally been considered essential to prolong service life. In 1991 Edgar Allen supplied new sets of points cast entirely in manganese steel to both the Beamish and Wirral heritage tramways.

Manganese steel special work is more expensive than plain steel, and W.S. Atkins Consultants, GMA's design consultants, did not consider that the extra cost of manganese steel could be justified for Metrolink's tramway point switches, which were ordered in rail steel from Kihn in Luxembourg. All switches are conventional, no advantage having been taken of modern pre-sorting techniques. Manganese steel crossings have been supplied by Edgar Allen and the differently-sourced components were first brought together in Piccadilly Gardens, not in a manufacturer's yard for trial assembly purposes as is normally the practice. Other rails within junctions have been cut, bent and fitted on site using plain Ri59 rail. Edilon encapsulation featuring tailor-made steel shuttering has been used for all the special work.

Metrolink's trams are fitted with powerful magnetic track brakes on each bogie to increase their emergency stopping-power. Manganese steel is non-magnetic, and this means that magnetic track brakes are ineffective on it. Magnetic track brakes should not normally be actuated when passing over pointwork because of the danger of their poleface-ends catching on a point blade tip and causing serious damage. The pros and cons are too complicated to discuss further here.

All point switches are electrically heated to prevent icing-up in frosty weather. Facing points are equipped with Hanning & Kahl HWE 60 VV-ZVV electro-hydraulic points setting machines and HNOF-1R 15 control equipment interfaced with GEC Alsthom Signalling Ltd selection and signal control systems. No mechanism maintenance is required other than cleaning out the drainage outlet every 6 months, inspecting the working parts once a year, changing the bellows every 3 years and generally overhauling every 6−10 years. No interim machine lubrication is necessary. Transponders buried between the rails on the approaches to facing points automatically determine the direction required by the tram as it passes over a detector loop; the route is coded into the tram's electronic recognition system at the start of each journey. More of this in Chapter 12.

Even when the points are "primed" to change, the blades will not actually move until the tram reaches a mass detection loop placed immediately before them. In this way the points cannot change until they are under the direct observation of the driver; the likelihood of anyone becoming trapped by or interfering with the moving switch parts is therefore minimised. The point blades are shifted powerfully enough to crush stones and other debris, but their movement is hydraulically damped to quiten them and to stop them throwing up little fountains of water in wet weather. Movement takes 0.6 seconds. Drivers will be responsible for seeing that points are properly set before going over them. Facing points are equipped with double interlocks; the position and locking of each set is monitored from the Queens Road operations and control centre.

A magnetic deadlock device located between the tracks just before the points prevents their changing while a tram is moving through them. All point mechanisms can be actuated manually by inserting a short red point iron, kept in a special locker attached to each points indicator signal pole, into a socket in the points. Wheels trailed through adversely-set powered points would displace knuckles in the interlock mountings, which would then have to be manually reset.

Trailing points are heated but unpowered, and are fitted, like the powered points, with lever sockets for manual setting. In normal running the trams' leading wheel flanges will shift the blades over if necessary as they trail through them. None of the points, except those at the Aytoun Street crossover, are being sprung to return automatically to one setting or the other; they will be held positively by the point

▼ Two Mowlem engineers are seen here carrying out a Quality Assurance audit on trailing pointwork in Mosley Street, Piccadilly Gardens, on 30th March 1992. Note tie bar encapsulation, pivotless point blades, point lever slot and herringbone-patterned block paving, with facing points control cabinets beyond. The instrument sitting on the rails is a combined spirit level and track gauge. *Author*

mechanisms in whatever position the previous tram set them at. Sprung points are hydraulically damped to stop them "clacking".

In railway practice, check rails are fitted opposite each crossing to keep the wheels away from the crossing nose (the point of the vee formed by the two merging rails). The positioning of the check rails is closely related to the back-to-back dimension of the wheelsets — in other words the distance from the back of one flange to the back of the other. Tramway wheels, because they roll in a relatively narrow groove (42mm on Metrolink), have to have thinner flanges than railway wheels. This gives a wider back-to-back dimension, which incidentally was one reason why the LRVs could not have been delivered across Europe by rail on their own wheels.

The wider tramway back-to-back dimension means that on railway sections the flanges would not engage the check rails sufficiently to keep them away from crossing noses, which they might strike. To overcome this difficulty Metrolink's wheels have thickened backs at a slightly smaller diameter than the tread to engage railway check rails specially raised to meet them, without affecting the passage of conventional railway rolling stock such as hopper wagons directly delivering ballast to Metrolink's trackside. In the street the thickened portion on the back of each wheel will run clear of the grooved rails, and the tramway-thickness flanges will fit the on-street flangeways. This technique was developed in Germany for use by Karlsruhe trams sharing DB main line tracks.

Tramway special work does not normally need to incorporate check rails because the continuous flange or lip on the grooved rail adequately serves the purpose. Modern practice, however, is to fit heavy sacrificial "nudge blocks" (author's terminology) opposite crossings, which can be adjusted laterally and renewed if they ever wear out — which, looking at them, seems most unlikely. Tramway crossings have traditionally featured grooves specially reduced in depth so that the wheels "tiptoe" on their flanges smoothly through them, avoiding the noisy impacts which occur when wheel treads ride heavily across an intersecting groove. In Manchester it is envisaged that the wheel treads will be sufficiently wide to span intersecting grooves even at acute angles; at the time of writing it remains to be seen how quiet the trams are when they negotiate the Delta Junction diamonds at normal running speeds.

SURFACING

Under the terms of the DBOM contract, the consortium was entitled to finish off most of the city centre trackwork layout with purely functional hot rolled asphalt ("tarmac") or concrete surfacing. While this was quite appropriate for carriageways like Mosley Street, it would not fit in with the aesthetic and safety requirements of the Manchester City Engineer and the Central Manchester Development Corporation in other locations. Surfaces are being "coded" by their treatment so that pedestrians and other road users can readily distinguish between tram lanes, bus lanes, pedestrian areas, cycle lanes and so on. This is especially important for visually-handicapped people.

Where the tracks run along Parker Street, Mosley Street from York Street to Market Street and along Market Street itself they are raised slightly above the level of the adjacent carriageways to form semi-segregated "trambaan" (Dutch spelling!) alignments along which pedestrians are not discouraged from walking. On London Road, Aytoun Street and High Street the "trambaan" alignments are level with the adjacent carriageways and are separated from them by continuous raised refuges. Stepping down into these faster "trambaans" — as into a roadway — will indicate to pedestrians that they ought to use due caution when crossing them, and that they should no more think of walking along them than they would along a roadway.

Road traffic does not normally have access to either type of "trambaan", but emergency vehicles can use them when they need to; the "trambaans" are bounded on either side by easily-climbed chamfered kerbs. For "trambaan" surfacing pale grey concrete paviors have been used, with red concrete paviors used for areas where servicing traffic can have access close to or across the "trambaans". Small local firms of paving contractors have been employed by Mowlem's to carry out all the block paving work to a common specification which calls for the blocks to be laid close-jointed on a bed of sand in a herringbone pattern. This has the advantage over coursed patterns that no matter which way the track turns as it negotiates bends and corners, the paving never looks noticeably out of alignment with it.

Where pedestrianised tramway surfacing meets ordinary footways, dark grey "key kerb" blocks have been used to distinguish the boundaries of the LRV "swept path" as required by the Department of Transport; the swept path is in this context taken to be the area within which a pedestrian could conceivably come into physical contact with

a tram, plus 380 mm as an extra safety margin. The "swept path" itself is derived from the Developed Kinematic Envelope (DKE) of the vehicle, which represents the extremities within which the bodywork will normally move, allowing for suspension displacement and so on. The DKE is widened on corners to allow for the centre-throw and end-throw of the tram bodywork relative to each track.

Balloon Street, accessible to road vehicles going to the Co-op Bank, has special treatment. The road vehicle accessible section is surfaced with granite cubes specially imported from Portugal while at the lower end, only accessible to pedestrians and trams, rustic "Tegula" paviors have been laid to indicate to drivers of road-only vehicles that a Prohibition of Driving order is in force for the section between the bank entrance and Corporation Street. As elsewhere, ornamental cast-iron bollards reinforce the message. "Tegula" blocks have also been used in the environmentally-sensitive St. Peter's Square together with stone flags. The reason for using new granite cubes on Balloon Street is that recovered granite setts ("setts", which have flat tops, should not be confused with "cobbles", which have rounded tops) would have been too deep to fit over the top of Metrolink's concrete track slab. Setts have been used open-jointed around pole bases on the footway as a tactile obstruction warning.

The difference between the cost of tarmac surfacing and the cost of block paving and stone flagging has been met by grants under the Urban Programme scheme, 75% of the extra cost coming from Central Government and 25% from the City of Manchester (or in some cases the PTE). At one time it had been hoped that the Aytoun Street track might be turfed, but it was unlikely that with spending cuts the City would have been able to afford the additional workload of keeping the grass looking decent.

MAJOR INTERSECTIONS

Tracklaying work at major intersections had to be carried out with the roads closed during four or five successive weekend occupations. After each tracklaying operation, temporary surfacing had to be put in place ready for the Monday morning rush hour traffic. At the busiest places precast slabs were installed to form the trackbases because there was insufficient time for reinforcing mesh to be assembled and for site-poured concrete to cure fully.

DRAINAGE

An important part of street tramway track installation is its effect on surface water drainage. When the tracks are laid close to kerbs, as on Mosley Street, the nests of ducts buried near to the outer rail of each track do not leave any space for conventional rainwater gulleys. Part of the Metrolink construction work has therefore included the provision of hollow kerbs having closely-spaced holes in their faces so that water is continuously gathered from the roadside channels and there is no opportunity for standing water to collect and spray passers-by. The hollow kerbs are constructed from "Beany Blocks", so called after their inventor Mr Neil Beanland.

The rail grooves themselves are efficient gatherers of surface water, and where necessary they have been fitted with polyconcrete drain boxes connected to the normal storm-water drains. Holes in the bottom of the rail grooves admit the rainwater into the boxes. All point-work incorporates storm-water drainage facilities. Pedestrian areas are drained for the most part by open polyconcrete channelling covered by continuous cast iron gratings.

ON-STREET PLATFORMS

The development of the profiled platform concept has already been dealt with. The platforms consist of reinforced concrete upstands backfilled with crushed limestone in preparation for block-pavior surfacing. Brick bases with cable duct access are provided for ticket machines at two locations on each platform, and there are also ducts to feed cables to lighting fittings and video surveillance cameras. Each platform has at least two British Telecom public payphones in distinctive housings supplied by Woodhouse of Warwick, manufacturers of street furniture and lighting.

All platforms have on their raised portions a J C Decaux "Murano" shelter similar to those already provided at city centre bus stops, while the Parker Street island platform has a longer "Standard" J.C. Decaux shelter. J.C. Decaux is a French-based street furniture firm which provides the shelters in return for enjoying the advertising rights associated with them. Shelter selection is one of the decisions which had to be left up to the consortium; the contractor could not under the loose terms of the DBOM Reference Specification be obliged to adhere to the shelter design which had been developed for the PTE by EGS Design.

11. OVERHEAD LINE EQUIPMENT

Manchester's pantograph-equipped trams are supplied at 750 V d.c. from overhead contact wires both on and off street, though the methods of construction vary according to location. All Metrolink's overhead line equipment has been installed to the requirements of GEC Alsthom by sub-contractors Balfour Beatty Power Construction Ltd. GECA, as the GMA consortium member responsible for power supply as well as vehicle provision and so on, had invited tenders for OHLE work and had duly appointed Balfour Beatty.

OFF-STREET OVERHEAD LINE EQUIPMENT

On the railway sections catenary construction (a catenary is defined as the geometrical shape of the sag in the upper wire, which by means of droppers gives enough support to the contact wire to keep it continuously level so as to maintain good pantograph contact at high speeds) is employed, with a considerably lower contact wire height than is used on street. On the Bury line the equipment is entirely new; there are two catenary wires per direction supporting a single hard drawn copper contact wire through dropper wires while on the Altrincham line the equipment remains, as in BR days, a fixed termination installation with single cadmium copper contact wires. Here conductivity has been improved for Metrolink's lower voltage operation by the addition of extra parallel feeders in each direction. On both lines the current distribution is improved by jumpers between catenary and contact wire. Some of the Bury line poles are cranked to avoid trackside drains, while some are fixed to trackside structures.

CITY-CENTRE OVERHEAD LINE EQUIPMENT

The city-centre overhead line equipment (OHLE) has prompted much passionate discussion. Numerous comments have been made about the number of traction poles, but it should be noted before we go any further that the criticism has not generally come from ordinary members of the public. Now that the poles look like an integral part of a finished transport system and appear mostly to be well loaded, it is instructive for us to consider the different factors which have contributed to the design as we see it.

At low on-street speeds there is no need for catenary construction, and in any case the greater support spacing possible with catenary cannot be exploited to the full on-street because extra structures are needed to register the wire accurately around tortuous alignments.

TROLLEY WIRE CONSTRUCTION

Except for some judicious use of cross-catenaries, modern trolley wire construction was therefore considered quite adequate for Manchester's city centre where speeds would be low due to the numerous curves,

the high level of pedestrian activity and so on. The performance of the overhead equipment was checked on a dynamic simulation computer program during the design process. The equipment's flexibility allows the tram pantographs to remain in good contact with the wires at all times. This is just as well because arcing in built-up areas can cause television interference. On-street the twin contact wires, each having a "cottage loaf" cross-sectional area of 120 mm ^{2}, are suspended at a nominal 6.05 m and never less than 5.5 m above each track; for comparison, the height of a double-decker bus is 4.42 m.

In the streets the copper-cadmium contact wires have been doubled to increase the current-delivering capacity and to meet the demands of the city centre section's designed ultimate throughput of 24 paired trams per direction per arm per hour. The increased aerial weight of the twin wires is partly what has brought about the large number of poles; the need for twin wires has been hotly questioned. The current drawn by each individual tram peaks briefly at perhaps 600 amps. This figure must be doubled for a coupled pair of trams, though it is to be hoped that trams are not going to be accelerated too hard in city-centre conditions. A single 120 mm ^{2} conductor can carry some amps continuously, and much more than that on a short-term basis depending on the wire's surface condition and state of wear and on the wind velocity. Additional currents can be safely delivered to trams by feeding sections from both ends and by inserting balancing links at regular intervals between "up" and "down" wires.

The city centre's fixed-termination construction without weight-tensioning means that any expansion due to heavy current demand or hot weather, or contraction due to cold weather, must be taken up by the wires and supporting structures. The twin contact wires look a little like those on an old postcard drawn in by a re-touching artist. At the delta junction the double wires cleverly divide into single wires to serve separate tracks before pairing up again at the layout's extremities. The contact wires have to be fixed over the tracks in positions which will ensure that they remain safely within the working width of the pantograph collector strips under all conditions including vehicle sway, temperature extremes and heavy winds.

The wires are fixed in place by tapered double phosphor-bronze clamps hammer-assembled to grip the top part of each wire firmly, leaving a space between the two wires approximately equal to their diameter and leaving the lower halves of the wires clear of obstructions. Two clamps are fitted at each support, one before it and one after. A bridle made from fibre-filled rope links the two clamps and passes over a bracket arm to support them flexibly, while a pivoting insulated cantilever arm registers the wire's lateral position. Where

▶ These strange-looking pole-top isolator switches were the preference of Manchester City Planning Department! Apparently they did not like the idea of the neat kerb-side metal boxes which the contractors offered!
Author

building-fixings are used, synthetic fibre-filled rope span wires are fitted, to which the contact wires are flexibly attached.

Each tram's single Brecknell-Willis pantograph is located immediately above a power bogie, ensuring that it remains vertically above the centre line of the track at all times — except on superelevated curves, when it will be displaced towards the inside of the curve by the tilt of the tram. On curves, the contact wires have to be "pulled off" laterally at intervals so that their path approximately follows the shape of the track beneath. On straight track, the wire is given a 250 mm lateral "stagger" at alternate supports so that it zigzags along the alignment, constantly wiping from side to side across the working width of the pantograph; this prevents the formation of grooves in the middle of the collector strips.

PULL-OFFS

The number of pull-off points on a curve is determined by the working width of the collector strip, being related to the amount by which the wires can be allowed to stray from a truly curved path. On railways, relatively large radius curves permit the pull-offs to be widely spaced. This means that is reasonable to use one pole per pull-off without the poles being sited ridiculously closely to each other.

Pull-offs at sharp tramway curves have to be more closely spaced than is the case with large-radius railway curves. In tramway practice, the minimum number of pull-offs needed at a right-angle double-track corner is five. Where building fixings are unobtainable, three strong poles set well back at a safe distance from the tracks are needed to support the five pull-offs; one opposite the first pull-off, one opposite the third and one opposite the fifth. The second and fourth pull-offs are each made via two spans, or "along-track pull-offs", one to each adjacent pole; this technique is known as "bridling", and can involve the calculation of interlinking triangles of forces.

Bridling is sometimes disparagingly referred to as "spider's webs"; the alternative is to put a support at every pull-off point, giving the OHLE rather a cluttered and uncompromisingly functional appearance in parts. Bridling has been used in Manchester wherever conditions would allow but if neither building fixings nor space for poles was available sufficiently far away from the outside of a curve, five poles had to be placed on the inside of the curve or close to its outside. The smaller the distance between tracks and pull-off supports, the less scope there is for bridling. It should be noted that in Manchester sub-surface statutory undertakers' plant had already been carefully moved away from the tracks in advance of the main contract, so that the space for pole foundations tended to be close to the tracks rather than at the distance from the outside of the curves preferred by the OHLE designers.

This has produced a functional power-supply system but has failed fully to reduce the visual intrusion of the tramway. There are thankfully a few notable exceptions: on Aytoun Street the line of evenly-spaced centre poles would make a good picture for an OHLE manufacturer's brochure; on Mosley Street next to the Peace Gardens the poles are hidden from view amongst trees; and on Market Street the wires are supported, along their straight portion only, entirely from the adjacent Lewis's and Debenham's department store buildings.

It is, though, impossible to admire the neat and agreeable-looking sections of OHLE in the city centre without being aware of the crowded clusters of poles nearby. We must not forget that initially Metrolink is the British LRT industry's shop window. Prospects for Metrolink's expansion depend on surrounding authorities' perception of the initial installation, and planners in Salford Quays, Trafford Park and Rochdale and Oldham might be slightly worried at the thought of inviting the erection of similar OHLE in their prestige development areas and streets. Prospects for LRT adoption elsewhere in the country will now depend on promoters' faith that they can secure a wider co-operative response from building owners and a willingness to pay for architectural embellishment of poles. It would indeed be tragic and ironic if Manchester's substantially-engineered street OHLE put people off LRT to an extent sufficient to cause empty order books in the future.

Having said that, the insertion of a modern tramway system into a mature city centre, with all its attendant difficulties — existing plant, awkward form of contract, extremely short timescale, etc. — really does represent a remarkable achievement by anybody's standards.

BUILDING ATTACHMENTS v POLES

One of the lessons learned by study teams from Manchester visiting overseas light rail installations had been the importance of minimising the visual intrusion of overhead line equipment (OHLE). With half an eye on the remarkably pole-free overhead equipment to be seen in Germany and Switzerland, the extensive use of building fixings to avoid a proliferation of unsightly traction poles was anticipated.

Comparisons with pole-free tramway scenes in Continental cities are, however, valid only up to a point. When those tramways were first constructed, perhaps around the turn of the century, they probably had profusions of poles just like Manchester has acquired today. The public at the time no doubt accepted the intrusion as part of a commitment towards clean, energy-efficient (and, then, cheap!) public transport. The same forbearance is apparent amongst the Manchester public in 1992. However, over the 80 or so years following those original tramways' construction, numerous building fixings were negotiated with owners and the complex geometry needed to make maximum use of them emerged progressively. In Manchester this process has already started and will continue in the future. Meanwhile we must be patient; after all, Rome wasn't built within two and a half years under a DBOM contract!

BUILDING FIXTURES

From a legal point of view, provision was made in Manchester's first light rail Act of Parliament for the street lighting building-fixture provisions of the Public Health Act 1961 to apply to the tramways. In practice, though, it has not been so easy to see through to reality all the good intentions. Several factors have conspired to cut down the number of opportunities for making fixings to buildings:

● In some locations there just aren't any suitably-located buildings, though it should be noted that fixings to further-off buildings can be mounted higher on the wall to retain their effectiveness over the longer span.

● Fixings to buildings can hamper routine window-cleaning operations by interfering with the use of suspended cradles.

● Some modern buildings consist of an inner framework with an outer non-structural cladding incapable of supporting OHLE.

● Some buildings do not have a secure enough future for it to be worthwhile fixing OHLE to them.

● Property owners' building surveyors may advise against attaching OHLE to particular buildings.

● Property owners may refuse to grant permission for fixings to be made or they may demand excessive wayleave rentals which would have been challengeable in a Magistrate's Court only with the luxury of a generous timescale.

● The annual wayleave payment exacted by frontagers for OHLE building fixings is under the DBOM contract the responsibility of GMPTE and is therefore a revenue burden on the public purse, even though those frontagers will theoretically benefit economically from LRT introduction.

● The line of communication between the OHLE designers and the frontagers was extended by the nature of the contract.

● Property owners are entitled under wayleave agreements negotiated with GMPTE to give notice of their intention to remove the fixings, for example to allow external work to be done; the period of notice varies, having been individually negotiated in each case. The consequence is that there are far more poles in the city centre than anyone can reasonably have envisaged. To some extent sensitively-designed OHLE can enhance a city-centre by silently advertising a strong commitment to public transport though not everyone will see it in that light. Some interesting cases of aesthetic dilemma have arisen; two examples occur close together on Mosley Street, an alignment where there has been considerable success in making fixings to buildings.

Two stone-built porticoed buildings on Mosley Street — the City Art Gallery and the Portico Library (now a pub) — are substantial and well-positioned enough to support OHLE. Even though the latter building bears a faint shadow high on its face where a first-generation tramway OHLE wall fixing was mounted, an advance fuss about the idea of attaching modern OHLE to the buildings got into the newspapers and so neither has nobly acquired a wire-supporting role today; it is the author's perception that the city-centre community, paradoxically, has shown more concern about building fixings than about poles. This is easily understood when one considers that in this country it is normal to clutter pavements with street light standards rather than follow continental practice by supporting the lights from span wires attached neatly to buildings; British people, therefore, do not expect buildings to serve additional community purposes but they readily tolerate poles. Perhaps it has something to do with our indigenous love of dogs.

Where attachments have been made to buildings, the fittings used have been modern masonry or through both types are used, eyebolts

"Pole Park" – a dog's paradise – seen from Piccadilly Gardens tram station on 30th March 1992; Car 1011, in the background, is heading down Mosley Street towards G-MEX on a driver training run. The diamond-shaped "10" sign indicates the tramway speed limit in mph and the designation "CC226" on the nearest pole is its identification number. A green "E" and green band – none of which had been applied when this picture was taken – on a pole indicates to firemen the location of trackside negative (*not* earth) access points (every 50 m) used when it is necessary in an emergency to apply a safety short-circuiting cable to the overhead line after the power has been switched off (see the text). At this time, the short polyconcrete (not plastic as stated in the text) base shrouds for the bolted-base poles were still awaited.   *Author*

► The two unpainted poles in the foreground were soon to be removed when this picture was taken on 11th February 1992. On the right, the wall of Lewis's department store is being diamond-drilled to take the anchorages which will render these two poles superflous. The remaining poles have been treated at the the expense of the Urban Programme scheme with six coats of paint, finishing with a black gloss. To the left of the picture the important bus lane is closed owing solely to final encapsulation work on the mass detector coil of the points badly situated within it; by the use of pre-sorting arrangement the point switches could have been moved clear of the bus lane, which was finally opened all the way from St Peter's Square to Piccadilly Gardens on 14th February. Visible aloft is the clever way in which the twin overhead contact wires separate to serve different arms of the triangular junction. *Author*

far simpler than the fancy tramway wall rosettes which were formerly used. Nowadays the wall fixings do not need the resilient rubber bushings which they used to have, because for one thing pantographs do not set up vibrations as much as trolley wheels could, and for another any vibrations are absorbed by the flexible form of suspension used for fixing the contact wires to the span wires. The electrical insulating properties of the non-metallic rope mean that no additional insulation is needed at the fixing point.

POLES

Where no fixings could be made to buildings, traction poles had to be used. At one time there was a British Standard Specification which featured three standard thicknesses of pole (type A, B and C), to which a fourth (type D) was later added. BSS poles were made up of three sections of uniformly diminishing diameter so that they had a uniformly tapered appearance and were capable of receiving uniform decoration no matter what their diameter.

Contrary to first impressions, Manchester's galvanized tubular steel poles are of only three different types, two of them being step-tapered (base diameters 219 mm and 273 mm, equivalent to the old B and D poles) and the third type being parallel sided (324 mm). In some cases the parallel-sided poles are used as anchor supports to take end strain off corners where the tension has been halved to reduce the radial load on poles or wall fixings, and in other cases they are used as "pull off" poles on full-tension bends. Neither struts nor backstays have been permitted in the city centre.

Most of the traction poles are bolted to gravity foundations, which are large blocks of below-ground reinforced concrete ranging in size from 1.2 m wide by 1.7 m long by 0.5 m deep (1.05 m^3) to 2 m wide by 3.5 m long by 0.7 m deep (5 m^3) depending on the loading on the pole. The reason for the use of gravity foundations rather than traditional pole-holes has been the amount of sub-surface pipes and cables remaining in place under the city pavements; their suspected or known presence would have made pole-hole auguring almost 2 m deep a risky business. In addition, the bolted base clearly meets the important requirement in a mixed traffic situation for damaged (and superfluous poles) to be easily replaced or removed. All pole bases have been positioned and cast by Mowlem. At some locations, underground ducts have been discovered and have had to be sleeved or brick-boxed before casting of the gravity base around them. As we have already observed, to some extent the positioning of poles close to the tramways has been dictated by the existence of displaced statutory undertakers' plant further away from the tracks.

All the bolted-based poles are being fitted with short moulded plastic pole base covers to shroud the threads and nuts which hold the poles in position. The pole bases have to be short because in some places the poles have had to be positioned so close to the track that higher bases would foul the passing trams. No other accoutrements will be added to the poles though Balfour Beatty and GMA did offer tasteful pole furniture in their successful bid for the Metrolink contract, as illustrated in a topic sheet produced as part of a set in 1990. Ornate pole bases, scrollwork and finials were proposed. Unfortunately, financial constraints did not permit the client, GMPTE, to take up this option. Painting of the poles with six coats of paint, the last being a smart glossy black, has been done under the Urban Programme scheme.

FIRE PROCEDURES

The presence in city streets of overhead line equipment energised at 750 V creates possible hazards for firefighters. Consultation between the Greater Manchester Fire Service, GMPTE, GMML and HM Railway Inspectorate has resulted in a set of procedures and a training programme to deal safely with fires or other incidents taking place adjacent to on-street alignments.

Whenever any hoses or high-level emergency access equipment have to be used at the scene of an incident adjacent to overhead line equipment, the fire service will inform the Queens Road Metrolink Operations Centre staff and ask for cessation of tramway operation past the scene of the incident together with disconnection of power from the section of overhead line involved. Having received confirmation of disconnection, fire officers will apply a short-circuiting cable to the overhead contact wires by means of a sectional fibreglass rod; the other end of the cable will already have been connected to the negative traction feeder pole via terminating points located at frequent intervals next to each track.

POLE-TOP ISOLATOR SWITCHES

Tramway or railway power supply systems have to be provided with a means of electrically isolating one section from the next as well as a means of switching off the power to each section when necessary. Electrical separation of sections is achieved on pantograph-equipped systems by means of section insulators in the contact wire having skids to permit smooth continuously-fed passage of the pantograph so that there is no need for drivers to shut off power when passing from one section to another. These are the "praying mantis" devices which sit on the wires here and there. The cables which feed power to the separate sections run from the trackside ducts up the inside of the feeder pole to, in Manchester's case, pole-top section isolator switches.

For sheer arrogance, Metrolink's pole-top section switches have to be seen to be believed. To a design evidently plucked from some remote railway embankment and plonked into the city's aesthetically cherished streetscapes, the Heath-Robinsonian tackle is jarringly functional and at considerable variance with established tramway practice. First-generation tramway section switches were housed neatly in ornate cast-iron boxes standing down-flow of the feeder pole on the footway.

Similarly, Balfour Beatty and GEC Alsthom offered metal kerbside enclosures within which the section isolator equipment would have been housed adjacent to the feeder pole bases. This was rejected in deference to the expressed wishes of the City Planning Department, anxious to avoid adding unnecessarily to the street furniture in Manchester's city centre; hence the pole-top contraptions. One can only reflect that while our forebears might not have spent much time talking about environmental awareness, they certainly knew how to go out and do it.

POWER SUPPLIES

Earlier plans envisaged two voltages for Metrolink — 1500 V d.c. off-street and 750 V d.c. on-street. Dual voltage trams would have been used, switching over at G-MEX and Victoria. The philosophy was that by doubling the voltage off-street the current drawn would be halved, thus reducing the number of substations and the size of the feeders. 1500 V d.c. would not at present have been acceptable in streets, hence the proposal for 750 V in the city centre.

Tenderers were free to offer to modify the power supply proposals put to them by GMPTE, and the GMA consortium successfully offered 750 V d.c. throughout. This simplified the trams' electrical systems at the expense of extra substations and feeders. Metrolink's substations are located at Bury, Radcliffe, Prestwich, Woodlands Road, Victoria, G-MEX, Trafford Bar, Dane Road, Timperley and Altrincham plus a track paralleling substation in the city centre. The substations are fed from the grid at either 6.6 kV or 11 kV through rectifier transformers rated at 600 kW. Connection to overhead wire sections is made via Whipp & Bourne type MM81 semi-high speed d.c. circuit breakers able to interrupt all values of current likely to be met with on an LRT system. The whole power supply system is monitored and controlled from Queens Road by GECA's SCADA (Supervisory Control And Data Acquisition) system. In addition there is a hard-wired trip system operating from Queens Road which can kill all tramway line power in the city centre.

It is important to note that the negative polarity is not directly earthed anywhere except Queens Road Depot. The rails alone carry the return traction current back to the negative feeder cable termination points, and are insulated from earth. In the city centre, as we have seen, the insulation is achieved by encapsulating the rails in polymer materials. In the concrete beneath the grooved rails the double layer of steel reinforcing mesh is and divided into electrically-separate sections at 50 m intervals to reliably intercept any wayward milliamperes. A leakage return cable connected to each section of mesh allows any leakage current to return harmlessly to the rectifier negative at the substation where its magnitude is monitored. There is bound to be some leakage, however small, but if it becomes excessive an alarm condition is originated.

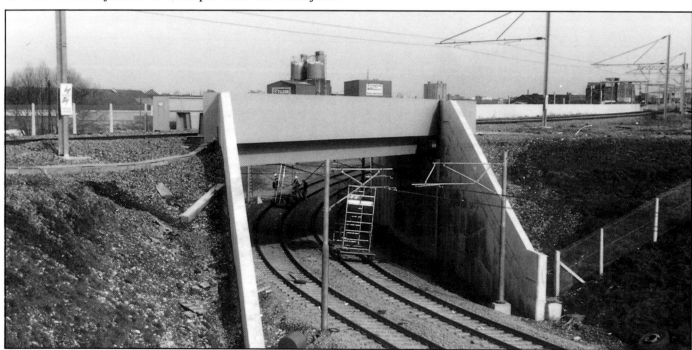

Work in progress on Metrolink's off-street overhead wiring at Cornbrook Underpass on 23rd February 1992. It is interesting to note that the "heavy" BR electrification to Trafford Park features tramway-style trolley-wire construction, while the "light" rail installation underneath features railway-style cantenary, compressed here to fit under the bridge. The gantry standing on the outbound track shows the amount of superelevation or "cant" which has been applied to this rather sharply-curved dip in the alignment between Old Trafford and G-MEX. The Trafford Park and Salford Quays LRT routes will branch off immediately on the other side of this underpass, and a Metrolink station may very well be installed opposite the concrete-producing plant visible in the background. *Author*

12. SIGNALLING & COMMUNICATIONS

Readers should note that this chapter carries a headache warning; the subject matter is technically complex. The apparent ease with which Metrolink trams slice through the city centre like knives through butter conceals a vast amount of behind-the-scenes activity on the part of the City Engineer's traffic signals staff working in close partnership with the PTE, the Department of Transport and GEC-Alsthom Signalling Ltd.

Metrolink's trams are able to run at speeds of up to 80 km/h on segregated railway alignments with automatic signal protection, or to obey new dedicated traffic signals in the street. Changeover between the two distinct modes will occur at G-MEX or Victoria station platforms while the vehicle is at a standstill. For the time being the whole of Piccadilly Undercroft is being treated for signalling purposes as "street".

Along the city streets the trams are driven on sight just like road vehicles, the important difference being that they cannot steer round obstructions and they have to negotiate a succession of sharp curves. Drivers on-street have to take more than average care to drive considerately and defensively to avoid giving passengers any nasty dynamic surprises. For example, standees lulled into daydreaming inattention during the long straight run into G-MEX from Cornbrook would not take kindly to being rudely awakened by a violent emergency stop when the tram arrives at its first road junction or to an over-fast passage through the sharp S-bends in St Peter's Square.

THE URBAN TRAFFIC CONTROL SYSTEM

The city's Urban Traffic Control (UTC) system, overseen by staff and equipment based in the PTE's headquarters building overlooking Piccadilly Gardens, has been especially helpful towards the implementation of Metrolink. The UTC system features computer-controlled co-ordination of all city-centre traffic signals. One of the county-wide initiatives inherited from the abolished Greater Manchester County Council, UTC also monitors the correct functioning of other traffic signals in the conurbation and is administered by Manchester's City Engineer.

The UTC system is supplemented by closed circuit TV cameras fitted with powerful zoom lenses mounted high above important city-centre intersections; they enable UTC staff to see hold-ups as they occur and to adjust signal timings if necessary to keep traffic on the move. The UTC computer holds signal plan programmes suited to traffic patterns prevailing at different times of the day and week such as morning peak, off peak, evening peak and overnight. The signal patterns can be overridden with special signal plans to cater for unusual circumstances like parades and tramway construction.

SIGNAL OPERATION PRINCIPLES

There is no link between the UTC computer and the Metrolink Operations Centre computers at Queens Road; all traffic lights interfacing is done via the Vehicle Recognition System (VRS, see later) supplied by GEC-Alsthom Signalling Ltd. VRS is responsible for generating LRT phase demands to individual traffic signals controllers. Roving Metrolink staff have exclusive local override access to Metrolink traffic signal equipment for emergency purposes. The Metrolink Operations Centre has no access to the closed circuit traffic surveillance TV system.

Certain characteristics of the Metrolink vehicles in the city centre are relevant to the operation of signals. Performance data supplied by GEC-Alsthom has been used to determine at what speed trams might be expected to approach each specific lights-controlled intersection. In many parts of the city-centre, speeds will be low due to movement amongst pedestrians, around sharply-curved track layouts or in proximity to stations. The service braking capabilities of the trams and the reaction time of the drivers are other factors which have been accounted for when determining detector positions and signal tim-

ings. Nowhere on-street will the vehicles exceed 30 mph, and in many places they will be moving much slower than that. Newly-developed diamond-shaped signs indicate maximum permitted speeds in mph to tram drivers. Trams may operate singly or in coupled pairs, or exceptionally in sets of up to four coupled together.

On some other systems, like the Utrecht "Sneltram", approaches to junctions are made via long stretches of reserved obstruction-free track; early detection of an approaching tram enables isolated traffic signals to commence a changing sequence leading to a green signal for the tram as it reaches the crossing. This impressive spectacle is not always possible in the constricted, unsegregated conditions found in Manchester but the principle will be applied where conditions permit.

Signals controllers are programmed to give the trams a degree of automatic priority at all intersections other than at five critical ones, where tram priority might seriously disrupt heavy conflicting traffic flows. The critical intersections are as follows: Portland Street/Aytoun Street, Nicholas Croft/Shudehill, Peter Street/Lower Mosley Street, Princess Street/Mosley Street and Cannon Street/High Street. At these intersections a tram demand is met at the next available "window" in the signal phasing pattern. The maximum waiting time for the trams is supposed to be of the order of 60 seconds.

LRT ON-STREET SIGNAL HEADS

Conventional road traffic signals in the city centre do not apply to trams. Instead there are separate distinctive signal heads obeyed only by tram drivers and ignored by others; these have been devised in conjunction with the Department of Transport. The LRT-specific signal heads consist of arrays of white lights illuminated so as to form vertical ("proceed"), horizontal ("stop"), single central cluster ("stop if it is safe to do so") or diagonal ("proceed to left or right") indications. The multi-lamp LRT traffic signal heads have been supplied by Forest City, a firm which started in business in 1902 as a supplier of tramway overhead line fittings and also manufactured electric points equipment for first-generation tramways including Manchester's.

There are enough lamps in each display to make quite sure that the failure of any two of them will not obscure the display's meaning; this is an improvement on Continental tramway signals having only five lamps. All unlit lamps appear black. The aspect of each signal head and the condition of all of its lamps is electronically monitored at all times so that faults can be rapidly attended to.

Another special signal head has been developed for places where the trams cross pedestrian or cycle routes. Featuring an illuminated outline of a tram and mounted in pairs one above the other these heads will flash alternately to warn of the approach of a tram. They have been supplied by GEC Traffic Automation Ltd. Other sub-contractors involved in the on-street signals provision have included Siemens Plessey Controls and Elequip Ltd. Prototype VRS equipment was tested at the Corporation Street crossing during the afternoon of Monday 2nd September 1991; the first tests for tramway operation took place with the VRS-fitted Metrolink Special Purpose Vehicle (SPV) on 17th October 1991. Full VRS commissioning took place on Monday 20th January 1992 using a test trolley, followed for the rest of the week by trial street running of trams both singly and in coupled pairs.

TRAM–TRAFFIC SIGNAL INTERFACING

All existing traffic signals equipment has been replaced at intersections where LRT has been introduced. Timings at neighbouring intersections without tram movements have been subject to adaptation to cater for changes in traffic flows brought about by Metrolink. The trams are being given as much priority as can be achieved within a traffic control system already featuring critical interlinking of successive road junctions to keep traffic moving; LRT is integrated into the operation of a total of 15 signals-controlled intersections in the city centre. Many different methods used overseas for interfacing trams to traffic lights were looked at before the appropriate solutions for the UK were arrived at.

For example, the "amber time" given to normal road traffic is 3 seconds, giving adequate time for road vehicle drivers to brake in anticipation of a red light. For LRT-specific signals the "amber time" is extended to 5 seconds, or to 7 seconds to permit comfortable braking at higher approach speeds. These longer periods will give drivers more warning in view of the large number of vulnerable mobility-impaired passengers likely to be sitting or standing on board the trams, making sudden brake applications inadvisable.

As with many other aspects of street-running LRT, Manchester's planners and engineers have worked in close partnership with the Department of Transport to set up what in effect are new UK standards for LRT. This has considerably increased the burden on the Manchester planners and engineers and has made things much easier for developers of following LRT schemes. The performance of the city centre signalling system will be kept under close review; fine tuning of timings and priorities in service will optimise performance and safety.

TRAM PRIORITY

Until the light rail system is extended, tram arrivals at intersections will only occur on average once every five minutes, a period which spans between 5 and 10 complete traffic signal cycles. It is this relatively low rate of demand which allows a high degree of priority to be given to trams when they do arrive.

Manchester's City Engineer is committed to promoting increased use of public transport and has endeavoured to ensure that every tram, in view of its high capacity and its likely carriage of mobility-impaired people, is given as clear a run as possible between one stopping-place and the next. To some extent special treatment of this kind can impose delays on conflicting traffic (including crowded buses), and is even better justified when trams are publicly subsidised within an integrated public transport network as originally conceived for Manchester's light rail system.

Thanks to conventional offsetting of successive traffic signals clocks and the careful positioning of VRS advance detector loops, trams running at design speed through a series of non-critical junctions will encounter a steady succession of "proceed" signals except when trams are obstructed between intersections; obstructing road vehicles are liable to be removed by the police. Generally it is expected that road and rail modes can work together equitably in the city centre.

THE VEHICLE RECOGNITION SYSTEM (VRS)

Every tram has a pair of VRS transmitter coils mounted one after the other underneath the unmotored centre bogie. Mid-way mounting ensures that the transmitter coil(s) faithfully reflect the tram's position regardless of its direction of travel, while duplication ensures that the transmitted data will span loop transpositions (see below) and that a journey can be continued on one coil should the other fail. Both coils on an tram transmit the same modulated carrier signal continuously; this is generated by the on-board vehicle recognition system and is picked up by detector loops buried between the rails, positioned to take account of the coils' 15 m distance from the front of each 30 m-long tram.

The detectors are designated advance detectors (AD), stop detectors (SD), train ready to start detectors (TRTSD) and cancel detectors (CD) and are formed over their active lengths directly on the surface of the concrete track slab before surfacing or slot-cut into the tarmac road surface if installed after surfacing. Every 5 m the loop wires are transposed to reduce noise pick-up. This creates a localised detection null where the wires cross, and is overcome by the pairing of transmitter coils referred to above.

Any detector can perform more than one function simultaneously — for example a cancel detector for one intersection can be combined with an advance detector for the next. The detectors are connected to cabinet-housed VRS Logic Units supplied by GEC-Alsthom Signalling Ltd, the company responsible for the signalling system's design, installation and testing as well as its final commissioning on 20th January 1992. In effect data is transferred from the on-board VRS equipment via the transmitter coil(s) and detector loop to the trackside VRS equipment, which is interfaced in turn to new signals controllers housed in the familiar cabinet adjacent to every set of traffic lights. Individual VRS units can be configured to respond to leading-edge signals arising from the entry of a tram into the loop's range or to

trailing-edge signals received as a tram leaves the loop's range.

The trackside VRS units are also connected via optical fibre links to the Metrolink Operations Centre at Queens Road. As well as signifying the tram's position the VRS equipment will also relay its service code and routing requirements, keyed in by the driver at the start of each journey, to the operations centre and to any facing on-street points controllers via the trackside VRS. Odd code numbers are given to southbound units, even to northbound.

When two trams are running as a coupled pair, only the transmitter coils on the leading tram will be active. All demands are therefore treated alike regardless of whether they come from a single tram or from a "train" of two or more units. In practice, even if the proceed indication were to expire before the whole "train" were clear, conflicting traffic would not be able to move off because of the highly-visible bulk of the tram(s).

Where a station is located in advance of a signalled intersection, a train ready to start detector is used as a special kind of advance detector or stop detector, depending on how far it is from the associated intersection stop line; the driver requests an LRT "proceed" indication when his doors have shut by pressing a "train ready to start" button to his right. This sends a demand signal via coil and loop to the trackside VRS.

TRAM CLEARANCE TIME

The duration of LRT "proceed" indications at different intersections is subject to a considerable degree of fine tuning to optimise signals performance in the light of operating experience. No more tram time than is absolutely necessary is being given at intersections, to minimise the time lost to other traffic. "Proceed" therefore runs for only a minimum period depending on factors like the width of the intersection and the expected speed of the trams across it.

There could be several reasons why a tram might fail to move off when given a "proceed" indication. At the Delta junction, for example, the driver of an Altrincham-bound tram coming from the Piccadilly branch might want to give way to another which is scheduled to arrive at Altrincham first but which he can see only just emerging from Market Street. Traffic engineers, though, dislike wastage of "green" time and it is unlikely that any such ignoring of "proceed" signals will be lightly tolerated; trams may have to go forward out of sequence and sort themselves out at termini by radioed arrangement with Controllers at Queens Road.

After timed expiry of the tram "proceed" indication there ensues what is known as an intergreen period consisting, say, of 5 seconds tram "amber" followed by a maximum of 6 seconds all red and 2 seconds conflicting traffic red/amber. In common with many other aspects of Metrolink, the length of the inter-green period is subject to fine-tuning in the light of experience, principally by altering the duration of the all-red period which in any case will be longer for LRT than it is normally.

Cancel detectors are sited so that they detect a tram's transmitted signal as its front end passes an imaginary line level with the back of the footway on the far side of the road being crossed. The signal controller's response will be to cancel the all-red extension period if it has not already expired. This is intended to ensure that other traffic is not detained after the tram has vanished up an intersecting street.

NON-CRITICAL INTERSECTIONS

Signals at the ten intersections granting full priority to LRT are set up to show LRT "proceed" exactly when required so that at those intersections the smooth progress of the trams is not interrupted at all. This is brought about in one of two ways. At six of these "non-critical" intersections absolute LRT priority is obtained by the "hurry call" method sometimes used near fire and ambulance stations by emergency vehicles. On the approach of a tram this causes the signals to immediately commence a sequence culminating in a quick "green" for the tram.

At these six absolute-priority intersections, the approaching tram's transmitted signal is picked up as it enters the buried detector loop's range some way in advance of the intersection. The VRS passes on the demand to the signals controller. The conflicting traffic signals immediately change from green to amber; meanwhile the tram signal head continues to show "Stop" (horizontal bar). 3 seconds later, the conflicting amber indications will change to red. There may then be an all-red clearance period of perhaps 4−5 seconds during which the tram will still be approaching the intersection at normal speed some way in advance of its own tram-specific signal, which will change to "Proceed" (vertical bar) while the tram is still far enough away to be able to service-brake smoothly to a standstill at the stop line if, in failure conditions, the signal stayed at "Stop". At small intersections like Mosley Street/Charlotte Street there will be no all-red period.

CRITICAL INTERSECTIONS

The signalling at each of the critical intersections is intimately linked to the operation of neighbouring road junctions. For example, the Princess Street/Mosley Street signals are co-ordinated with the preceding Princess Street/Cooper Street and succeeding Princess Street/Portland Street signals so that road vehicles, including buses, receive a "green wave" and do not have to wastefully stop and start more than is absolutely necessary. Absolute tram priority across one junction in a chain might unduly disrupt traffic flows in a wider area.

In some respects, tram operation of traffic signals at the critical intersections can be compared to push-button actuated pedestrian phases at or near to intersections; each demanded phase occurs at the next available opportunity or "window" in the signalling cycle.

A tram's approach to a critical intersection is picked up by an advance detector loop which transmits the received signal to the trackside VRS. The VRS puts in a demand to the traffic signals controller which in turn deals with it at the next available opportunity in the signalling cycle. Meanwhile the tram may have to come to a standstill at the

▲ This tramway-only signal at the York Street end of the Mosley Street profiled platform is showing a "Proceed" indication called by the driver when he was ready to depart. A "green wave" demand will at the same time have been made to the signals controllers at the next two non-critical intersections, Charlotte Street (see page 57) and Nicholas Street so that if the tram proceeds at the design speed for the section it will not have to stop until reaching the critical intersection with Princess Street, though with a considerable slice of luck the signal there will be favourable too, giving the tram a clear run all the way through to St Peter's Square. *Author*

▲ Finishing touches: "TRAM ONLY" wording being applied to the road surface on the outbound track at the junction of Mosley Street and York Street on 9th February 1992. The surface has been flame-dried before spraying the outline of the letters onto the road through large stencils; the stencils are then removed and the hot marking material deposited by machine as shown. Signs like this leave no-one in any doubt about the correct name to use when referring to Metrolink's tramway vehicles. *Author*

▶ Metrolink's off-street signals are of the simple two-aspect type as illustrated in this view looking towards Manchester from Besses o' th' Barn station platform during driver training in March 1992. The unusual cross-section of the bridge is discernible here, as is the Automatic Train Stop between the rails adjacent to the signal post. *Author*

More than just the ticket.

*B*y supplying Manchester Metrolink with their Automatic Fare Collection Systems, including Ticket Vending Machines complete with a Computer Data Link, to the Central System Network, we are supporting Britain's latest Light Railway Project with proven sophisticated technology.

Our track record shows we're capable of keeping people on the move anywhere, a fact which will prove of great benefit to Metrolink and the people of Manchester.

THORN
Transit Systems International
Wookey Hole Road Wells
Somerset BA5 1AA England
Tel: +44 (0) 749 672081
Fax: +44 (0) 749 679363

stop line, where its presence will be registered by the stop line detector loop. trams are not automatically stopped if an on-street signal is over-run; their drivers all have road vehicle licences subject to endorse-ment for such ordinary traffic offences.

It should be noted that, for reasons of clarity, the foregoing ac-count has been exceedingly simplified. In practice, traffic signals operation does look simple to passers-by, belying the fact that tim-ing calculations down to one second and distance measurements down to one metre are the tolerances within which traffic engineers have to work if they are to fully optimise the capacity, safety and conflic-ting needs of roads, tramways, cycle ways and pedestrian crossings interlinking across the city centre.

FACING TRAMWAY POINTS

Tram-activated setting of powered tramway points has already been dealt with in Chapter 9. There are three sets of facing points, all located in the Piccadilly Gardens area. Each has an adjacent square signal head to show which way the points are set and to confirm that their interlocks have operated properly. Settings indications and in-terlock operation are relayed to ''control'' at Queens Road. Tram drivers must ascertain that points indicators, traffic signals and blade positions agree before proceeding.

OFF-STREET SIGNALLING

Metrolink's off-street signalling system is not so innovatory or com-plex as its on-street counterpart. There is full track-circuit block work-ing and two aspect red/green colour-light signals are employed throughout, except when line-of-sight is limited in which case yellow/green ''distant'' signals are employed to give advance warn-ing of the state of the signals beyond. Trams passing a red signal off-street are automatically brought to a standstill by a trainstop. State-of-the-art SSI (Solid State Interlocking) technology is used. The Queens Road based Controller operates the automatic signalling system using manual route-setting and, in particular instances, addi-tional automatic route setting so as to ease the workload. Vehicle posi-tions off-street are relayed from the track circuits to screen-based train describer displays on the signalling workstation in the control centre.

If a driver overruns a red signal off-street at a speed above 3 km/h, the vehicle's Automatic Train Stop (ATS) system will bring it to a halt and increment a signals overrun counter in the cab; the driver would then have to give an explanation for the overrun. The ATS system is activated magnetically.

On the approach to each off-street station a yellow station warn-ing board is positioned at least at service braking distance from the station stop line to warn the driver of a station ahead so that he can take appropriate action to bring the vehicle to a satisfactory stand-still. The level crossing at Hagside, where Warth Fold Road crosses the Bury line, is remotely controlled from Queens Road with the assistance of closed circuit TV surveillance. The section of line singled near Altrincham between Deansgate Junction and Navigation Road is controlled exclusively by BR from Deansgate Lane signal box, which has full communication with Metrolink's operations centre staff.

COMMUNICATIONS

The absence of permanent staff at stations and amongst passengers on the vehicles is offset by the presence of roving customer services inspectors and transit police officers, by the physical openness of the system and its vehicles, and by comprehensive communications and video surveillance facilities using reliable fibre optic transmission and multiplexing techniques. Supervision of the system is centred on the control room at the Queens Road operations and maintenance cen-tre, where as we have already seen all vehicle movements are monitored.

In addition, every tram is fitted with driver-to-base radio equip-ment working via on-board aerials. In tunnels there are ''leaky-feeder'' cables to maintain radio contact, normally maintained via tall fixed aerials one of which can be seen at Queens Road. Controllers at the Queens Road operations and maintenance Centre can converse individually with specific drivers or transmit a broadcast message to all units. Control can also address all passengers on the system or just those on a specific vehicle via on-board public address equip-ment. In the event of radio equipment failure, staff can use strategically-placed telephones at every station and on the lineside to contact the duty controller. Roving customer services staff have portable radio units by means of which they retain contact with the operations and maintenance centre at all times.

The controller can speak to the passengers at any station, or make a broadcast to all stations, through the station public address system. At each important interchange the public address system is sup-plemented by TV-like monitor facilities which the controller can use to relay service information to passengers.

On every station platform there is a video camera operating per-manently. Other video surveillance cameras are located at tunnel mouths, at Hagside level crossing and at the few passenger subways on the system. A bank of screens in front of the controller will nor-mally display pictures from surveillance cameras cyclically because it would be impossible to provide a monitor for every camera. The controller can watch for anything unusual, lock a monitor onto any particular camera and initiate a video recording if necessary.

Also on every station platform, including those on street, there is an emergency panel which passengers can make use of by pressing a button. This attracts the attention of the controller and at the same time causes the video surveillance picture from that platform to ap-pear directly in front of the controller. Via a microphone and loudspeaker the passenger can then converse with the controller, who can see him or her on the monitor. It is intended that during the late evening, passenger lifts at outlying stations will only be made available by the controller when has received a genuine request from a passenger via the panel. This is intended to cut down on misuse and vandalism.

All ticket vending machines (TVMs) are connected to a central com-puter located in the control room at Queens Road. Ticket stocks, cor-rect functioning and cash receptacle contents are monitored and an audible alarm gives warning of attack. Fares amendments can be made globally by downloading information from control to the TVMs.

▶ It is vitally important for tram drivers to switch over from off-street to street mode (and to conscientiously remain in on-street mode while they are driving on-street) and vice-versa when stationary at Victoria or G-MEX platforms. The upper sign here at the Bury end of Victoria's Platform ''A'' refers to the speed limit in mph applying for the sharp curve forward into Platform ''B'', while the one below it draws at-tention to the two rectangular notices giving specific changeover in-structions to the driver.   *Author*

13. THE OPERATIONS AND MAINTENANCE CENTRE

During the tendering process for Metrolink, the GMA consortium engaged the services of Brown & Root Ltd to prepare concepts for certain aspects of the maintenance part of the contract, or the "M" in DBOM. This in turn enabled other disciplines to correctly estimate their costs for the construction project. Brown & Root and W.S. Atkins looked at Bury BR depot for GMA, decided that it would not be suitable because of its location, its layout and the condition of its buildings, and recommended instead that the seat of Metrolink's operations should be at the Queens Road site. Brown & Root then set out the requirements and design concepts for the site taking account of the facilities needed, the functions to be fulfilled and the activities which would be based there. These concepts — shed size, number of roads, equipment, etc — have remained virtually unchanged. W S Atkins Consultants did the detailed design work including site layout and detailed building layouts and AMEC, better known in the North West as Fairclough Civil Engineering, carried out the landscaping, civil engineering and building works. Balfour Beatty installed the track and overhead line equipment.

LOCATION

Metrolink's £8 million Operations and Maintenance Centre is located on four hectares of land adjacent to the railway chord which linked Cheetham Hill Junction on the "Manchester Loop" line with Queens Road Junction on the Bury line. Part of the site was latterly used for landfill purposes (for bricks and soil rather than rubbish), and extensive landscaping had to be done before construction by Faircloughs of the main workshop and headquarters buildings could begin. Every effort was made to incorporate current maintenance technology and practices, and to permit expansion, as the system ridership increased, creating a need for additional vehicles. The procurement, installation, testing and commissioning of all plant and equipment was undertaken by Brown & Root.

The Operations and Maintenance Centre lies at the geographical centre of the system both present and conceivable in the future. This will minimise dead tram mileage. It is situated in an area of the City of Manchester having high unemployment and therefore in need of a new major employment input. The site's road access is from the adjoining Queens Road; the new junction with the access road has been constructed to allow tramcar deliveries to be made by road, and the contractors' temporary site accommodation was located nearby; it was within this "Portakabin City" that Greater Manchester Metro Limited began life. One of the first jobs after landscaping and planting the main headquarters site was the realignment of the existing railway chord to allow construction of the main workshop building to start. The chord itself had to retained so that the Bury EMU trains could be extracted from the line when it closed in August 1991.

The main building on the site is the purpose-built 70 m x 40 m x 6 m high steel-framed workshop, which as well as accommodating three inspection and maintenance roads also houses associated offices and workshops as well as a training room, where safety both in the workplace and out on the "road" is regarded as by far the most important subject on the curriculum. Plenty of daylight is let into the maintenance building by glazing materials built into the wall and roof cladding. Other buildings house the offices and control room and the Queens Road substation. All the buildings have been provided by Fairclough's. There is a gatekeeper's lodge on the access road to keep

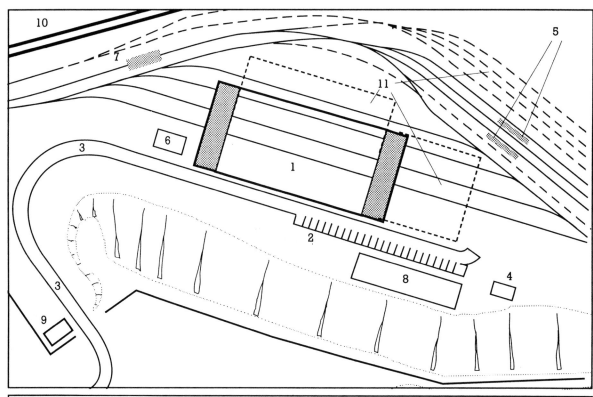

1. Workshop	5. Cleaner access points	9. Gatehouse
2. Car park	6. Sub-station	10. Metrolink's main line
3. Access road	7. Washer	11. Future extension
4. Emergency generator	8. Offices & control room	

site access under control, and the whole site is securely fenced to exclude graffitists and thieves.

It should be emphasised that the maintenance building is in no way a running shed. Stabling of the fleet will take place in the open on three tracks designated 5, 6 and 7; track designations 1—4 are reserved for future growth, 8 is an access road and future storage track, 9 gives access to the workshop roads which are numbered 21, 22 and 23, and 10 is a through road running past the maintenance building. All the roads unite at the Manchester end of the site into a headshunt which no longer connects with BR. There are two sidings, one of which is unwired and serves a PW yard.

THE WORKSHOP ROADS

Of the three workshop roads, only the one nearest the Bury line — road 21 — is wired for traction. This is the multi-access service road, equipped with a very wide maintenance/inspection pit running the full length of the building; this pit has ramped access at both ends and is so large that it has been referred to as the "swimming bath". The pits on the other two roads — 22 and 23 — only give access between the running rails. The floors either side of these two roads are specially strengthened to allow co-ordinated sets of powered lifting jacks to be positioned for lifting bodies off bogies. Not being wired for traction, these two roads are equipped for electric capstan and rope haulage of "dead" vehicles. Both are served by an eight tonne travelling overhead crane. All maintenance equipment has been supplied under sub-contract to GMA by Brown & Root Limited.

Road 22 is in the middle and is designated the unscheduled lifting road. It is provided with a large square pit housing a Hegenscheidt underfloor wheel lathe capable of re-profiling the steel tramcar tyres in situ without any dismantling work. The most westerly road is designated the scheduled lifting road and is the area in which routine interchange of bogies will take place; one complete car set (two power, one centre) have been supplied under the contract as a "float" for rotation purposes. Thus no car will have a particular set of bogies to remain with it always, but will have its bogies changed for overhauled ones when due. Without the "float" system, trams would have to be kept out of service during bogie overhaul. Many other tramway operators, notably the London County Council, based upkeep of major detachable parts like bogies (or, in tramcar terminology, trucks) on rotation principles. Other Metrolink tramcar parts, from pantographs down to electronic slide-in-units and brake pads, are held in heavy and light store rooms adjacent to road 23.

CLEANING ARRANGEMENTS

Under the terms of the DBOM contract, each tram must be cleaned daily. External cleaning is taken care of by an Dawson Aquamatic Modular Train Wash positioned on the main through access track from the Bury line; trams are driven slowly through on entry or exit from service or at any other convenient time. The daily wash is given by a partially-recirculated detergent solution followed by a rinse. An acid wash can be substituted periodically to clear heavier deposits of dirt. A water lance is on hand nearby to clean the vehicle ends thoroughly. The internal cleaning, which will be less onerous on Metrolink than on a smoking-allowed system, is carried out on the storage roads 5, 6 and 7 where access on and off the vehicles can be made via raised walkways. Steam-cleaning facilities are provided in a special area where bogies can be thoroughly de-greased ready for inspection and attention.

METROLINK HOUSE

Originally GMA had hoped that Metrolink House, GMML's headquarters building, could be constructed to a design which would allow it to be easily expanded in the future. The design did not, however, meet with City Planning approval. The finished structure bears a strong resemblance to the Cheltenham GCHQ building best known as the site of so much controversy over trade union representation in Margaret Thatcher's '80s.

Apart from Greater Manchester Metro Limited's HQ offices, staff training and visitor reception facilities, the staff canteen and a police station for the 30-strong transit police team, the building also houses Metrolink's Control Centre; this is the nerve centre of the whole system from where a network of radio, fibre optic and hard-wired communications links radiate to all points on the system. The Control Centre is also the main staff signing-on point.

Controllers have banks of video monitors displaying pictures from remotely-located cameras and visual display units (VDUs) which can show vehicle locations, signalling states, track circuits, points and route settings, power supply status and so on. The Control Centre computers use software developed for railway applications by GEC and previously used only overseas. The SCADA (Supervisory Control And Data Acquisition) system enables staff to monitor and control critical parameters including signalling, traction power, fire and intruder detection. There is a radio base station for communication with drivers; announcements to passengers can also be made via PA systems or by updating the visual display units located at principal stopping places. Radio communication with the teams of roving Customer Services Inspectors can be made from Queens Road. There are "hot line" telephone links with the police, the fire brigade and Deansgate Lane BR signal box on the Altrincham line.

The operational role of the Control Centre is further dealt with elsewhere in this book. As far as the Queens Road site is concerned, all vehicle movements are for safety reasons under the control of one individual, the Person In Charge Of Possession (PICOP). The PICOP is in direct radio contact with Control. Vehicles under repair or defective are immobilised and/or clearly marked and all staff receive thorough training in everything concerning safety.

▶ Metrolink's trams are normally stabled out in the open on storage tracks situated towards the Manchester end of the headquarters site. Seven cars are visible here, with 1008 speeding Bury-bound off the bridge which carries the Metrolink tracks over BR's adjoining "Manchester Loop" line to Rochdale. Earlier on this momentous day — 6th April 1992 — No 1008, operating as a coupled pair with 1004, had carried Metrolink's first fare-paying passengers from Bury to Victoria. *L A Nixon*

◄ Cars 1001 and 1005 are seen here on the Queens Road depot (or, more correctly, workshop) fan on 13th January 1992. The workshop building itself is in the background. The raised check rails which engage the thickened portions on the backs of the wheels, illustrated on page 51, can be seen in the foreground here. *Colin J Marsden*

◄ Metrolink's headquarters is served by its own small staff halt, seen in use her on the occasion of a major press event on 13th January 1992. Paul Neal, GMML's Operations Manager, is welcoming guests aboard No 1007 for a demonstration run to Bury. *Colin J Marsden*

▼ In this interior view of the main workshop building numbers 1004 and 1012 are standing on the unscheduled lifting road (Road 22). The 8 tonne overhead travelling crane is used for lifting various components rather than whole tram bodies. *Colin J Marsden*

▶ Each vehicle in service will, under the terms of the DBOM contract, can be cleaned inside and out on a daily basis. Exterior cleaning of the car sides is taken care of by fixed automatic washing equipment. The tapered ends are dealt with separately, using high-pressure water lances, though initially the trams often seemed to have "runny" noses streaked with roof and pantograph run-off marks. Internal sweeping-out is done at least once an hour during terminal layover times by the driver. And if you should see any ladies with brooms boarding the trams, be assured that they are not employed as well-armed passenger-loaders to pack 'em aboard at busy times. More thorough internal cleaning, made easier because the system is smoking-free, is down on the stabling tracks on a daily basis. This view, taken from the tram-spotter's eyrie next to the Queen's Road overbridge, shows a tram lined up to pass through the washing plant on 23rd February 1992.   *Author*

▶ In the frontispiece of this book we featured a remarkable scene on the Brenner Pass, showing Car A of units 1009 and 1010 (with strikingly appropriate destination displays) stranded in the snow en route to Manchester on 3rd January 1992. This photograph, taken a few days later on 13th January 1992 in the Queens Road workshops, testifies to 1010's safe arrival. Re-united with its other half, it stands above its three bogies on a set of tower jacks during commissioning work. Also visible is one of the winches used for shifting the trams around on the unwired workshop roads.   *Firema*

▶ Metrolink's Hegenscheidt wheel lathe is installed in its own pit at the Bury end of Road 22. It is used for re-profiling the tramcar wheels in situ without any dismantling work, and has proved itself especially useful for dealing with the many wheel "flats" afflicting the cars during the "running-in" period. During reprofiling, wheel diameters must be closely matched throughout all the axles in a car-set so that any slight diameter differences do not exceed the working tolerance of the electronic slip/slide control equipment.   *Author*

14. OPERATING METROLINK

Metrolink's operation and maintenance have been franchised under a novel Design, Build, Operate and Maintain (DBOM) form of contract to Greater Manchester Metro Ltd (GMML) for a concession period of 15 years, though the whole system remains publicly owned by GMPTE. The guarantee period of the 15-year contract lasts for three years, during which GMML is firmly committed to operate and maintain the system no matter what. After expiry of the guarantee period the Concession Agreement can be determined (ended) at any time. This could happen, for instance, if the enterprise proved unprofitable. In the event of determination the responsibility for operation and maintenance of the system would revert to GMPTE, with GMML liable to pay between £0.5 million and £1 million to rectify wear and tear and bring the system up to a condition satisfactory for handover.

Metrolink is based technically on LRT installations whose operation is publicly subsidised. Nobody asked Greater Manchester's taxpayers whether they would like to support Metrolink in the same way; instead, the view imposed from Westminster was that a publicly-built and publicly-owned light rail system should stand on its own feet and be profitable as well as paying off its start-up costs and part of its capital debt. If profits rise sufficiently, GMML will under a "super-profits" clause have to pay GMPTE a portion thereof. The Department of Transport has indicated that it would also expect a share. Profitability is dependent to some extent on outside influences beyond the operator's control, such as the viability, pricing and attractiveness of alternative road-only travel as well as shifts in employment, commercial, retail, leisure and educational activity. Efficient management, careful planning, staff commitment and non-farebox income (advertising, duct rental, special events, consultancy, etc) will help keep the books healthy, but all the same there are fears amongst the public of fares escalation should demand build up to levels which cannot readily be met. Worries about high fares have been most prevalent in the Bury line's area, where the theme has been pursued in the local press.

PATRONAGE BUILD-UP

The DBOM contract embodies a penalty clause, similar to the BR Passenger's Charter, which will be invoked if there is a failure to meet 98% of the specified capacity over a 28 day period. The first six months of operation are, however, being regarded as a settling-in or "honeymoon" period during which the performance clause is not being applied. Metrolink's subsequent fares trends may not follow inflation as closely as we have come to expect of public transport tariffs. The new concepts launched with Metrolink are so diversified and so jointly complex that it is hard to predict trends with any certainty. These are just a few of the system's interacting novelties:
- mixture of on-street and conventional railway running with system-wide access for mobility-handicapped people
- first modern on-street LRT in a British city centre
- first use of on-street profiled platforms
- DBOM (Design, Build, Operate and Maintain) form of contract involving franchising the system to a private operator for 15 years
- a new LRT system shoehorned into a deregulated public transport regime
- initial fleet size reduced below the preferred minimum level
- a greater ratio of seats to standing space than is conventional with mass transit vehicles
- "honour" system of fares payment combined with open on-street stations

INITIAL FARE LEVELS

The initial fares structure for the entire Phase 1 system between Bury, Manchester and Altrincham was announced by GMML on 17th March 1992. Mechanisation of ticket sales and anticipated expansion beyond a simple linear system has required the two lines to be divided up into seven zones — three for the Bury line (each with 3 stations), three for the Altrincham line (each with 3 stations) and one for the city centre (with a total of 8 stations). This coarse zoning introduces some pricing anomalies which depend on where in the zone an originating or destination station lies; for instance, the standard single fare from Bury to Manchester is, at £1.80, around 5% dearer than the equivalent BR fare (and a thumping 63% dearer than a similar journey on the subsidised Tyne & Wear Metro) while the Metrolink fare from Whitefield to Manchester, also £1.80 because it's in the same zone, is 15% up on BR.

The flat fare of 70p within one zone means that the cost of tram travel within the city centre is rather expensive compared with 30p on the Centreline bus. Some users, though, strike lucky with the fares structure; for example, from Stretford to Piccadilly Gardens will cost 90p by tram compared with 95p by bus. In contrast, the tram fare from Old Trafford to G-MEX (one stop) is the same 90p for something like only half the distance. Between Stretford and Manchester the standard (peak) return tram fare is discounted to £1.70 compared to £1.90 at all times on the bus. Off-peak "Cheap Day Returns" are available on Metrolink after 09.30 on weekdays and all day on Saturdays and Sundays. These offer some real bargains and are already helping spread loadings throughout the operating periods; for example, taking the Stretford to Manchester journey again, the return fare on Metrolink is only £1.10 off-peak compared with £1.90 at all times by bus. "Half" fares apply at all times for children between the ages of 5 and 15, and Local Education Authority free passes are accepted for travel to and from school.

Through tickets are available to 115 local BR stations grouped into 16 zones. The initial through fare levels, being tied to local BR fares, are only valid until 10th May. Generally, the premium for city-centre penetration appears to be 50p, taking a journey from Trafford Park (BR) to Piccadilly Gardens (Metrolink) as an example. No bus/tram through fares have yet been established, not surprisingly as deregulation dictates that negotiations must be conducted with every bus company in the vicinity.

CONCESSIONARY ARRANGEMENTS

Under the terms of the DBOM contract, GMML must participate in GMPTA/E's concessionary fares scheme whereby pensioners and some disabled or visually-handicapped people benefit from lower-priced or free travel. Concessions based on those already applying on Manchester's local railways are being applied to Metrolink. Different rules apply according to whether travel takes place in the peak or off-peak. In the peak, concessionary riders pay half fare and in the off-peak a low flat single fare, initially set by GMPTA at 25p. The difference between the half or flat fare paid and the full ordinary fare is made good to the operator by the PTE out of the concessionary budget, which in turn competes for PTA funds also needed for bus and BR-operated rail service subsidies and for other purposes. The easy-access light rail system is bound to attract a far higher volume of subsidised travel than is the case on less accessible buses and trains. Concessionary consumption of scarce PTA resources will need to be carefully watched and it is the PTE's firm intention not to allow Metrolink's concessionary top-up to become a hidden operating subsidy to GMML.

PERIOD PASSES

GMML envisage that at least 50% of passengers will pay in advance for their travel, by means of Weekly, Monthly, Quarterly or Annual Period Passes offered at discounted prices. Period Pass users must have a Metrolink Travel Club membership card. Pass sales and Travel Club enrolment (free of charge) are available at participating Post Offices, BR ticket offices and PTE Saver Sales outlets or by postal application from GMML at Queens Road. So far, no Period Passes giving through travel to or from BR are being offered. Metrolink's manually-sold Period Passes follow an even coarser zonal pattern than the TVM tickets, with travel between Bury and Altrincham costing the same as travelling half the distance between, say, Whitefield and Trafford Bar thanks to amalgamation of the price bands for crossing five, six or seven zones. The maximum Annual tariff is £729, though GMML has given the value of an Annual Season Ticket as "as much as £1,000 each". Period tariffs for travel within one, two, three or four zones are individually priced. Period Passes are not being

On Metrolink's first day of passenger service, 6th April 1992, No. 1005 takes schoolchildren on board at Heaton Park under the watchful eye of a customer service inspector. *Peter Fox*

priced individually per actual station-to-station distance travelled even though they are manually sold.

TICKET SALES

No tickets are normally sold on the vehicles; non-holders of season tickets or passes are required first to obtain tickets from automatic Ticket Vending Machines (TVMs) situated at each station. The TVMs, supplied by Thorn-EMI, accept all existing coins with values of 5p and above and will give change. They do not accept notes; people will have to remember to put enough coins aside if intending to use the system. One of the enhancements of which the TVMs are capable is the acceptance of banknotes. TVM design development is discussed in more detail in Chapter 5. There is no separate validation of tickets before boarding, nor are there any all-day multi-ride tickets.

All TVMs, as well as being within the field of view of video cameras, are connected by fibre optic links to Control at Queens Road. By this means, cash contents can be monitored, statistics polled, attacks alarmed and new fare levels centrally downloaded to every machine on the system. Passengers using the TVMs will follow a five-step procedure: select the zone required from an alphabetical list of 141 Metrolink and local BR stations; press the appropriate zone button; press another button selecting type of ticket required (adult/child/OAP/single/return); insert coins up to or in excess of the fare displayed; collect ticket and any change from the delivery tray; hop on the tram in the fairly near future — the ticket is valid for outward travel for 1½ hours from the moment of issue. Return journeys are not subject to a time limit but must be made on the same day. Breaks of journey and necessary transfers are permitted, in contrast to the archaic situation carried on by competing bus operators.

Because Metrolink stations are unstaffed and the system operates on the "honour" principle, revenue protection is important. Passengers must be in possession of a valid ticket, pass or permit when making or intending to make a journey, otherwise they will be liable to pay a standard fare of £10. This figure is related to the planned frequency of inspection and to the mean ordinary fare level, such that it acts as a workable deterrent to "freeloading". Teams of uniformed Customer Services Inspectors (CSIs), in radio contact with Control, are on hand around the system to assist passengers, give information and carry out ticket inspections — standee conditions permitting.

FLEET SIZE

One-man operation of coupled units is one of the ways in which light rail can fully realise its staffing economies and efficiency. Paired operation at peak times was projected by GMPTE for Metrolink, but widespread coupling will not yet be seen for two reasons. One is that there are insufficient vehicles in the inaugural fleet and the other is that, with understandable thrift, the substation capacity needed to feed an entirely coupled-pair peak service has not initially been provided.

Of Metrolink's 26 cars, up to 23 will be required for service at peak times with the remaining 3 standing by or being maintained. 14 will be required off-peak, releasing up to 12 for regular maintenance attention in the inter-peak period. Initially it was estimated by GMPTE and its advisers that to strike the right capacity balance between rolling-stock and infrastructure provision and to fully realise Phase 1's objectives, 36 trams would be needed. Under the

◄ Following the opening of the Bury-Victoria section, driver training continued on the street section between Victoria and G-MEX. This involved end-on interfacing at Victoria between revenue and non-revenue workings using the same crossover. Here on 9th April No. 1005 swings around the curve from Victoria's Platform "C" towards G-MEX while No. 1006 waits to move forward from Platform "A" towards the crossover and reversing stub/siding beyond the Cheetham Hill Road overbridge at the Bury end of the station. 1005 and 1006 are both on driver training runs. *Peter Fox*

▲ Commissioning work on Metrolink wa a phased process. Here, on 11th Decembe 1991, No. 1003 is being towed through the city centre under police escort while final pan tograph alignment checks are made before the power was switched on shortly after wards. Contact wire alignmnet had already been checked by Balfour Beatty Power Con struction staff using stagger-gauges. The bit terly cold air temperature on the day of the test subjected the overhead line equipmen to one of the lowest temperature extreme ever likely to be met with in the city. The SPV's cab-top platform provides a chilly bu useful vantage-point for the engineers anc HM Railway Inspector. *Autho*

◀ Metrolink was opened for fare-paying passengers between Manchester Victoria anc Bury on 6th April 1992. On that long-waitec day one of the trams is seen here calling a Woodlands Road Station. *Peter Fo*

◀▲ During the extended changeove periods on the Bury and Altrincham lines a range of substitute bus services had been pro vided. Here on 21st August 1991 one of the Bury line's Rail Replacement busses pauses or Shudehill while the Italian Rotra Metro rail grinding unit carries out one of its 6 or 7 passes across the busy junction, moving at its working speed of between 500 and 800 metres per hour. *Autho*

◀ Here a Manchester-bound tram makes a brief appearance in the grounds of Heaton Park, where Manchester's "other" working tramway is to be found not far away. The tram is about to enter Heaton Park Tunnel, or "Covered Way" as it was originally known in view of its construction method. Height within the tunnel is at a premium and that is why the tram's pantograph is compressed so close to its roof, making an interesting com parison with the considerable reach of the pantographs in the street. *Author*

On 27th April 1992, Metrolink opened its city-centre tramway to fare-paying passengers between Manchester Victoria and G-MEX. The first journey was made by No.1007. Before that, an intensive programme of driver training and ghost-running took place. Here No. 1002 "Manchester Arndale Voyager" moves forward on 9th April 1992 across Corporation Street as the double-headed tram signal flashes a warning to pedestrians. Also depicted are a "TRAMWAY CROSSING" sign as well as 1002's folded rearview mirror, opening cab window, marker/indicator light and, below it, one of the jacking points. *Peter Fox*

At the same location seen from a different angle on the same day, Victoria station can be seen in the background as No. 1005 on a driver training run accelerates out of Halliwell Street and crosses Corporation Street on its way towards the city centre and G-MEX. *Peter Fox*

▼ A little further on, at the top end of Balloon Street a tram waits for signal clearance to cross Dantzic Street en route to G-MEX during driver training. Hill starts at locations like this are accomplished with the aid of a push-button which holds the wheel brakes applied until the motors start to "pull". *Peter Fox*

terms of the DBOM Reference Specification, however, the PTE was not allowed by the Government to prescribe fleet size; otherwise, a fleet of 32 vehicles may well have been the bare minimum called for. If GMPTE had been allowed to demand compliance with expertly-advised fleet size requirements, all tenderers would have competed on a firm footing but the private sector would not have been given the level of risk-taking freedom demanded on its behalf by the Government. During the Stage 1 tendering process, one (unsuccessful) consortium went so far as to offer a fleet of only 22 vehicles.

If, let us say, GMML now had at its disposal a substantially larger fleet, demand could be liberally fuelled until Metrolink amply fulfilled all the wider purposes in the community for which the system was first planned. Thanks to light rail's efficiency and economies of scale coupled with the great marketing benefit of built-in street penetration, a profitable situation might then be reached more quickly and easily and with more public forebearance than is likely with the present constrained fleet. As it is, GMML is having to test out one of the Government's railway privatisation options with one hand tied behind its back, starting life disadvantaged by a Westminster-imposed fleet size handicap. Immediate instructions from the Government to order at the very least ten additional trams would begin to rectify the deficiency and allow GMML to truly show its paces by coping with burgeoning demand when it arises, as it surely will, rather than being overwhelmed by it. For fares to be used instead to suppress demand would be a shameful example of theme park economics applied to a respectable public transport system.

SERVICE PATTERNS

GMPTE, as the client acting on behalf of the public, was permitted to specify a minimum service pattern, basically 5 minutes peak, 10 minutes off-peak and Saturday and 15 minutes Sunday. GMPTA/E was also allowed to impose a limit of 15 minutes (for example Victoria to Prestwich) on the time any passenger would have to travel standing outside the city centre, and a requirement that the number of passengers on board should not exceed 130% of the nominal 206 passenger load in the peak period. Substation constraints have imposed limits on the number of units employed simultaneously in service. Initial service intervals, due for review one month after opening, were set at 12 min off-peak and 6 min peak with no Sunday service. The principal reason given for the slightly extended service frequencies beyond the specified 5 and 10 minute intervals was the additional turnback time needed at Victoria; the use of the constricted Victoria crossover involves observation of a 10 mph speed limit followed by operation down a longish single track stub into the platform. During the first weeks of the Bury–Victoria service, cars involved in on-street driver training were turning back at the same crossover.

9 units were diagrammed to operate the inaugural Bury-Victoria services. The first departure from Victoria at 05.57 was followed by a departure from Bury at 06.00, with units then entering service every 12 minutes alternately from each end so that by 07.24 a 6 min service using all 9 units would be in place. The reverse would happen towards the end of the morning peak, with cars selectively running into the depot leaving in place, by 09.48, the inter-peak 12 min service pattern. In the evening peak a similar build-up and decay would occur between 16.30 and 18.30, giving a 6 min service in the main part of the peak.

STAFFING PHILOSOPHY

GMML employs between 190 and 200 staff; of these, 10 are administrative, including managers and executives, 100 are engaged on operations, including 60 Drivers, 20 Customer Service Inspectors and 20 Controllers, 40 are involved in vehicle maintenance and 30 deal with signals and permanent way maintenance. Originally it had been intended that all maintenance except that of the trams themselves would be done by outside contractors. Instead, all regular maintenance is now being kept in-house thus keeping closer control over standards.

In addition to the GMML staff proper, there is a special Greater Manchester Police (GMP) Metrolink police team consisting of one Inspector, 3 shift sergeants and 26 constables. All have been voluntarily transferred from other duties within GMP and the team is based in a small new police station within Metrolink House where the police officers can mingle with GMML staff, using the same staff canteen and other facilities. Still part of GMP, the transit police team will maintain strong links with the rest of the Manchester police force. An offer by GMML to allow free travel to Manchester's 7000 police personnel was declined by GMP.

For Phase 1 GMML has recruited 60 drivers, but in addition to

that number other operations staff have been trained to drive the trams. In due course it is envisaged that staff in other departments may also qualify to drive. Meanwhile, Customer Services staff have during system commissioning found themselves gainfully occupied as transit ambassadors doing jobs like visiting local schools to tell the children about Metrolink. Safeguards are built in to maintain quality and to prevent abuses of staffing flexibilities. There must be a break of at least 12 hours between shifts. All staff qualified to drive will have to do so for at least 8 hours per month. The Queens Road site has been declared "dry" in that no alcohol will be allowed on the premises. Like airline pilots and train drivers, all Metrolink staff are required to abstain from alcohol consumption for at least 8 hours before signing on for a shift, so that they present themselves for duty completely drink-free; this is legally enforced by the Transport and Works Act 1992.

RECRUITMENT

Following the early appointment of executives, recruitment of GMML's Engineering Team began on 14th June 1990 when several management and maintenance posts were advertised nationally. Salaries were negotiable according to experience and potential. A relocation package was available as it was not supposed that all the required staff could be recruited locally; in contrast to the stay-put tenacity of PTE staff, which had been crucial to the successful pursuit of the LRT scheme over the years, Metrolink's successful operation depended on recruiting suitably experienced staff willing to re-locate if necessary to take on an exciting new challenge. Most of Metrolink's managers have railway experience where appropriate; street tramway experience, interestingly, was not sought.

Recruitment of operations staff began on 21st February 1991 with advertisements in the local press for the first 130 supervisory and technical staff, controllers, customer service inspectors, drivers and commercial assistants. The fields covered were operations, vehicle maintenance, signalling and telecommunications maintenance and track, bridge and building maintenance. No fewer than 9004 enquiries were received, showing both the level of interest in the new venture and also the high level of unemployment in the area. Initially a paper sift narrowed down the number of candidates to be interviewed. The only stipulations for applicants were a minimum age of 21 years and an ability to pass a PSV medical and a railway-standard eyesight test. No rigid upper age limit was applied and no particular group was targetted; an important selection requirement was an enthusiasm for the new concepts represented by Metrolink.

STAFF REPRESENTATION

Talks were held by GMML with seven different trades unions with a view to selecting a single one to represent Metrolink staff, but an alternative consideration, the establishment of a separate Metrolink staff association, was in the event chosen.

TRAINING

All staff completed a two weeks' induction course on joining GMML. It was necessary to look overseas for somewhere to train the first drivers partly because initial training was expected to peak in the summer season and that was when Blackpool could least afford to spare the time and resources to commit to the training of a large number of new tram drivers. Brussels was chosen because of its attributes as a large mixed-alignment modern tramway system not too far from Manchester and already equipped with driver training facilities which included a simulator. The Operations Manager and his Assistant sampled the training facilities and were first to pass the tram driving course. Eight drivers subsequently passed their tests in Brussels, the first two in June 1991.

Back in Manchester, driver training started on the Bury line and was increased as vehicles and track became available. Practical experience was backed by theory; trainees have had to pass a one and a half hours' examination on aspects such as vehicle component location and function, emergency procedures, communications, safety and so on. Earlier trainees "cascaded" their driving skills and knowledge to later recruits, bringing the disconcerting sight of drivers apparently receiving on-street instruction one week and giving it the next. Driving examinations have been conducted by a member of the Operations Management staff.

All staff have been encouraged to take First Aid training. While self-defence instruction is not being given, the Metrolink police officers have given operations staff some hints about avoiding trouble on and around the system by correctly interpreting aggressive body language and reacting calmly.

Coupled operation is fully provided for in the design of Metrolink's stations and platforms, though it is unlikely to be seen on any widespread scale in the immediate future. This shows what a coupled pair of trams, 1001 and 1005, look like when calling at the High Street profiled platform. The trams were paired on this occasion, 22nd January 1992, to take part in parking brake tests on Balloon Street. This elevated view shows the trams' roof-mounted braking resistor frames and pantographs (CAR A), saloon ventilation units and articulation-arch location arms. Also visible is the intense activity at "Debenhams' Corner", amongst which the trams have to turn left into Market Street. The fat traction poles detract slightly from what is otherwise a neat if rather profuse line of centre-poles. Note the surface treatment of the "trambaan" section of track. *Author*

THE ROLE OF HER MAJESTY'S RAILWAY INSPECTORATE

Under Sections 11 and 12 of the Greater Manchester (Light Rapid Transit System) Act 1988 and Section 7 of the No 2 Act, the approval of the Secretary of State for Transport was required before the system could be opened for traffic. This role is delegated by the Secretary of State to HM Railway Inspectorate (HMRI) of the Health and Safety Executive. HMRI's Inspecting Officer of Railways has exercised continued surveillance from the design stage onwards, will take a close interest in the system's operation and must be advised of all incidents reportable under the Railways (Notice of Accidents) Order 1986. HMRI's involvement continued throughout commissioning, with frequent visits to observe various tests carried out both on and off street. Several incident simulations were undertaken including a full-scale disaster scenario on Friday 13th March in Heaton Park Tunnel. This involved all the emergency services and was one of the stringent requirements imposed on new or reopened railways.

Final opening of the Bury to Manchester section was delayed by a fortnight pending completion of necessary physical works and because of a shared lack of sufficient confidence in communications, control room procedures and staff awareness on some points; these matters had to be remedied to the satisfaction of the Inspecting

Officer of Railways. The necessary certificate was issued on Friday 27th March to allow inauguration to take place on Monday 6th April. There then remained the task of opening the city-centre section, the Altrincham line and Piccadilly Undercroft to the public. As a major step forward, test running and driver training on-street without police escort between Victoria and G-MEX were approved following an inspection on 24th January. Gauging trials as far as Altrincham took place during the week immediately preceding the Bury line's inauguration (see later) and the first powered run to Altrincham was made shortly afterwards.

CHANGEOVERS

The projected opening date for Metrolink started receding shortly after the scheme was first conceived nine or so years before inauguration; at its worst the slippage was counted in whole years, wasted in overcoming various obstacles originating from Westminster. Latterly the delays have been reckoned only in months and finally in weeks as the big day reluctantly approached, the culmination of a design and construction period lasting only about two and a half years.

When work started in earnest it had been clearly projected that the Bury line would open to passengers in September 1991, followed by the on-street sections and then the Altrincham line. In due course these dates slipped two months to November 1991 for Bury, "just before Christmas" for G-MEX, early in the New Year for Altrincham and 2nd June 1992 for Piccadilly Undercroft, delayed by BR's structural requirements. With this schedule in mind, the Bury line was closed for conversion on 16th August 1991 and the Altrincham line closure was fixed rigidly at 24th December 1991.

Then the projected opening dates slipped again because, it was explained, of unforeseen additional work on the Bury line including "concrete cancer" in Besses o' th' Barn motorway bridge, undergrowth clearance on embankments (!) and the renewal or repair of much of the track. The wide range of work continuing on-street well into 1992 coupled with the achieved vehicle delivery rate made it questionable whether the earlier timescale was ever feasible. The new promised dates were: 21st February 1992 for Bury, 20th March 1992 for the street section to G-MEX, 17th April (Good Friday) 1992 for the Altrincham line and an unchanged 2nd June for the undercroft.

Even though a couple of weeks had been the changeover time predicted for the Altrincham line by the PTE, Barfoot Bridge across the River Mersey at Stretford had to receive remedial attention to its foundations lasting much longer than that. Detailed exploratory inspection of both Besses and Barfoot bridges was only possible after BR shutdown, revealing the need for more substantial attention than had been predicted. A range of substitute bus services, carefully planned by GMPTE, was provided to cover each line during its shutdown period. Some rail replacement bus services are being continued, this being the commercial prerogative of bus operators under deregulation.

◀ A near miss on Market Street at "Lewis's Corner" in late March 1992; for this to have happened one of the drivers must have failed to comply with an adverse signal. *Author*

▲ The trams do not have as much priority in the city centre as some would like, but all the same a balance does not have to be struck between the needs of bus and tram passengers. Here No. 1005 waits at an adverse signal on Snow Hill for a bus and car to clear the junction of Nicholas Croft and Shude Hill. *Peter Fox*

◄ At important locations, elevated monitors give passengers who notice them up-to-date information about services and so on. This monitor at Victoria is displaying a test message on the first day of passenger-carrying operation, 6th April 1992. *Peter Fox*

▼ On-street driver training runs continued after the inauguration of passenger services between Victoria and G-MEX on 27th April 1992. Two trams, both on driver training duties, are seen here passing each other at the Mosley Street profiled platform on 1st May 1992. *Author*

► This G-MEX tram is approaching the Mosley Street stop as it runs through the junction special work en route to G-MEX on 1st May 1992. Note how the vans on the left are correctly parked clear of the swept path as defined by the key-kerbs. The fence on the left has been installed to control pedestrian movements in this large open space. *Author*

► At dawn on the opening day of the city-centre street tramways between Victoria and G-MEX on 27th April 1992, several GMML personalities line up at Victoria for a group photograph alongside No. 1007, fresh from the inaugural run. Nearest the camera are Amanda Best (the former bank employee who took such a leading role in driver training), Chelvin Hibbert (Chief Executive), and Paul Neal (Operations Manager). 1007's roof board says it all. *Author*

▼ With the Bridgewater Canal in the foreground No. 1020 crosses Hawthorn Lane Bridge, Stretford at speed during driver training on 11th May 1992. No wonder the trams run so quietly along here; according to British rail the line does not exist! A new timetable for the BR Chester – Manchester (via Altrincham) service, effective from the day this photograph was taken, made no mention of Metrolink/BR connection possibilities at Altrincham and Navigation Road. This particular consequence of lack of co-ordination turns back the clock 150 years to the days when the canal wouldn't have mentioned the railways. *Author*

PASSENGERS AT LAST

With the approval of the Inspecting Officer of Railways, passenger services on Metrolink were inaugurated on Monday 6th April 1992 with the 6am departure of cars 1004 and 1008, operating as a coupled pair, from Bury bound for Manchester Victoria. Simultaneously and with equal ceremony, 1012 set off as the first working from Victoria to Bury. Both services were well filled with PTE, GMA, GMML and other officials and staff, councillors, media representatives and many ordinary members of the public who had risen early to take part in the historic occasion. Many of 1012's passengers alighted at Bowker Vale, crossed to the inbound side and boarded 1004/1008 so as to have sampled both inaugural workings.

Commemorative first-day tickets, entitling holders to ride-at-will travel all day on the 6th, had been on sale in advance at £3.50 each; similar issues were planned for the street, Altrincham and whole system openings. These were to be the only ride-at-will tickets available on Metrolink, at least for the foreseeable future. In addition, everyone who had registered as a user of the former BR Bury service received free of charge a ticket entitling the holder to unlimited first-day travel. On the first day, 11 000 passenger journeys were made and it was evident that these included a good many ordinary commuting trips. On Tuesday 7th, the first day of operation without special tickets, 6500 known passenger journeys were made; this was in addition to any trips made by Period Pass holders. Ridership after that showed a steady upward trend. The system's first Saturday in operation saw loads reaching well over 100 passengers, many of whom travelled standing quite happily. Peak patronage established itself more slowly than had been expected. There could be several reasons for this. Off-peak travel tends to be optional and even happy-go-lucky, but commuters need reliability to maintain their own punctuality; many would therefore have postponed a change in their travel habits until Metrolink had proved its dependability. Also we must not forget that Metrolink was inaugurated in a recession. Travel and economic activity were correspondingly depressed and it is relevant to note that in 1991 Greater Manchester had seen a 3% drop in road traffic, which in passing helps to explain how city centre tramway installation was achieved without too many traffic problems. Another reason for the slow build-up of peak travel may have been that some commuters were already using monthly tickets not valid on Metrolink and were waiting for them to expire. Others may have been making use of GMPTE TravelCards bus/train multi-ride facilities and will postpone migration to Metrolink until the PTE-owned tram routes appear on the PTE TravelCard validity map. Then again some may have been waiting for Metrolink to be extended through the streets and to Altrincham and Piccadilly BR.

The important street section from Victoria to G-MEX was opened to passengers on 27th April 1992 when at 05.40 No. 1007 broke a ceremonial tape as it moved off into the streets carrying various officials as well as members of the press and several keen members of the general public. Later that day many people sampled the novelty of a tram-ride through the city streets and after that patronage settled

down in the same way as it did on the Bury—Victoria section. Again, the first Saturday saw capacity loads with some people occasionally having to wait for the next car.

Accounts of journey quality vary, with the liveliest rides occurring towards the Bury end of the line where fast running results in a certain amount of bogie hunting. The ex-BR jointed track gives the cars' suspension systems plenty to do. Those who have experienced continental LRT operation — such as Utrecht's "Sneltram" — on entirely new welded track would find Metrolink's Bury line ride less sophisticated, with articulation arches performing some especially telling gymnastics at speeds said to reach as much as 59 mph. The bogies and air suspension, however, seem to absorb the greater part of the wheelset activity so that ordinary passengers perceive a remarkably smooth and quiet ride, which just goes to prove the adaptability and versatility of good modern light rail vehicles.

Inauguration of the Altrincham line was expected in late May with the Undercroft opening unchanged at 2nd June. As the grand finale to a Manchester's tremendous achievement, Her Majesty The Queen will officially open Metrolink on Friday 17th July, after which she will ride from St Peter's Square to Bury — and hopefully be persuaded, like other members of her family before her, to try her hand at the controls.

▲ Customer Services Inspectors made themselves available from the beginning to acquaint passengers with the Metrolink way of doing things. Here at Victoria's Platform "A" on the first opening day — 6th April 1992 — a CSI explains a Ticket Vending Machine to a group of intending passengers.
Peter Fox

◄ On the Wednesday of the first week of on-street operation, 29th April, a good crowd of inter-peak passengers prepare to board a tram arriving at Market Street for all stations to Bury. The distribution of waiting passengers along the platform is most interesting; the first ones to arrive have clustered at the highest part of the profiled platform where there is level boarding deterring access to the front end of the platform for passengers who had arrived later via the Ticket Vending Machines, located towards the trailing end of the platform. This will usefully help to fill up the backward-facing seats in the rear half of the arriving tram. A competing express GM bus passes by empty in the bus lane. *Author*

15. EXTENSION PROSPECTS

AN EXPANDING RAIL NETWORK

Light rail has given Manchester the basis of an expanding rail network. Extension prospects have gone a long way towards sustaining support for Phase 1 from districts gaining on the face of it no direct immediate benefit from Metrolink. Light rail had, however, the potential to bestow indirect benefits, regardless of extension prospects, on the whole region. These include: city-centre rail penetration involving one easy interchange, Park and Ride possibilities, enhanced quality of life in and access to the city centre, leading to inward investment and resistance to inner city decay, and increased city-centre road and car park space potentially freed by modal shift to public transport.

To what extent these indirect region-wide benefits are realised will depend on Metrolink fare levels and passenger capacity as well as on public perceptions. But most of all the way in which Metrolink-supporting Districts could benefit from light rail would be for them to be connected to the system itself. Through the county-wide policy-forming PTA all Districts have had the opportunity to seek Metrolink penetration of their own areas, and most of them have done so.

THE ORIGINAL "NAMED SCHEME" NETWORK

As mentioned in Chapter 1, Metrolink had been originally conceived, like Newcastle's Tyne and Wear Metro and Manchester's abortive Picc – Vic proposals, as a "named scheme" within the meaning of the Transport Supplementary Grant mechanism then in use for allocating funds under Section 56 of the 1968 Transport Act. This meant that Manchester's light rail scheme was intended to qualify for a phased release of funds over a number of years so that it could be constructed and equipped in manageable chunks, the first one of which was to have been what we now know as Phase 1 (Bury and Altrincham plus the city centre section).

In the event, the "named scheme" philosophy had lapsed from use before Manchester's first Section 56 Application was submitted to the Government, dealing purely with Phase 1. Subsequent phases involving conversion of the Oldham/Rochdale, Glossop/Hadfield and Marple/Rose Hill lines plus reinstatement of the Midland line to East Didsbury were referred to in the submission document for illustrative purposes only, to show the extent of the potential for future growth. In point of fact Phase 1 stood on its own two feet as a robust case in its own right apart from any growth possibilities. It is from the local political and strategic planning points of view that Phase 1 does not stand alone.

The five existing lines featured in the original plans shared some common characteristics. Each was supported by the PTE under Section 20 of the Transport Act 1968 and each could be sufficiently segregated from BR services to overcome inter-running constraints. Each line's conversion to LRT would be justified largely because of the savings in operating subsidies and renewal costs which could be shown to be possible. The Didsbury line was included to balance up the projected six-line network, with each of Phase 1's three legs splitting into two separate routes beyond the city-centre.

THE NEED FOR A FRESH APPROACH

Even though a six-line network had been provisionally mapped out, it had not been carved indelibly on a tablet of stone. Phase 1 featured street-compatible LRT standards lending themselves to flexible growth. This gave the PTE what was in effect a blank sheet of paper on which to plan future network expansion. It is appropriate at this stage to remind ourselves that GMPTA and GMPTE are not charged primarily with any narrow objective like expanding the LRT system but with maintaining an overview of the locally subsidised rail network to ensure that it provides value for money and serves the community in the best way. There may always be other ways of bringing this about besides LRT conversion. The rail network was at all times looked at objectively, with LRT conversion rated as only one of a range of options. The possibilities for extending LRT into new areas had also to be evaluated.

Accordingly in Autumn 1988 GMPTE initiated an extensions priority study to attempt to put in ranking order the candidate lines for the next stage of Metrolink's expansion. Changes in circumstances together with new opportunities needed to be looked at and a new set of priorities identified. What has been the nature of the changes calling for this fresh approach?

THE EASTERN SECTOR

All the surviving railways running out of Manchester in an easterly direction were connected in their heyday with Yorkshire via trans-Pennine routes. Only two of the three through routes survive: one runs through Standedge Tunnel from Victoria to Leeds via Ashton, Stalybridge and Huddersfield; the other, from Piccadilly to Sheffield, runs through Totley Tunnel via Chinley and Edale. A third, the electrified Woodhead line, has been abandoned beyond Hadfield, leaving the electric Section 20 supported Glossop/Hadfield commuter trains in sole possession of the line inwards as far as Hyde North, from where the tracks are shared by other BR services running into or through Manchester.

The eastern sector presented different problems to Phase 1 so far as LRT conversion was concerned, and as time went on these difficulties became more apparent. Although in network terms it seemed logical to extend the Piccadilly Undercroft stub-end over local rail service routes, when detailed planning commenced the difficulties of running alongside BR operations loomed large. This was the critical distinction from Phase 1, both lines of which are almost totally segregated from the BR network. The kind of joint running then being experimented in Karlsruhe, Germany, was clearly far from BR's considerations, and segregation of any eastern sector LRT system from BR was envisaged.

MAKING THE EASTWARD CONNECTION

The conclusions of the early studies were that LRT routes serving the eastern sector would join the Phase 1 network by means of an end-on connection to the Metrolink headshunt tracks located in the diagonal cross-tunnel linking Sheffield Street with Piccadilly Undercroft tram station. Coming from Glossop, Marple or Ashton, the trams would have approached Piccadilly on the extreme right of the multi-track layout before descending to ground level and swinging left into the cross-tunnel, thence running forward into the Undercroft station and on into the streets.

GLOSSOP/HADFIELD AND ASHTON/STALYBRIDGE

Though the Glossop/Hadfield line had been featured in the proposed ultimate network, subsequent events began to dilute the case for conversion to LRT. The 1500 V d.c. system was converted to 25 kV a.c., thus removing the non-standard electrification which had been part of the case for LRT conversion. In its North Trans-Pennine Rail Services Strategy, BR had in 1989 diverted east – west express services to Piccadilly over the Guide Bridge – Ardwick section of the route and this meant that segregation would be needed between intensive long-distance passenger services as well as from freight operations.

Though the line is well-patronised and has plenty of potential, it has been found that much of any projected growth in patronage would be achieved in off-peak periods. The Department of Transport's view was expected to be that benefits close enough to those accruing from LRT conversion would be achieved by an increased off-peak frequency of conventional trains coupled with Metrolink's city feeder/distributor facilities.

Investigations were also undertaken into the feasibility of augmenting the Glossop/Hadfield conversion with an LRT route to Ashton and Stalybridge so as to create a more attractive package. This route would branch northwards off the Metrolink Glossop line at Audenshaw and join the alignment of the BR freight line from Denton Junction to Ashton Moss South Junction, which it would have to cross by flyover or underpass somewhere along its length. A single track for LRT and a single track for BR would provisionally run along this alignment.

LRT would run with BR as far as a point near Wellington Road, where the LRT line would diverge to the right onto its own alignment because of development which has taken place on the abandoned eastern leg of Ashton Moss triangle. The alignment near to the course of Wellington Road would take the line to Ashton town centre, from whence it could run onto the existing BR line between Ashton and Stalybridge which might be freed of BR services by diverting them to Piccadilly via Guide Bridge. The LRT line would terminate and interchange with BR at Stalybridge, substantially improving rail services in the Tameside area.

The problem with this route is that it would have tended to duplicate the Glossop service west of the Audenshaw curve, and that the traffic potential between this point and the outskirts of Ashton was questionable because the area was destined to be developed for motorway-related employment uses rather than patronage-generating residential use. A possible solution could take the form of a new alignment from Ashton to Manchester through major regeneration areas, but this must remain an option for the future. Meanwhile, support for LRT in districts like Tameside is not entirely universal; there is a school of thought which maintains that strengthened commuter links with the regional core would turn outlying districts into characterless dormitories by pulling shopping trade and social activity away from district centres into Manchester.

MARPLE/ROSE HILL

Marple suffers from poor road access and has had one of the most persistently unreliable train services in the region. The BR Marple/Rose Hill line, DMU operated, shares tracks with the Glossop/Hadfield line from Piccadilly as far as Ashburys East Junction, where the two lines part company. These tracks are also used by BR freight trains. Retention of freight capacity from Piccadilly as far as Hyde would be required in the event of LRT conversion. Inter-running between LRT and conventional trains would require automatic train protection (ATP), but this may not necessarily be the most cost-effective solution. The original plan was to run as two single lines from Romiley to Marple.

Because the section between Piccadilly Station and Ashburys East Junction would possibly have to feed up to at least three routes in the future, separate double track for LRT and double or single track for BR would be required between Piccadilly and Hyde with different grade-separated crossings according to which lines were converted to LRT. These complications dictate that conversion of the

Glossop/Hadfield and Marple/Rose Hill lines would best be done as a package. Failing conversion to LRT, electrification of the Marple/Rose Hill line at 25 kV a.c. could be done by making use of substation equipment released from the LRT-converted Altrincham line.

EAST DIDSBURY

The ex-Midland main line as far as East Didsbury was one of the lines featured in the original proposals for the 6-line LRT network. At Old Trafford — renamed Trafford Bar with conversion to Metrolink — the line would branch off from the LRT tracks to Altrincham by means of a grade-separated junction. Here until recently the remaining ex-Midland track passed diagonally beneath the Altrincham tracks and the adjacent Elsinore Road just south of the station. The Didsbury-bound track would swing left to cross Elsinore Road at grade before descending into the cutting. Coming back from Didsbury, the other track would remain at low level to pass under the existing road and railway bridges before swinging sharply right and climbing to join the inward LRT track from Altrincham just before reaching the station platform.

Stopping places on the East Didsbury LRT line have yet to be fixed but will probably include Manchester Road, Chorlton-cum-Hardy, St Werburghs Road (near where the new Arrowfield housing estate encroaches on the alignment, necessitating a short length of single track), Withington Hospital, West Didsbury, Didsbury Village and East Didsbury. Continuation of the line beyond East Didsbury to Stockport or even Marple or Romiley would be an attractive option were it not for the fact that the trackbed has been built on and obliterated where it traverses the Mersey Valley. Notwithstanding the Didsbury line's difficulties, Parliamentary powers to construct it have now been obtained.

ROCHDALE/OLDHAM

Rochdale lies on Manchester's third and most northerly trans-Pennine route, running from Victoria to Halifax and Bradford via Summit Tunnel and the Calder Valley. This railway is used both by Section 20 supported trains and by BR Regional services and so is not available for LRT conversion. But Rochdale has another surviving railway. The town is the terminus of the "Oldham Loop" line which runs from Victoria through Oldham and onwards via Shaw and Milnrow

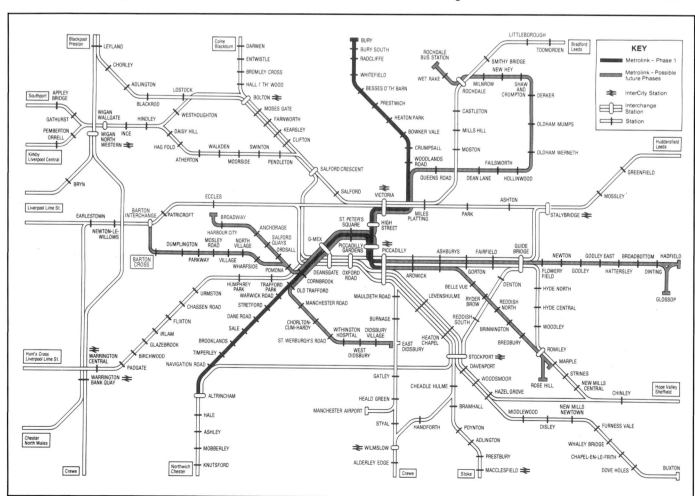

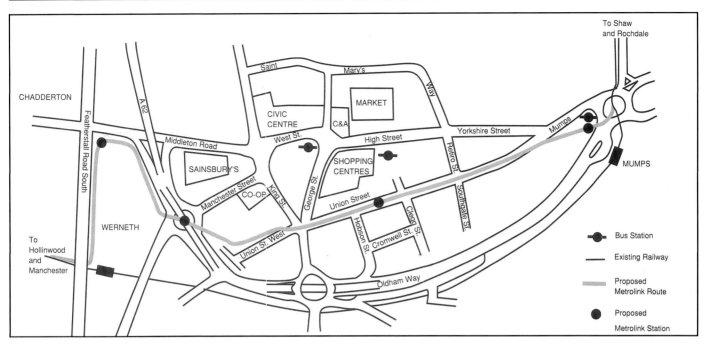

<table>
<tr><td>●—</td><td>Bus Station</td></tr>
<tr><td>—</td><td>Existing Railway</td></tr>
<tr><td>▬</td><td>Proposed Metrolink Route</td></tr>
<tr><td>●</td><td>Proposed Metrolink Station</td></tr>
</table>

to Rochdale, where loop trains join the line coming in from Yorkshire and finish their journeys facing Manchester. The Oldham loop is eligible for LRT conversion because it carries only PTE-supported services and can be physically separated from BR operations.

Connection with Phase 1 of Metrolink would be made by reinstating a former junction close to GMML's Queens Road headquarters. Rochdale-bound trams climbing away from Collyhurst Tunnel will leave the Bury line at Irk Valley Junction just before Smedley Viaduct, which carries the Bury line Manchester Loop from Victoria to Thorpes Bridge Junction. The Rochdale trams will descend via a reinstated chord to reach this line which they will follow as far as Thorpes Bridge where the loop line presently joins up with the direct line from Victoria. Instead of connecting with the direct line, the LRT tracks will reach the Oldham–Rochdale line via a new underpass.

After a few hundred metres the trams will pass the Greater Manchester Waste Disposal Authority's Dean Lane plant, where refuse trains are unloaded. These trains will have continuing access to the plant via an independent single track. From Dean Lane the trams will continue towards Oldham on substantially unmodified BR alignment, though extra stations may be added. At Oldham, it was initially intended that the trams would follow the existing tunnelled line between Oldham Werneth and Oldham Mumps stations, neither of which is particularly near to the town centre. Following overtures from Oldham Metropolitan Borough Council and considerable planning and consultancy work it is now intended to divert the LRT line via Oldham town centre as shown on the sketch map.

Just north of Oldham Mumps the trams will regain the railway alignment, which will take them to Rochdale via Shaw and Milnrow. At the point where the Oldham loop presently joins the Calder Valley line from Yorkshire, the single LRT track will cross by a flyover to the Rochdale side of the BR line, alongside which it will run in the Manchester direction towards Rochdale Station. Instead of entering the station, which is located half a mile or so from the town centre, the tracks will swing right off the railway alignment into the streets where they will become double. The sketch map shows how the on-street alignment continues all the way to the centre of the town.

Penetration of the town centres of both Rochdale and Oldham has helped strengthen the case for conversion of the Oldham–Rochdale Loop to LRT. Gradients of up to 6% in both towns will be within the climbing and descending capabilities of the trams but would take some getting used to as far as disabled passengers are concerned. The Rochdale town centre extension gained Parliamentary approval when GMPTE's No 5 LRT Bill was enacted in 1991.

SALFORD QUAYS

Salford Quays is the new name for the old Manchester Ship Canal docks complex which has been revitalised out of all recognition; the area now resembles London's Docklands, though on a much more human scale. The whole complex is located in Salford, Manchester neighbouring city, which originally had no prospects of benefitting directly from the light rail proposals. Following a suggestion by a member of the public in June 1985, Salford City Council asked

GMPTE to consider the prospects for LRT penetration of the redeveloping area.

An engineering feasibility study confirmed that a junction could be made with the LRT Altrincham line at Cornbrook and that the line could then cross the Pomona Docks complex of the Ship Canal before entering the Quays area itself, through which it would run at grade as far as Eccles New Road at its junction with Langworthy Road. Continuation of the line through Weaste to Eccles is featured in the Unitary Development Plan proposals for the area; the alignment is protected by Order of Council.

Parliamentary approval for the Salford Quays extension from Cornbrook Junction as far as South Langworthy Road's intersection with Broadway was secured when GMPTE's No 3 LRT Bill and what was known as the "1988 Bill" were enacted in 1990. The sketch map shows the authorised and protected route. It is possible that track foundations and ducts across Trafford Road will be installed soon as part of the dualling of the carriageway, to avoid having to disrupt traffic twice.

TRAFFORD PARK

Trafford Park is a sprawling industrial estate created at the turn of the century on the other side of the Ship Canal from the main Docks complex. Laid out very much according to American ideas, every firm on the estate was offered rail access by means of sidings branching off a comprehensive network of roadside freight lines. These were linked both to the main line railways and to the Ship Canal Company's own extensive system of dock and canalside railways. Much of the track mileage remains in place to this day and is seeing ever-increasing use by Trafford Park Estates Company locos hauling a variety of BR freight wagons at-grade into the far reaches of the Estate.

In 1984, when Trafford Metropolitan Borough Council received its copy of the Second Report of the Rail Study Group for consideration, Trafford Park's fortunes were at a low ebb. Many premises and large plots were vacant or derelict and the whole area had a run down feel to it; moves were, however, afoot to do something positive to give the area an uplift, and the receipt of the Study Group Report recommending pursuit of the LRT option could not have come at a more opportune time. It was suggested to Trafford MBC by a resident that LRT could be extended through Trafford Park to a large Park and Ride facility near to Dumplington Circle and the motorway network. The Council agreed and added to its endorsement of the LRT proposals a request for consideration to be given to extending LRT into Trafford Park.

Trafford Park Development Corporation soon afterwards took over direct responsibility for the revitalisation of the area, and of its own accord asked for the extension of LRT into the Estate. It has been in conjunction with that body and with Trafford Metropolitan Borough Council that GMPTE has worked up detailed proposals for LRT penetration of Trafford Park with Dumplington as a projected destination. Dumplington-bound trams would leave the Altrincham line at Cornbrook Junction and share tracks with the Salford Quays route as far as a new bifurcation to be known as Ship Canal Junction. Their route from there onwards to Dumplington is shown on the sketch map.

Dumplington itself was chosen as the projected terminus because of plans to construct a major out-of-town shopping centre there, similar to Gateshead's Metrocentre. The impetus and financial support generated by serving the new complex with light rail would support the route's provision through Trafford Park, which could not have justified light rail penetration on its own. The route has been projected to run possibly as far as a new station called "Barton Interchange" on the Manchester – Liverpool (via Earlestown) line west of Patricroft.

CORNBROOK JUNCTION

The site of Cornbrook Junction, where both the Salford Quays and Trafford Park extensions would diverge from the Phase 1 Altrincham line, is exceedingly cramped and inaccessible. Bounded immediately on the one side by BR's Manchester – Liverpool (via Warrington) line and immediately on the other by the Bridgewater Canal, construction of an underpass beneath the BR tracks to carry trams from the G-MEX approach viaducts towards Altrincham was going to be bad enough on an initially vacant site, but the later insertion of substantial junction works close to the LRT Manchester – Altrincham and BR Manchester – Liverpool traffic would be even worse.

The awkwardly inaccessible nature of the site meant that a temporary bridge had to be thrown across the Bridgewater Canal from Pomona Docks for construction traffic access. Now that the access bridge has been removed, it cannot in the future be re-erected because of redevelopment work which is taking place in the former Pomona Docks area. This effectively landlocks the Cornbrook Junction site and perhaps provides the most compelling reason of the lot for doing all the work while the site could be easily accessed. As a consequence, abutments for the Trafford Park/Salford Quays line have been put in place ready for bridge deck installation at a later date.

MAKING A CASE FOR METROLINK EXTENSIONS

We have seen in earlier chapters what a merry dance the Government led GMPTE before permitting Phase 1 of the LRT proposals to proceed on an operationally franchised footing. Deregulation had by the late 'eighties made it anathema to even think of subsidising the operation of light rail services despite the fact that subsidy is the norm on the overseas systems on which Metrolink's is technically based. GMPTA and GMPTE have therefore had to accept that no extension is likely to go forward unless it can be shown to be operable against bus competition without subsidy. This drastically reduces the scope for using electric light rail transit in the UK whatever the wider community, strategic planning, congestion relief, improved accessibility, economic revitalisation and ecological considerations might be.

GMPTA and GMPTE have put together and thoroughly examined a richly varied range of extension options. Parliamentary powers have been obtained. The cost of all the extensions studies and associated Parliamentary Bill promotions has run into several millions of pounds with, as Phase 1 goes into operation, no definite prospect of success. At this point we should again remind ourselves that the Phase 1 infrastructure, particularly in the city centre, will remain a grossly-underutilised piece of public capital investment as long as it is only carrying Phase 1 services.

THE USER PAYS – CONGESTION STAYS

The Government's current criteria for making Section 56 grants available for public transport schemes originated in 1985 in conjunction with bus deregulation, from which the criteria are directly derived. As a consequence the Government's present LRT funding philosophy suffers from being negatively-inspired, being based on the Spartan view that it would be unfair on struggling bus operators to publicly subsidise the operation of a more attractive mode of public transport on busy corridors.

Using that as a starting point, the list of grant-qualifying requirements can only go from bad to worse. In effect, promoters can only look to the Government for Section 56 grant when all other possibilities for funding have been exhausted. Most disturbing is the requirement that the user must be seen to be made to pay in full for the benefits he receives from using new rail services in preference to some other form of transport; in other words, if you want to go "green" you must pay for the privilege. This diminishes concern for the environment to the level of political hot air.

The implication is that the pinnacle of perfection would be reached if the attractiveness of the new service could be completely cancelled out by fare-raising until it had zero net appeal in comparison to

other modes including car, bike and bus. In neighbouring Continental countries you pay the same per kilometre whichever mode of public transport you have to use, whether it be bus, train, tram or ferry.

DEVELOPER CONTRIBUTIONS?

Another source of funding favoured by the Government is the developer contribution. Here it is instructive to note that in reality some provincial frontagers, far from being eager to contribute financially to light rail because it will do them good, have shown themselves content to profit directly from it by negotiating wayleave rentals for graciously accepting overhead wire attachments. In spite of this cold reality, circumstances elsewhere in the country directed attention in 1987 towards the use of private capital as a possible source of funds for new public transport schemes. It was at this time that private funds came in prospect for rectification of Docklands Light Railway capacity constraints as well as provision of extensions to Bank, Beckton and Lewisham and for the separate Jubilee line extension project.

This lavish availability of private funds was and always will be peculiar to the Capital, but all the same the theme was taken up vigorously in the provinces by a couple of other light rail promoters who have since had to change their tune. Avon was first, echoed not long afterwards by West Midlands. Promoters in both places made bold noises about using private capital to fund their schemes and this led the Department of Transport, no doubt with the Treasury's hand working its mouth, to say in effect to GMPTE: "These other promoters say they can attract private capital; now you do it. We'll wait here while you go away and work out how. Only when you come back with the soles of your shoes and the knees of your trousers worn through will we consider helping you".

Phase 1 of the Manchester scheme had already been proved sufficiently sound on its own merits not to need any extra fund-raising of the hat-passing kind, but for the time being some of the extension proposals look vulnerable to funding restrictions. The Oldham/Rochdale line still looks a good prospect for LRT, with penetration of Oldham and Rochdale town centres added to the saving of Section 20 support together with the dubiously-worthwhile prospect of some premium fares tolerance.

PHASE 1A

During the run-up to Phase 1's implementation it was envisaged that any extension of Metrolink which could be authorised and funded within two years of the completion of Phase 1 would be constructed as Phase 1A by GMML, and subsequently operated by the same company. This would have maintained the construction and supply momentum and was an ojective pursued enthusiastically by David Graham, Director General of GMPTE until his untimely death in mid-1991 denied him even the satisfaction of seeing Phase 1 inaugurated. There is now no hope of any extension being funded soon enough to meet the two-year Phase 1A deadline. The consequence is that extensions when approved could be thrown open to tender and may be operated other than by GMML.

When the Government insisted on the franchising of Phase 1's operation to the private sector, the possibility could be foreseen of different operators being allowed in the future to provide services over the same lengths of track. This would fall in line with Government ideas on deregulation and railway privatisation, but could in practice stir up the sort of arguments and rivalries that so beset railway operation around Manchester in Victorian times. An indication that some judicious back-tracking might be taking place was given on 10th November 1991 when Mr Malcolm Rifkind, Secretary of State for Transport, was quoted as saying "We do not envisage the whole of the railways being privatised. A substantial proportion of the railways are providing a social service rather than running a business". Wise words indeed!

DEVELOPER DISTORTION

Allowing developer involvement to influence or overwhelm strategic county-wide planning initiatives may be the Government's way of pursuing its desire to take power away from local authorities. If so, it would be accomplished at the expense of distorting those initiatives. History shows us that in the last century the private sector did not always limit itself to giving the country the railways it needed; any railway historian can rattle off a list of superfluous routes set up purely because of inter-company jealousy or cut-throat competition.

The misfortune with ill-conceived and transient public transport routes – bus, rail, ferry and so on – is that people's ways of life come to depend on them while they're there. Society's patterns of employment, education, leisure activity and habitation will always revolve to a great extent around public transport provision which is not something to be lightly tinkered with or left without a structured planning overview to make sure that what is provided is enduringly robust, justifiable and properly-conceived.

Thus it is that in the case of the Trafford Park extension, the light rail route is needed to help revitalise the area, yet it will only go ahead if it is partly funded by the developers of the out of town shopping centre at Dumplington if and when that development is given the go-ahead by the Environment Minister. The PTEs are not developers' agents, they are public bodies endeavouring to organise public transport for the good of the whole community rather than for the benefit of a minority; the Government ought to back them fully in pursuit of that objective and no other.

THE EFFECTS OF METROLINK'S INAUGURATION

Once Phase 1 of Metrolink is in full operation between Bury, Altrincham and Piccadilly BR there is no doubt that a much better picture will emerge of the true prospects for extensions. All of the possibilities mentioned in this chapter will be seen afresh in the light of experience and it is quite likely that new opportunities for making use of light rail in the region will be identified.

THE EAST LANCASHIRE RAILWAY CONNECTION

The East Lancashire Railway currently operates a heritage railway service from Bury Bolton Street to Rawtenstall, with much potential as a weekend and holiday traffic generator for Metrolink. The Bury electrics used to run into Bolton Street station before the construction of the present Bury Interchange. The ELR may take over the old Bury electric depot, now a listed building. As Metrolink's inauguration approached the premises were being used by Firema to carry out modifications to the new trams. Though a physical link between the two railways may be retained and even, who knows, electrified through to Bolton Street, the East Lancs was deprived by the Bury line's LRT conversion of a full loading gauge stock-transfer link to the BR network. Consequently the ELR is in the process, with local authority assistance, of reinstating the Bury to Heywood (BR) line via a new bridge over Metrolink close to Bury Interchange.

During GMA's work on the Bury line, an East Lancs industrial diesel loco and a flat wagon were borrowed to assist with tidying up; in return, GMML donated obsolete recovered material to the ELR. The associated movements made use of the surviving link between the Bury line and the ELR. Other links between the two neighbouring railways exist in the persons of some Metrolink staff who also belong to the East Lancs railway society. Who knows, perhaps one day there may be potential for commuter services to be jointly provided by the two privately-operated railways with cross-platform transfer facilities and through-ticketing. This would be a cost-effective way to extend Metrolink's catchment area all the way beyond the County boundary to Ramsbottom and Rawtenstall and perhaps, by a very fanciful stretch of the imagination, to Holcombe Brook as well.

▶ Metrolink's Oldham/Rochdale line will branch off from the Bury line at Irk Valley Junction, seen here on the occasion of the December 1988 Sunday inspection visit to the line by tendering consortia during the first stage of the Phase 1 tendering process. The intended trackbed can be seen in the right background. No doubt the engineers were somewhat fascinated at the state of the third rail equipment, which nevertheless was still sustaining a remarkably good train service at the time.   *Mick Crabtree*

▶ Another of the more viable prospects for Metrolink growth is the line through Trafford Park to Dumplington. We have already seen where this line would bifurcate from the Altrincham route (page 72), and here we see the open fields presently occupying the site where the line would terminate at the new out-of-town shopping development planned for Dumplington. The area is already accessed by a Manchester Ship Canal roadside freight line which sees heavy use on a daily basis by trains operating from the Container-base (on the right) to Southampton Maritime. The immensely long trains are hauled by the MSC's Sentinel or Hunslet industrial locomotives. Trafford Park has its own well-used roadside freight network.   *Author*

ACKNOWLEDGEMENTS

I could not have written this book in isolation. The help, support and encouragement I have received from others has been tremendous, especially considering the demands already bearing down on those from whom I have sought assistance, which almost always has been generously given. The following individuals or groups of people have all helped beyond the call of duty either by giving information or be commenting on drafts, though it should be emphasises that no responsibility for inaccuracies or imbalance can rest with them:

Tony Young, David Tibke (GMPTE) and Martin Arthur (formerly GMPTE, now with Tameside District Council), Bill Tyson, Liam McCarthy, John Berry, Richard Naylor, Connor McGuinness, (all GMPTE), David Rumney (GMPTE/Mott Macdonald), Bill Maddocks and Jack Flanagan (GMPTA), Keith Williams (City Engineers traffic management), Bill Usher (Manchester City Council), Tony Fletcher, Martin Williams and Mick Crabtree (all BR), Ivor Thomas (Mowlem), David Cox and Jim McDermott (GMA), Eric Black (GMA/GMML), Bob Hall, Roger Benton and Geoffrey Claydon (National Tramway Museum), John Trebacik (RFS), Roger France (Balfour Beatty Power Engineering), Renia Bisewska (Balfour Beatty Engineering), Roger Hull (W S Atkins), Chris Cobb (Brown Root), Scott Hellewell, Paul Neal, Don Kenny and Nick Donovan (all GMML), Sergio Vigano (Firema Engineering), David Russell (SAB WABCO), M N Oliver (M N Oliver, Surveyors), Graham Stevenson (T&GWU), David Banbury (Geismar), Richard Barton (Sika), W P Schram (Edilon), G J Dunbavin (Whipp & Bourne), Tony Johnson (Huck UK Ltd), Wolfgang Helas (Hanning & Kahl GMBH), Robert Prosser (National Diamond Drilling Services), Tim Baynes (GMTCC), Harvey Scowcroft (NWTUCC), Dennis Gill (Martic Proposal) and finally, too many staff at GEC Alsthom to name individually.

Liam McCarthy of GMPTE contributed the section "Public Expenditure Provision" and Major C B Holden of HMRI gave guidance specifically with "The Role of Her Majesty's Railway Inspectorate. Also, Peter Fox, the publisher contributed the section on comparison between modes, as well as numerous other small pieces of text and was responsible for the selection of the photographs. To anyone I have missed, my sincere apologies. It is important to stress that the inclusion of individuals' or companies' names here in no way implies their endorsement of anything said in this book, responsibility for which rests entirely with the author and publisher.

My thanks also go to my family — my wife Nicolette, my 11-year old daughter Alexandra and my 8-years old son Gregory — to whom I was a little more than the wrong side of a study door for ten months during my work on this book.

LIGHT RAIL TRANSIT & TRAMWAY TITLES FROM PLATFORM 5